DESSERTS
AND
PUDDINGS

CRUIK £2.25

366

RECIPES

DESSERTS
AND
PUDDINGS

SUNBURST BOOKS

CONTENTS

FRUIT DESSERTS

COINTREAU APRICOT SURPRISE
Serves 4

15 oz (425 g) can of apricot halves
2 level tsp cornflour
4 tbsp Cointreau
¼pt (150 ml) double cream
6 pistachio nuts

Drain the apricots, but reserve the syrup. Arrange the apricot halves in four glasses, reserving four halves for decoration. Sprinkle the cornflour in a small saucepan and blend with a little of the apricot juice. Heat gently, stirring in the remaining juice and the Cointreau. Bring to the boil over a medium heat and stir in 4 tablespoons of the cream. Pour over the apricots and leave to cool. Put the nuts in a small basin and pour over boiling water. After 20 seconds strain the nuts and remove the skins. Halve the nuts. Whip the remaining cream until it just holds its shape and pipe a swirl on top of each glass. Decorate with a fan of sliced apricot and a few pistachio nuts.

NECTARINE TRIFLE
Serves 4

4 trifle sponges
1 tbsp sweet sherry
10 fl oz (300 ml) thick cream
1 oz (25 g) caster sugar
3 tbsp orange juice
3 tbsp brandy
4 tbsp lemon juice
6 nectarines

Arrange the trifle sponges over the base of a flat dish. Pour on the sherry and leave to soak for 2 hours. Whip the cream and caster sugar together until thick. Beat in the orange and lemon juices and the brandy. Stone the nectarines and roughly cut up the flesh. Drain the sponges from the sherry and cut into cubes. Place a little of the cream mixture into the bottom of four glass dishes. Divide the sponge cubes and nectarine pieces between the dishes, then top with the remaining cream. Chill for at least 3 hours before serving.

GERMAN APPLE PUDDING
Serves 6

3 oz (75 g) raisins
3 fl oz (75 ml) orange juice
grated rind of 1 small lemon
4 tbsp melted butter
8 oz (225 g) breadcrumbs made
  from pumpernickel bread

6 oz (175 g) brown sugar
4 oz (110 g) almonds, chopped
1 tsp ground mixed spice
4 tbsp butter, softened
1½ lb (675 g) cooking apples, peeled,
  cored and thinly sliced

Place the raisins in a bowl together with the orange juice and lemon rind and leave for 30 minutes. Preheat the oven to 350°F/180°C/ Gas Mk 4. Add the breadcrumbs, sugar, almonds, mixed spice and melted butter to the raisins. Grease a 3 pint (1.8 ltr) ovenproof dish and put in one-third of the breadcrumb mixture. Place half the apples on top, another third of the breadcrumbs and then the remaining apples. Sprinkle the last of the breadcrumbs on the top. Dot with the softened butter. Cook in the oven for 35 minutes.

APPLE & CHOCOLATE CLOUD
Serves 6

6 slices white bread
3 oz (75 g) butter
chocolate spread
1½ lb (675 g) cooking apples, cooked, puréed and sweetened
1 oz (25 g) plain chocolate, grated
5 fl oz (150 ml) double cream, whipped

Cut the slices of white bread in half diagonally and fry in the butter on one side only. Spread the unfried side with chocolate spread. Lightly butter a 1½ pint (900 ml) ovenproof dish and spread a layer of the sweetened apple purée on the bottom. Cover with some of the bread slices, fried side up, and scatter grated chocolate over. Repeat the layer of apple purée and so on until all is used up, ending with a layer of apple. Chill in the refrigerator then cover with whipped cream and more grated chocolate. If a hot dessert is preferred, beat 2 egg yolks into the apple purée before using it. Then whisk 2 egg whites with a pinch of salt until they hold their shape. Whisk in 2 tablespoons of caster sugar until the meringue is stiff. Gently fold in an extra 2 tablespoons with a metal spoon and pile on top of the last layer of apple purée. Bake at 350°F/180°C/Gas Mk 4 in a preheated oven for about 30 minutes until golden brown.

HOT RASPBERRY TRIFLE
Serves 6

4 oz (110 g) butter, cut into small pieces
4 oz (110 g) caster sugar
2 eggs, beaten
4 oz (110 g) self raising flour
8 oz (225 g) canned or frozen raspberries, drained of juice
7 fl oz (200 ml) double cream
2 tbsp dry sherry
glacé cherries, for decoration

Preheat the oven to 375°F/190°C/Gas Mk 5. Cream the butter and sugar in a bowl until light and fluffy. Beat in the eggs, little by little, adding one teaspoonful of flour with each addition. Fold in the remaining flour. Place the raspberries in the bottom of a 2 pint (1.2 ltr) ovenproof dish. Arrange the egg mixture evenly over the top making a small well in the centre. Bake in the oven for 45 minutes until the sponge is risen and set. Meanwhile, whip together the cream and sherry until thick. When the sponge is ready, spread this mixture over the top and decorate with cherries. Serve immediately.

UPSIDE DOWN PEAR RING
Serves

3 oz (75 g) butter
2½ oz (60 g) caster sugar
14 oz (400 g) can of pear halves, drained and sliced
1 tbsp chopped nuts
1 oz (25 g) soft brown sugar

1 egg, lightly whisked
2½ oz (60 g) self-raising flour
½ oz (10 g) cocoa
½ tsp instant coffee granules
1 tbsp milk

Preheat the oven to 350°F/180°C/Gas Mk 4. Grease and base line a 7 in (18 cm) sandwich tin. Melt 2 oz (50 g) of the butter and the sugar. Spread over the base of the tin. Arrange the pear slices around the edge of the tin and spoon the nuts into the centre. Cream the remaining butter, cut into small pieces, and the brown sugar together until light and fluffy and then beat in the egg. Sieve in the flour, cocoa and coffee. Fold in the milk. Spread the mixture over the pears and smooth the top. Bake for about 25 minutes in the oven until springy to the touch. Let it cool in the tin for about 5 minutes before turning out and gently removing the paper. Can be served hot or cold with whipped cream.

PEARS IN BUTTTERSCOTCH
Serves 4

10 fl oz (300 ml) water
4 tbsp golden syrup
3 in (7.5 cm) cinnamon stick
zest of one small lemon
4 dessert pears, slightly under–ripe,
  peeled and cored
4 tbsp demerara sugar

1 oz (25 g) butter
1 tbsp lemon juice
10 fl oz (300 ml) thick cream
2 egg yolks
1 oz (25 g) walnuts, finely chopped,
  to garnish

Place the water into a saucepan together with 2 tablespoons of the syrup, the cinnamon stick and lemon zest. Cook over a low heat until the syrup has melted. Bring to simmering point, add the pears and poach for about 30 minutes until they are tender and transparent. Remove from the heat and allow to cool in the syrup. Place the demerara sugar, remaining syrup, butter and lemon juice into a saucepan over a low heat until the mixture has melted. Remove from the heat. Scald the cream and stir into the sugar mixture. Beat the egg yolks in a small bowl. Beat in 6 tablespoons of the cream and the sugar mixture then stir this back into the saucepan. Place over a low heat and stir with a wooden spoon until thick. Remove from the heat and allow to cool completely. Remove the pears from the syrup and arrange on a serving dish. Spoon over the sauce and garnish with the walnuts.

APPLE ROLY POLY
Serves 6

8 oz (225 g) self-raising flour
pinch of salt
4 oz (110 g) shredded suet
water
2 tbsp demerara sugar
2 cooking apples, peeled, cored and sliced

Preheat the oven to 400°F/200°C/Gas Mk 6. Place the flour, salt and suet in a bowl. Add sufficient cold water to make a soft dough. Knead lightly. Roll out on a floured surface to a 10 in (25 cm) square and spread over the sugar leaving a 1 in (2.5 cm) clear edge all round. Arrange the apple slices on the dough and then roll up loosely, sealing the edges well. Lay on a lightly floured baking sheet and cook in the oven for 40 minutes until golden brown. Cut into slices and serve on a warm dish.

RHUBARB CRUMBLE
Serves 4–6

1½ lb (675 g) rhubarb, trimmed and cut into 1½ in (4 cm) lengths
1 tsp grated orange zest
6 oz (175 g) sugar
6 oz (175 g) flour
pinch of salt
3 oz (75 g) butter, cut into small pieces

Preheat the oven to 375°F/190°C/Gas Mk 5. Place the rhubarb and orange zest in a large bowl, add the 4 oz (110 g) of the sugar and mix. To make the crumble, sift the flour and salt into a mixing bowl. Add the butter, and lightly rub in until the mixture resembles fine breadcrumbs. Add 2–3 tbsp of the crumble to the rhubarb and mix well. Place the rhubarb into a greased 2 pint (1.2 ltr) ovenproof dish, levelling the surface. Sprinkle the crumble over the top and the remaining sugar. Bake in oven for 30–40 minutes until the crumble is golden brown and the rhubarb is soft.

PLUM CRUMBLE
Serves 4

1½ lb.(675 g) plums, halved and stoned
1 tbsp water
4 oz (110 g) butter
4 oz (110 g) caster sugar
6 oz (175 g) plain flour

Preheat the oven to 350°F/180°C/Gas Mk 4. Put the plums, 1 oz (25 g) of the butter and 2 oz (50 g) of the sugar into a saucepan and add the water. Bring to the boil gently, cover with a lid, then simmer for 5 minutes, or until plums are tender. Spoon the fruit mixture into a buttered 1½ pint (900 ml) baking dish. Choose one that is shallow rather than deep so you get a good area for the crumble. To prepare the topping, sift the flour into a mixing bowl, add the remaining butter in pieces and rub in with the fingertips. Add the remaining sugar and continue to rub in until mixture is breadcrumb-like in appearance. Spoon crumble evenly over the fruit and press gently. Bake in the top half of the oven for 40 minutes. Serve with cream or vanilla ice cream. Variation: Raspberry Crumble – Put 1 lb (450 g) fresh raspberries in the greased baking dish. Sprinkle over 3 oz (75 g) caster sugar and add 1 tbsp water. Omit the butter.

BANANAS BRAZIL
Serves 4

8 fl oz (225 ml) thick cream
2 tbsp strong black coffee
1 tbsp dark rum
4 large bananas, sliced thinly

juice of ½ small lemon
1 tbsp soft brown sugar
1 tbsp sultanas

In a bowl, whip the cream, coffee and rum until thick. Arrange the bananas in a shallow dish and pour over the lemon juice. Sprinkle the sugar and sultanas over the fruit. Spread the cream mixture on top and chill thoroughly before serving.

KENTISH STRAWBERRY TRIFLE
Serves 4–6

8 oz (225 g) strawberries
4–6 tbsp sweet sherry
1 large packet (8)
  trifle sponge cakes
strawberry jam
4 standard egg yolks

1 rounded tbsp caster sugar
½ level tsp vanilla essence
1 pt (600 ml) milk, plus 2 tbsp
8 blanched almonds
5 fl oz (150 ml) carton
  double cream

Reserve 6 strawberries for decoration. Hull and slice the remainder, then place in a small basin. Add the sherry and mix lightly. Split the trifle sponge cakes in halves, sandwich together with strawberry jam. Cut into small pieces, and place in a 3 pint (1.8 ltr) glass bowl. Add the strawberries and sherry, and mix together lightly. To make custard, place the egg yolks and caster sugar together in a large basin. Add the vanilla essence and beat with a wooden spoon. Bring 1 pint (600 ml) of the milk to the boil in a small saucepan, and gradually stir into the egg mixture. Place the basin over a saucepan of boiling water over a moderate heat (or pour the custard mixture into the inner pan of a double boiler). Stir frequently until the custard thickens and coats back of spoon. Remove the custard from the boiling water. Leave the custard to cool slightly, stirring occasionally. Pour into the glass bowl and leave in a cool place until the custard has set. Preheat a grill to a moderate temperature. Shred the almonds, spread out in the grill pan and brown under the grill. Place the cream and the remaining milk in a bowl and whisk until thick. Pile 12 dessertspoonful of cream around the edge of the bowl. Place a reserved strawberry on each alternate peak of cream. Arrange 'spikes of shredded almonds on remaining peaks of cream. Keep cool until ready to serve.

FRUIT SAVARIN
Serves 6

7 oz (200 g) plain flour
¼ level tsp salt
½ oz (10 g) fresh yeast
  or ¼ oz (5 g) dried yeast
4 tbsp tepid milk
¼ oz (5 g) caster sugar
4 oz (110 g) butter, softened
  and cut into small pieces

4 eggs, beaten
4 oz (110 g) granulated sugar
½ pt (600 ml) water
2 tbsp sherry
½ small pineapple, peeled and cubed
¼ lb (110 g) strawberries,
  hulled and sliced
1 kiwi fruit, peeled and sliced

Preheat the oven to 400°F/200°C/Gas Mk 6. Lightly grease and flour
an 8 in (20 cm) ring cake tin. Sift the flour and salt into a mixing bowl.
Cream the yeast with a little of the tepid milk and then stir in the
remaining milk. If using dried yeast, sprinkle a level tsp of caster sugar
onto the tepid milk and yeast and leave for 15 minutes until frothy.
Make a well in the centre of the flour and pour in the milk and yeast
mixture. Add the butter, eggs and caster sugar. Beat in the flour from
the sides of the well until all is incorporated and then beat well until
you have a smooth batter. Pour into the prepared mould, and leave in
a warm place for 30 minutes or until the mixture has risen two-thirds
up the sides of the tin. Bake the savarin for 25 minutes, or until firm
and golden. Cool in the tin for a few minutes and then turn out onto
a rack set on a tray. Heat the granulated sugar in a saucepan with the
water, stirring until dissolved. Bring the syrup to the boil and boil for
7 minutes or until the syrup thickens. Stir in the sherry and leave to
cool. Prick the savarin with a skewer and pour the syrup slowly over
so that it becomes completely absorbed. Place on a serving dish and
fill the centre with the fruit.

ALMOND FRUIT PUFF
Serves 6

2 oz (50 g) butter,
  cut into small pieces
2 oz (50 g) caster sugar
2 eggs, beaten
¼ tsp almond essence
½ oz (10 g) flour
2 oz (50 g) ground almonds
2 oz (50 g) maraschino
  cherries, halved

8 oz (225 g) can of sliced peaches
8 oz (225 g) can of sliced apricots
8 oz (225 g) can of sliced prunes
1 small eating apple, peeled
  and finely chopped
1 lb (450 g) puff pastry

Preheat the oven to 450°F/230°C/Gas Mk 8. Cream the butter and sugar together until light and fluffy and beat in the almond essence, 1 egg, flour and ground almonds. Lightly fold in the cherries, well drained canned fruit and the apple. Thinly roll out a quarter of the pastry and trim to an 8 in (20 cm) diameter circle. Place on a baking sheet and prick all over with a fork. Brush a 1 in (2.5 cm) rim around the edge with the remaining beaten egg. Divide the remaining pastry into two portions. Roll out one piece and trim into a 9 in (23 cm) circle for a lid. Roll out the remainder to a strip 1 in (2.5 cm) wide and 14 in (35 cm) long. Divide in half. Lay these strips over the egg glazed rim to form a 'wall'. Leave the pastry to relax for 30 minutes. Pile the fruit mixture within the wall. Brush the wall with the egg and place the lid on top. Press the edges together lightly and glaze with beaten egg. Bake for 15 minutes. Reduce the heat to 350°F/180°C/ Gas Mk 4, cover the puff with dampened greaseproof paper and cook for a further 45 minutes. Serve warm, in wedges, with thick cream.

BLACKBERRY AND BANANA PUDDING
Serves 4–6

For the sponge:
3 oz (75 g) margarine,
  cut into small pieces
3 oz (75 g) sugar
1 large egg

3 oz (75 g) self-raising flour
1 level tsp ground cinnamon
1 tbsp milk

For the base:
1 oz (25 g) butter
2 oz (50 g) sugar

½ lb (225 g) blackberries
1 large banana

Preheat the oven to 350°F/180°C/Gas Mk 4. To make the sponge, cream the margarine and sugar together until light and fluffy, then add the egg and beat thoroughly. Mix the flour and cinnamon together and fold them into the creamed mixture with the milk. Leave on one side. To make the base, melt the butter, stir in the sugar and the blackberries. Slice the banana into the pan and heat for 1 minute, then transfer to a 2 pint (1.2 ltr) greased ovenproof dish, reserving a large tablespoon of the mixture for decoration. Spoon the sponge mixture over the top of the fruit in the dish and spread it level. Stand the dish in a baking tin, in case the fruit boils over, and bake just above the centre of the oven for 50–60 minutes. Serve decorated with the reserved fruit mixture, and with custard.

CHERRY ALMOND CREAMS
Serves 4

15 oz (425 g) can of creamed semolina pudding
½ tsp almond essence
8 oz (225 g) can of red cherries
1 tsp arrowroot
1 rounded tbsp flaked almonds

Mix ¼ tsp of the almond essence with the creamed semolina and pour into four individual glass dishes. Chill. Strain a little of the cherry juice into a small bowl and strain the rest into a saucepan. Blend the arrowroot with the juice in the bowl and pour into the saucepan with the remaining juice. Heat gently, stirring, until thick, and then simmer for 3 minutes. Stone the cherries if necessary and add to the cherry sauce together with the remaining almond essence. Stir well and allow to cool. Spoon over the semolina and chill for 45 minutes before serving. Toast the almond flakes under a moderate grill until lightly browned and leave to get cold. When serving sprinkle the almond flakes over the top of each dish.

APPLE BROWN BETTY
Serves 4–6

4 oz (110 g) butter
4 oz (110 g) fine brown breadcrumbs
4 oz (110 g) soft light brown sugar
½ level tsp ground cinnamon

1 lemon, finely grated rind and juice
1½ lb (675 g) cooking apples, peeled,
cored and sliced
3 tbsp water

Preheat the oven to 350°F/180°C/Gas Mk 4. Generously grease a 2 pint (1.2 ltr) baking dish. Melt the butter in a saucepan over a low heat. Remove from the heat and stir in the breadcrumbs. Mix the brown sugar, ground cinnamon and grated lemon rind together in a small bowl. Sprinkle a third of the buttered crumbs over the base of the prepared baking dish. Cover with half the apple slices and sprinkle over half the sugar mixture. Add another layer of the buttered crumbs, then the remaining apples. Sprinkle over the remaining sugar mixture and cover with the remaining buttered crumbs. Spoon the water and lemon juice over the top. Cover the pudding with buttered greaseproof paper or kitchen foil. Bake in the centre of the oven for 30 minutes, or until the apples are tender and top is golden brown and crisp. Serve hot or cold with cream.

ORANGE DESSERT
Serves 4

3 large oranges
1 small pineapple
2 oz (50 g) caster sugar
5 oz (150 g) desiccated coconut

Peel the oranges, carefully removing all the pith, then cut into thin slices. Peel, slice and core the pineapple and cut each slice into 8 pieces. Mix together the coconut and sugar. Arrange the orange and pineapple in layers in a serving bowl or individual dishes sprinkling each layer with the coconut mixture, leaving a little to sprinkle on the top. Chill for at least 2 hours before serving.

TOFFEE APPLES & BANANAS
Serves 4

2 large apples, peeled and cored
2 firm bananas
1 oz (25 g) plain flour
1 oz (25 g) cornflour
1 large egg

3 tsp sesame oil
½ pt (300 ml) groundnut oil
(or another vegetable oil)
6 oz (175 g) caster sugar
2 tbsp white sesame seeds

Cut each apple into eight thick chunks. Peel the bananas and cut them into 1½ in (4 cm) chunks. Mix together the sifted flour and cornflour, the egg and 1 tsp of the sesame oil in a wok or a strong large saucepan. Heat the batter until it is moderately hot. Carefully put the fruit into the batter and when the batter is beginning to cling to the fruit lift out with a slotted spoon and let the excess batter drain off. Heat the groundnut oil and deep-fry the pieces of fruit for about 2 minutes until they are golden. Remove with the slotted spoon and drain on kitchen paper. When ready to serve have ready a large bowl of iced water filled with ice cubes. Reheat the oil and deep-fry the fruit a second time, for about 2 minutes. Remove and drain on kitchen paper as before. Put the sugar, sesame seeds and 2 tablespoons of the frying oil into a pan. Heat it gently until the sugar begins to caramelise. Watch to prevent burning. When the caramel is light brown add the fruit sections just a few at a time and stir around until coated. Remove with a long fork if possible and plunge into the iced water to harden. Remove from the water and place on a serving dish. Serve at once.

LEMON PUDDING
Serves 4

4 oz (110 g) self-raising flour
pinch of salt
4 oz (110 g) butter or margarine,
  cut into small pieces
8 oz (225 g) caster sugar

1 lemon, finely grated rind and juice
2 eggs
1–3 tbsp milk
2 level tbsp cornflour
hot water

Preheat the oven to 375°F/190°C/Gas Mk 5. Generously grease a
2 pint (1.2 ltr) baking dish. Sift the flour and salt on to a plate. Cream
the butter or margarine, half the sugar and the grated lemon rind in a
mixing bowl until fluffy and light. Lightly whisk the eggs and
gradually beat them into the creamed mixture. Add a little of the
sifted flour along with the last addition of egg, then fold the
remaining flour into the mixture and add sufficient milk to make
a medium-soft consistency. Spoon the mixture into the prepared
baking dish and spread level. Blend the cornflour with the remaining
sugar in a small bowl. Make the lemon juice up to ½ pint (300 ml)
with hot water and stir into the cornflour mixture. Pour the lemon
sauce over the pudding mixture. Bake the pudding in the top half of
the oven for 40 minutes. During baking the sauce will sink to the
bottom and thicken. Serve hot with cream or ice cream.

AUTUMN APPLE PUDDING
Serves 6

8 oz (225 g) apples. peeled, cored
  and diced
2 oz (50 g) currants
2 oz (50 g) sultanas
1 oz (25 g) mixed peel
1 oz (25 g) glacé cherries, quartered
1 oz (25 g) stoned dates, chopped
2 level tbsp demerara sugar

1 level tsp ground cinnamon
4 oz (110 g) soft margarine
4 oz (110 g) caster sugar
2 eggs, beaten
6 oz (150 g) self-raising flour
1 level tsp baking powder
2 tbsp milk

Put the diced apple, fruit, demerara sugar and spice in a bowl. Beat
the margarine and sugar together in another bowl until soft and fluffy,
then beat in the eggs and fold in the flour and baking powder. Beat
until smooth, adding the milk. Place half the fruit mixture in a lightly
greased 2 pint (1.2 ltr) basin. Spread half the creamed mixture on top.
Add the remaining fruit and then the remaining creamed mixture.
Cover with greased greaseproof paper, pleated in the centre, then with
foil, doubled. Steam for 1½ hours.

APPLE AND BANANA FEAST
Serves 6–8

8 oz (225 g) plain flour
2 tbsp baking powder
½ tsp salt
4 oz (110 g) butter, cut into
small pieces
2 oz (50 g) brown sugar
1 beaten egg
whipped cream

1 tsp grated lemon rind
3 bananas, peeled and mashed
2 oz (50 g) sultanas
3 dessert apples, cored and
thinly sliced
2 oz (50 g) soft light brown sugar
½ tsp ground cinnamon
1½ oz (35 g) melted butter

For the filling:
12 oz (350 g) cottage cheese

Preheat the oven to 375°F/190°C/Gas Mk 5. In a bowl, mix together
the flour, baking powder and salt. Add the butter and rub in until
mixture resembles fine breadcrumbs. Mix in the sugar and add the
egg. Beat until the mixture forms a stiff dough and knead lightly.
Place the dough on a floured surface and roll out to line a greased
11 x 7 in (28 x 18 cm) baking tin. Place the cottage cheese and lemon
rind together in a bowl and mix well. Spread over the bottom of the
pastry. Mix the banana and sultanas together and spread on top of the
cottage cheese mixture. Evenly lay the apple slices on top of the
bananas and sprinkle with sugar and cinnamon. Pour the melted
butter on top. Bake in oven for 35–40 minutes until the top is crunchy
and golden brown. Cool in the tin and serve with whipped cream.

JELLIED RASPBERRY MELON
Serves 4–6

10 fl oz (300 ml) sieved raspberry purée
juice of 1 lemon
1 tbsp caster sugar

2 tsp gelatine
2 tbsp hot water
1 medium–sized honeydew melon

Place the raspberry purée into a small pan, add the lemon juice and
sugar to taste. Heat gently, stirring to dissolve the sugar. Remove
from the heat. Dissolve the gelatine in hot water, then pour in the
warm purée stirring constantly. Turn into a dish and chill for 35–45
minutes until the jelly has thickened but not set. Cut the melon in half
lengthways. Scrape out and discard the seeds. Scoop out some of the
flesh to enlarge the centres. Pour the jelly into the centres. Chill for
about 2 hours until set. To serve cut the melon into slices lengthways.

PEACH AND STRAWBERRY SURPRISE
Serves

1 oz (25 g) cornflour
2 eggs, separated
3 oz (75 g) caster sugar
1 pt (600 ml) milk
½ oz (10 g) gelatine

3 tbsp hot water
1 tbsp vanilla essence
1 large can of sliced peaches
12 oz (350 g) fresh strawberries

In a bowl, place the cornflour, egg yolks and 2 oz (50 g) of the sugar. Add a little cold milk and mix well. Heat the remaining milk in a saucepan over a low heat and stir in the cornflour mixture. Boil for 3 minutes stirring constantly. Remove from the heat. Dissolve the gelatine in the hot water, then stir into the milk and cornflour mixture. Add the vanilla essence. Put aside to cool. Drain and chop the peaches, but keep a few whole slices for decoration. Just as the milk mixture begins to thicken, stir in the chopped peaches. Beat the egg whites and remaining sugar together and fold into the mixture. Pour into a dampened 2 pint (1.2 ltr) ring mould and leave to set. When ready, turn out onto a serving dish and pile some strawberries in the middle. Place the remaining strawberries and peach slices alternately around the top.

BLACKBERRY AND PEAR COBBLER
Serves 4

1 lb (450 g) blackberries
1 lb (450 g) ripe cooking pears, peeled,
   cored, and sliced thickly
1 lemon, finely grated rind and juice
½ tsp ground cinnamon
8 oz (225 g) self-raising flour

pinch of salt
2 oz (50 g) butter or block margarine,
   cut into pieces
1 oz (25 g) caster sugar
¼ pt (150 ml) milk plus extra to glaze

Preheat the oven to 425°F/220°C/Gas Mk 7. Wash the blackberries. Put the blackberries and pears into a saucepan with the lemon rind and the cinnamon. Poach gently for 15 or 20 minutes until the fruit is juicy and tender. Meanwhile place the flour and salt into the bowl. Rub in the fat, then stir in the sugar. Gradually add sufficient milk to mix to a fairly soft dough. Roll out the dough on a floured work surface until ½ in (1.5 cm) thick. Cut out rounds using a 2 in (5 cm) fluted pastry cutter. Put the fruit in a pie dish and top with overlapping pastry rounds, leaving a gap in the centre. Brush the top of the pastry rounds with milk. Bake in the oven for 10–15 minutes until pastry is golden brown. Serve hot.

PINEAPPLE CREAMS
Serves 4

1 tbsp gelatine	*grated zest of ½ lemon*
2 tbsp hot water	*1 tbsp lemon juice*
15 oz (425 g) can of pineapple chunks	*12 oz (350 g) natural cottage cheese,*
2 eggs, separated	*sieved*
4 oz (110 g) caster sugar	*¼ pt (150 ml) double cream*

Melt the gelatine in the hot water. Drain the syrup from the pineapple. Whisk the egg yolks and sugar together until thick, then gradually whisk in ¼ pint (150 ml) of the pineapple syrup. Place this mixture in a saucepan, add the gelatine and stir well over a low heat until the gelatine has dissolved. Add the lemon zest and put aside to cool. Stir in the cottage cheese and lemon juice and leave until just beginning to set. Beat until smooth. Beat the cream and fold into the mixture. Whisk the egg whites until stiff. Finely chop half of the pineapple chunks. Fold the chopped pineapple and egg whites into the mixture. Put into individual serving dishes and decorate with the remaining pineapple chunks. Chill well before serving.

APPLE AND BLACKBERRY TRIFLE
Serves 6

1 lb (450 g) cooking apples, peeled,	*2 tbsp cornflour*
cored and sliced	*¾ pt (450 ml) milk*
8 oz (225 g) fresh blackberries	*2 eggs, separated*
4 tbsp water	*¼ tsp vanilla essence*
4 oz (110 g) sugar	*2 tbsp mixed nuts, chopped*
6 trifle sponges	

Place the apples and blackberries in a saucepan with the water and cook gently until fruit is tender. Stir in 3 oz (75 g) of the sugar and cook until dissolved. Crumble the sponges into the bottom of a large glass bowl. Arrange the fruit on top and leave aside to cool. Mix the cornflour together with a little of the milk to a paste, then stir in the remaining milk. Pour the mixture in to a saucepan over a low heat, stirring constantly, until the mixture has thickened. Remove from the heat, add in the beaten egg yolks, return to the heat and cook for 2 minutes, stirring. Remove from the heat and set aside, cover and leave to get cold. Stiffly whisk the egg whites, fold into the milk and cornflour mixture, adding the vanilla essence. Pour over the fruit and sprinkle with the chopped nuts and remaining sugar. Chill and serve.

APRICOT CUSTARD CREAMS
Serves 4

2 level tbsp custard powder
3 level tbsp granulated sugar
1 pt (600 ml) milk

¼ pt (150 ml) double cream
8 oz (225 g) ripe apricots
2 level tbsp caster sugar

In a basin, blend the custard powder, sugar and a little of the milk together to a smooth paste. Heat the remaining milk and when boiling, pour onto the blended custard powder, stirring all the time. Return the custard to the pan and bring back to the boil, stirring. Cook for half a minute. Remove from the heat and leave to cool for 5 minutes, stirring occasionally to prevent a skin forming. Stir in 4 tablespoons of the cream. To remove the skins easily, plunge the apricots into boiling water then into cool water. Peel off all the skins, cut in half and remove the stones. Mash the halved apricots, then stir them into the custard. Pour into 4 sundae glasses and sprinkle with the caster sugar to prevent a skin from forming . Place in a refrigerator until well chilled. To serve, whip the remaining cream until stiff and either spoon or pipe it on to the centre of each dessert.

STRAWBERRY SALAD
Serves 6

8 oz (225 g) fresh strawberries
3 kiwi fruits
½ ripe melon
orange juice (optional)

Hull the strawberries and slice down the middle. Thinly peel the kiwi fruit and cut into horizontal slices. Chop the flesh of the melon in to cubes. Mix together all the fruits and place in serving dish. If desired, the orange juice can be poured over the fruit.

AVOCADO WITH STRAWBERRY CHEESE
Serves 4

2 oz (50 g) fresh brown breadcrumbs
1 tsp ground nutmeg
1 egg, beaten
2 avocados, peeled and halved

6 oz (175 g) fresh strawberries
4 oz (110 g) cream cheese
1 egg white

Preheat the oven to 375°F/190°C/Gas Mk 5. Place the breadcrumbs and nutmeg in a bowl and mix well together. Place the beaten egg in a bowl and dip in the avocado halves making sure they are well coated. Dip the avocados in the breadcrumb and nutmeg mixture. Place each avocado half in individual ovenproof dishes. Put aside four large strawberries and chop up the remainder. Place in a bowl together with the cream cheese and mix well. Whisk the egg white until stiff and fold it in the strawberry and cheese mixture. Pile on top of each avocado leaving a small margin clear around the edges. Cook in the oven for 15 minutes. Place one reserved strawberry on top of each avocado and serve immediately.

PLUM CRISP
Serves 4–6

8–10 large ripe plums
6 slices bread, buttered
3 oz (75 g) brown sugar

1 oz (25 g) butter
caster sugar, to garnish
ground cinnamon, to garnish

Preheat the oven to 375°F/190°C/Gas Mk 5. Slice the plums in half and remove the stones. Cut off the crusts from the bread, then place the bread butter-side down in a shallow casserole dish. Sprinkle over half of the brown sugar. Lay the plums on top and sprinkle over the remaining brown sugar. Place dots of butter over the top. Cover with greased foil and bake in the oven for 25–30 minutes until the top is crisp and the plums are soft. Sprinkle with caster sugar and cinnamon and serve at once.

BRANDY ORANGES
Serves 6

3 oz (75 g) raisins
2 tbsp brandy
1 medium-sized melon

6 oranges, peeled and segmented
grated rind of 2 oranges
sherry

Place the raisins and brandy in a bowl and leave to soak. Halve the melon, remove seeds and scoop out the flesh in small balls. Place the orange, brandy raisins, melon balls and orange rind in a bowl, cover and place in refrigerator to chill well. To serve, pile the mixture into individual glass dishes and pour a little sherry over the fruit mixture.

SESAME TOFFEE APPLES
Serves 4

1 tbsp sesame seeds
4 dessert apples, peeled, cored, diced
1 tbsp cornflour

2 tbsp sugar
2 tbsp corn oil

Spread out the sesame seeds on some foil and toast under a hot grill until golden brown. Toss the apples in the cornflour. Place the oil in a small saucepan add the sugar and cook slowly until becoming a thick syrup with the little oil floating on the top and golden brown in colour. Stir in the sesame seeds. Drop in a few apple chunks at a time, remove and place on a warm serving dish. To serve, dip the apple chunks into a bowl of iced water and remove with a slotted spoon.

APPLE AND BLACKCURRANT CLANGER
Serves 6

8 oz (225 g) plain flour
4 oz (110 g) shredded suet
6–8 tbsp water
1 lb (450 g) cooking apples, peeled,
  cored and finely sliced

6 oz (175 g) blackcurrants,
  topped and tailed
3 oz (75 g) caster sugar
milk and sugar for glazing

Preheat the oven to 400°F/200°C/Gas Mk 6. Place the flour and suet in a bowl and mix with sufficient water to form a soft dough. Place the apples, blackcurrants and sugar in a bowl and mix well. Place the dough on a floured flat surface and roll out to a 10 x 8 in (25 x 20 cm) rectangle. Spread the fruit mixture over the pastry and roll up the pastry from one of the narrow ends. Place the pastry roll, seam at the bottom, on a greased baking sheet. Brush over some milk and sprinkle on a little sugar. Make three slits in the top and cook in the oven for 30–40 minutes until golden brown.

SUMMER PUDDING
Serves 6–8

8 oz (225 g) red or black currants
12 oz (350 g) cherries, stoned
8 oz (225 g) raspberries

¼ pt (150 ml) water
4–6 oz (110–175 g) sugar
6 thin slices white bread

Place all the fruit with the water and sugar in a saucepan and simmer until the sugar melts. Trim the crusts from the bread, cut each slice in half lengthwise. Line the sides of a bowl or soufflé dish with some of the bread. Cover the bottom of the dish with triangles cut from the remaining bread, reserving some for the top. Fill the dish with the fruit mixture. Cover the pudding with the last of the bread. Place a flat plate on top of the pudding, weight it down and chill in the refrigerator overnight. When ready to serve, invert onto a dish and serve with whipped cream.

PEAR CRUMBLE WITH CHEDDAR CHEESE
Serves 6

2½ oz (60 g) self-raising flour,
* plus 2½ tbsp*
5 oz (150 g) light brown sugar
2 oz (50 g) rolled oats
¼ tsp cinnamon
¼ tsp nutmeg, freshly grated
5 oz (150 g) grated mature
* Cheddar cheese*

Topping:
4 oz (110 g) unsalted butter,
* cut into bits*
pinch of salt
2 oz (50 g) chopped walnuts,
* toasted lightly*
6 firm ripe pears, peeled, cored
* and sliced*

Preheat the oven to 375°F/190°C/Gas Mk 5. Combine 2½ oz (60 g) of the flour, 3 oz (75 g) of the sugar, the oats, cinnamon, nutmeg, Cheddar cheese, butter, and salt until it is in fairly fine lumps. Stir in the walnuts. Put the pears into a bowl and stir in the remaining flour and brown sugar. Spread the mixture evenly in the base of a medium-size buttered baking dish. Sprinkle the cheese mixture over and bake in the top part of the oven for 30 minutes, or until the topping is crisp and brown. Serve warm with cream.

RASPBERRY AND MELON SALAD
Serves 8

1 lb (450 g) fresh raspberries
2–4 oz (50–110 g) caster sugar
2–3 tbsp Grand Marnier
1 ripe melon, peeled, seeded and diced

Sprinkle the raspberries with the sugar and Grand Marnier. Leave in a cool place for 1 hour. Stir the melon into the raspberries and chill well before serving.

PINEAPPLE CONDÉ

Serves 4–6

2 oz (50 g) short-grain rice
2 oz (50 g) sugar
1 pt (600 ml) milk
3 tbsp water
1 tsp powdered gelatine
15 oz (425 g) can of
 pineapple chunks

2 tbsp Kirsch
¼ pt (150 ml) whipped
 whipping cream
angelica, to decorate

Place the rice, sugar and milk in a saucepan and cook over a low heat, stirring from time to time, until the sugar has dissolved. Bring to the boil, lower the heat and simmer for 30 minutes, stirring occasionally, until all the milk has been absorbed. Remove from the heat and set aside to cool. Place the water and gelatine in a bowl standing in hot water and stir until gelatine has dissolved. Drain and reserve the syrup from the pineapple, chop up about three-quarters of the chunks. When the rice is cool, mix in the whipped cream, Kirsch and chopped pineapple. Mix together the gelatine and 8 tbsp of the pineapple syrup and leave for about 20 minutes. Place the pineapple mixture in individual glass bowls. Decorate the top of each bowl with whole pineapple chunks and pour over the gelatine mixture. Chill and decorate the top with angelica.

CRUNCHY RHUBARB LAYERS

Serves 4

1½ lb (675 g) rhubarb,
 cleaned and trimmed
3 oz (75 g) sugar
4 tbsp water
1 tsp lemon juice

½ level tsp ground ginger
1 tbsp strawberry jam
8 oz (225 g) stale cake, of any variety
whipped cream to decorate

Cut the rhubarb into 1 in (2.5 cm) pieces. Place the sugar, water, lemon juice, ginger and jam in a saucepan and heat gently until the sugar has dissolved. Add the rhubarb and simmer gently for 7–10 minutes. Stir as little as possible to prevent it from breaking up. When the rhubarb is tender, remove from the heat, pour into a bowl and leave to cool. Grate the cake into crumbs and either toast under the grill until crunchy or dry-fry the crumbs in a heavy-based frying pan until dry and crisp. Layer the rhubarb and crumbs in four individual glasses, beginning with a layer of rhubarb and top with a large swirl of whipped cream. Serve chilled.

PLUM NUT CRUNCH
Serves 6

1½ lb (675 g) plums
3 tbsp water
3–4 oz (75–110 g) soft
  brown sugar
4 oz (110 g) butter

3 oz (75 g) porridge oats
4 oz (110 g) demerara sugar
1 tsp ground cinnamon
4 oz (110 g) crushed walnuts
2 oz (50 g) sesame seeds

Preheat the oven to 350°F/180°C/Gas Mk 4. In a saucepan, cook the plums and brown sugar together with 3 tablespoons of water over a low heat until the plums are soft. Remove the plum stones and place the fruit in an ovenproof dish. Melt the butter gently in a saucepan. Stir in the porridge oats, demerara sugar, cinnamon, walnuts and sesame seeds and cook over a moderate heat for 3–4 minutes. Arrange the mixture on top of the plums and bake in the oven for 20–25 minutes until the top is golden brown.

GINGER PEARS
Serves 6–8

2 lb (900 g) fresh pears, peeled, quartered, cored, and cubed
4 pieces preserved stem ginger, halved and thinly sliced
4 tbsp syrup from the ginger jar
10 fl oz (300 ml) dry white wine
5 fl oz (150 ml) soured cream

Preheat the oven to 350°F/180°C/Gas Mk 4. Place the pears in an ovenproof dish. Mix the ginger into the pears, spoon over the syrup and pour in the wine. Bake in oven for 45–60 minutes until the pears are soft and transparent. Serve hot with the soured cream.

STUFFED PRUNES
Makes 10

10 large prunes, cooked
2 oz (50 g) ground almonds
1 oz (25 g) soft raw cane sugar

1 egg white
juice of ½ lemon

Carefully remove the prune stones leaving a pocket. Mix together the almonds, sugar, egg white and lemon juice and spoon into the prune pockets. Place in petit four paper cases or arrange on a serving dish.

GINGER FRUIT SALAD
Serves 4

2 fresh apricots
boiling water
2 dessert apples, cored and diced
1 orange, peeled and segmented
8½ fl oz (235 ml) bottle of ginger ale

2 bananas, peeled and sliced
2 tbsp lemon juice
2 oz (50 g) white seedless grapes,
   halved and seeded

Pour some boiling water in a bowl, dip in the apricots for a few seconds, drain and peel off the skin. Cut them in half, remove the stones and dice the flesh. Place the apricots, apples and orange into a bowl, pour in the ginger ale, stir lightly. Cover and leave for 1 hour. Place the banana in a bowl with the lemon juice. Add the grapes and bananas to the other fruits in the bowl and serve.

FRUITY BAKED APPLES
Serves 4

4 Bramley apples
4 tbsp chopped raisins
½ tsp ground cinnamon
1 tbsp chopped nuts

2 tsp lemon juice
2 oz (50 g) butter
2–3 tbsp brown sugar
water

Preheat the oven to 350°F/180°C/Gas Mk 4. Remove all the core from the apples. Make a cut on the peel of each apple to prevent splitting when cooking. Mix the raisins, nuts, cinnamon and lemon juice in a bowl. Stuff the mixture into the middle of each apple and arrange them on a lightly buttered shallow ovenproof dish. Place a knob of butter on top of each apple and sprinkle over some brown sugar. Pour sufficient water into the dish to cover the bottom. Place a small piece of foil on top of each apple. Bake in the oven for 40–60 minutes until soft, adding extra water if necessary. Serve at once.

CHOCO PEARS
Serves 4

½ pt (300 ml) water
juice of 1 lemon
2 oz (50 g) caster sugar
4 pears, peeled, leaving
   stalks intact

2 oz (50 g) plain chocolate,
   broken into squares
½ oz (10 g) margarine or butter
4 level tbsp golden syrup
a few pistachio nuts, optional

Place the water, lemon juice and sugar in a saucepan. Bring to the boil, add the pears, reduce the heat and poach until tender. Carefully lift out pears and drain on kitchen paper on a plate. Leave to cool. Place the chocolate and the margarine in a small basin. Measure the syrup into the basin, levelling off the spoon with a knife and making sure there is none on the underside of spoon. Place over a saucepan of boiling water for 4–5 minutes or until the chocolate has melted. Stir until smooth. Remove the pistachio nuts from their shells and chop finely. Arrange the pears in a dish. Pour a little chocolate sauce over each pear and serve the remainder separately. Sprinkle a few chopped nuts over each pear, if desired.

BANOFFEE TRIFLES
Serves 8

8 trifle sponges
3 fl oz (75 ml) sweet sherry
3 large ripe bananas, mashed
14 oz (400 g) can of sweetened
    condensed milk
¼ pt (150 ml) single cream

3 eggs
3 tbsp coffee essence or strong
    black coffee
½ pt (300 ml) double cream
some fresh fruit for decoration

Preheat the oven to 325°F/170°C/Gas Mk 3. Pour the sherry in a bowl and dip in the trifle sponges. Place the sponges in the bottom of eight individual ovenproof dishes. Add the condensed milk to the bananas, then beat in the single cream, eggs and coffee. Pour this mixture over the sponges and bake in the oven for 30 minutes until the custard has set. Remove from oven and leave to stand for 5 minutes. Whip the double cream until thick and pile on top of each trifle. Arrange some fresh fruit on top and serve at once.

CHERRY CREAMS
Serves 4

½ pt (300 ml) double cream
½ pt (300 ml) natural yoghurt
14 oz (400 g) can of stoned black cherries
caster sugar

In a bowl, whisk the cream and yoghurt together until thick. Drain the cherries and fold into the mixture. Spoon into four individual glass dishes, sprinkle with some caster sugar and chill until ready to serve.

BLACKBERRY AND APPLE SPONGE
Serves 6

8 oz (225 g) cooking apples, peeled,
  cored and sliced
8 oz (225 g) blackberries
2–3 oz (50–75 g) granulated sugar
4 oz (110 g) soft margarine

4 oz (110 g) caster sugar
2 eggs
4 oz (110 g) self-raising flour
1 tsp baking powder

Preheat the oven to 350°F/180°C/Gas Mk 4. Place the apples and blackberries in a greased 2 pint (1.2 ltr) ovenproof dish and sprinkle with granulated sugar. Place in the oven until the sponge is prepared. Beat the margarine, caster sugar, eggs, flour and baking powder until all the ingredients are well blended. Remove the dish from oven and arrange the sponge mixture over the fruit. Bake in the oven for 1 hour or until the sponge is golden brown and well risen. Serve hot.

BAHAMA BANANAS
Serves 6

6 firm ripe bananas
juice of ½ lemon
3 oz (75 g) soft light brown sugar
pinch of ground cinnamon

1 oz (25 g) butter
2–3 tbsp rum
whipped cream

Preheat the oven to 400°F/200°C/Gas Mk 6. Peel the bananas and cut in half lengthways. Arrange close together in a well-buttered baking dish and sprinkle over the lemon juice, brown sugar and cinnamon. Top with the butter in flakes. Place in the centre of the oven and bake for 15 minutes. Remove from the oven and spoon over the rum. Bake for a further 5 minutes, until bananas are soft and glazed. Serve from the dish with chilled whipped cream.

RHUBARB AND ORANGE FUDGE CRUMBLE
Serves 6

1½ lb (675 g) rhubarb
5 oz (150 g) soft brown sugar
juice of 2 oranges
4 oz (110 g) butter

4 oz (110 g) demerara sugar
10 digestive biscuits, crushed
few drops of vanilla essence
grated rind of 1 orange

Preheat the oven to 350°F/180°C/Gas Mk 4. In a saucepan, cook the rhubarb, brown sugar and orange juice over a medium heat for 15 minutes until the rhubarb is tender. Arrange in an ovenproof dish. Heat the butter and demerara sugar together in a saucepan until the butter has melted. Stir in the crushed digestive biscuits (the best way to crush the biscuits is to put them into a plastic bag and use a rolling pin). Add some vanilla essence to taste and the orange rind. Blend thoroughly. Arrange the mixture on top of the rhubarb and bake in the oven for 20–25 minutes.

PEACH & ALMOND UPSIDE DOWN
Serves 4

butter, for greasing
½ oz (10 g) caster sugar
15 oz (425 g) can of peach halves
½ oz (10 g) whole almonds, blanched and toasted
6½ oz (185 g) pkt sponge mix
1 level tsp cornflour

Preheat the oven to 375°F/190°C/Gas Mk 5. Butter a 7 in (19 cm) round ovenproof dish. Sprinkle caster sugar around the dish, leaving any surplus in the base. Drain the peaches, reserving the syrup, and cut each in half again. Arrange with the almonds over the base of the dish. Make up the sponge according to the directions on the packet. Spoon this over the fruit and bake in the oven for 35–40 minutes until golden brown and firm to the touch. Invert onto a serving plate and top with a peach glaze made from ¼ pint (150 ml) of the reserved syrup blended with the cornflour. Bring gradually to the boil, stirring continuously. Pour over the pudding.

LEMON SYLLABUB
Serves 4

½ pt (300 ml) double cream   *icing sugar to taste*
grated rind of half a lemon   *2 tbsp white wine*
juice of 2 lemons   *2 egg whites*

Whip the cream with the grated lemon rind, adding the lemon juice and wine and sifted icing sugar at intervals. When stiff, whisk the egg whites and fold in. Spoon into four individual serving glasses.

PEACHES IN BITTER-SWEET CREAM
Serves 4

¼ pt (150 ml) water
4 oz (110 g) granulated sugar
4 large peaches, peeled and sliced
2½ fl oz (75 ml) double cream

¼ pt (150 ml) natural yoghurt
1 oz (25 g) demerara sugar
1 oz (25 g) moist brown sugar,
   mixed

Heat the water and granulated sugar gently in a saucepan, stirring until sugar has completely dissolved. Simmer the syrup for 5 minutes. Add the peaches, cover and cook gently for about 5 minutes until tender. Remove the peaches from the syrup with a slotted spoon. Place in a 1½ pt (900 ml) dish or four individual dishes. Whip the cream until it is the same consistency as the yoghurt. Stir the yoghurt and cream until well mixed. Spread the yoghurt cream smoothly over the peaches. Mix the demerara and brown sugar then sprinkle over. Cover, then chill for several hours.

APPLE CHARLOTTE
Serves 6

4 tbsp demerara sugar
6 oz (175 g) shredded suet
6 oz (175 g) fresh white breadcrumbs
2 lb (900 g) cooking apples, peeled, cored and sliced

Preheat the oven to 375°F/190°C/Gas Mk 5. In a bowl, mix together the sugar, suet and breadcrumbs. In a greased ovenproof dish, place layers of apples and breadcrumb mixture alternately, starting with the apples and finishing with a top layer of breadcrumb mixture. Bake in oven for 45 minutes until top is golden brown and crisp. Serve hot.

SUNRAY FRUIT SALAD
Serves 14

½ pt (300 ml) unsweetened
   pineapple juice
8 oz (225 g) clear honey
3 x 1 lb (450 g) cans of lychees
3 large pineapples, skinned,
   cored and diced
1 lb (450 g) canned cherries,
   drained and stoned
12 kiwi fruit, peeled and
   thinly sliced

1 lb (450 g) black grapes, seeded
1 lb (450 g) blanched
   almonds, halved
4 fl oz (120 ml) lemon juice
¼ pt (150 ml) sweet white wine
2 lb (900 g) red dessert apples,
   thinly sliced
2 lb (900 g) bananas,
   peeled and sliced

Mix the pineapple juice and honey together in a large bowl. Pour in the lychees with their juice. Add the pineapple, cherries, kiwi fruit, grapes and almonds. Cover the bowl and leave overnight in a cool place. When preparing to serve, mix the white wine and lemon juice together in a bowl and dip in the prepared apples and bananas until the fruit is well coated. Add to the bowl and stir well.

BANANAS CACAO
Serves 4

3 oz (75 g) butter
3 level tbsp demerara sugar
½ large lemon, grated rind and juice
4 cardamom seeds, crushed

4 bananas, peeled
3 tbsp Crème de Cacao
cream for serving

Melt the butter in a frying pan. Add the sugar and heat gently until the sugar dissolves and caramelises to a deep golden brown. Stir the lemon rind, juice and cardamom into the pan. Cut the bananas diagonally into thick slices. Toss quickly in the pan to heat through. Pour Crème de Cacao over the bananas and ignite. Serve at once with lightly whipped or pouring cream.

CHARLOTTE MALAKOFF
Serves 6

6 oz (175 g) caster sugar
6 oz (175 g) unsalted butter,
  cut into small pieces
6 oz (175 g) ground almonds
2 drops vanilla essence
½ pt (300 ml) double cream,
  whipped

2 tbsp Kirsch or rum
24 Boudoir (or sponge finger)
  biscuits
Fruit (for example strawberries,
  peaches etc.) if desired

Line a 6 in (15 cm) loose bottomed cake tin with buttered greaseproof paper. Cream the butter and sugar together until pale and fluffy. Add the ground almonds, vanilla essence, Kirsch and fold in half the whipped cream. Dip the biscuits in the mixture and stand them up around the sides of the tin, trimming to fit. Place biscuits across the bottom of the tin, also trimming to fit. Fill with the cream mixture and chill for at least 3 hours. Remove from the tin carefully and place on a serving plate. Lay fruit on top of the filling if desired, and decorate with the remaining whipped cream. Tie a length of ribbon around to keep the gateau upright.

BANANA AND HONEY BOLSTER
Serves 6

10 oz (300 g) self-raising flour
4 oz (110 g) shredded suet
2 oz (50 g) sugar
3 oz (75 g) desiccated coconut
water or milk to mix

1 lb (450 g) bananas,
  peeled and sliced
3 tbsp thin honey
1 oz (25 g) sugar

Preheat the oven to 400°F/200°C/Gas Mk 6. Mix together the flour, suet, sugar and coconut. Stir in enough milk or water to make a soft not sticky dough. On a floured working surface roll out the pastry to a rectangle about 9 x 16 in (23 x 40 cm). Spread the bananas over the suet pastry. Spoon over 2 tablespoons of the honey and sprinkle over the sugar. Dampen the edges of the pastry with water and roll up, starting from one of the shorter sides. Place in a 2 lb (900 g) greased loaf tin and cut the top at intervals with a sharp knife. Bake in the top half of the oven for about 50 minutes. Remove from the oven and brush over the remaining honey. Serve with custard.

BAKED PEARS WITH BROWN SUGAR
Serves 6

6 firm dessert pears
3 tbsp soft light brown sugar
1 oz (25 g) butter
¼ pt (150 ml) double cream

Preheat the oven to 400°F/200°C/Gas Mk 6. Peel the pears, cut in half lengthways and scoop out the cores with a tsp. Arrange the pear halves in a buttered baking dish cut side down. Sprinkle over the sugar and top with flakes of butter. Cover with buttered greaseproof paper or kitchen foil. Bake in the centre of the oven for 20 minutes, or until the pears are tender. Remove the buttered paper, pour the cream over the hot pears and serve.

GLAZED APPLE SLICE
Serves 4

1 lb (450 g) cooking apples, peeled, cored and thinly sliced
7½ oz (210 g) pkt frozen puff pastry, just thawed
2 oz (50 g) caster sugar
3 tbsp apricot jam

Preheat the oven to 400°F/200°C/Gas Mk 6. Place the apples in a bowl of cold water to prevent browning. Roll out the pastry on a lightly floured surface to a 8½ in (22 cm) square. Transfer to a dampened baking sheet. Prick over the base with a fork. Drain the apples and arrange attractively over the pastry to within 1 in (2.5 cm) of the edge. Sprinkle with the caster sugar and bake for about 25 minutes until the pastry is cooked and the apples are tender. Melt the apricot jam and brush over the top. Serve warm or cold with whipped or clotted cream.

RASPBERRY RING
Serves 8–10

4 tbsp water	*1 lb (450 g) fresh or*
½ oz (10 g) gelatine	*frozen raspberries*
8 oz (225 g) cottage cheese	*1 tbsp clear honey (optional)*
¾ pt (450 ml) thick natural yoghurt	*8 oz (225 g) fresh raspberries*

Place the water in a bowl and stir in the gelatine. Stand the bowl in a pan of boiling water to dissolve the gelatine. Remove from the heat and leave to cool. Press the cottage cheese through a sieve into a large mixing bowl and stir in the yoghurt. Press the raspberries through a sieve into a separate bowl, discarding the pips. Stir the cooled gelatine into the raspberry purée and carefully fold into the cheese and yoghurt mixture. Add the honey if desired. Pour into a 2 pint (1.2 ltr) wetted ring mould and put into the refrigerator to set. Before serving, remove from mould and fill the centre of the ring with fresh raspberries.

LAYERED GOOSEBERRY BAKE
Serves 6

6 oz (175 g) fresh white breadcrumbs	*butter, for greasing*
2 oz (50 g) shredded suet	*4 fl oz (125 ml) golden syrup*
1 lb (450 g) gooseberries	*2 fl oz (60 ml) water*
3 oz (75 g) demerara sugar	

Preheat the oven to 350°F/180°C/Gas Mk 4. Mix the breadcrumbs and suet together, and the gooseberries and sugar together separately. Butter a pie dish and put the breadcrumb mix and the fruit mix in layers in the pie dish, finishing with a layer of the breadcrumb mixture. Warm the golden syrup with the water and spoon carefully over the pudding. Bake for 50 minutes until golden and crispy on top.

FRUIT IN BUTTERSCOTCH SAUCE
Serves 4

2 oz (50 g) butter
6 oz (75 g) soft light
   brown sugar
4 oz (110 g) golden syrup
¼pt (150 ml) whipping cream

½tsp vanilla essence
1 lb (450 g) strawberries,
   washed and hulled
2 bananas, sliced
whipped cream, to serve

Place the butter, sugar and syrup in a small saucepan and cook over a very low heat until the sugar has melted. Simmer for 5 minutes. Add the cream and vanilla essence, stir well and simmer for 2 minutes. Beat the mixture and pour into a container, cover and leave to cool. Store in a refrigerator for a few hours before using. Place the strawberries and bananas in a serving bowl. Stir the sauce until well blended and pour some over the fruit. Leave the remainder to be served separately together with the whipped cream.

PEAR AND GINGER PUDDING
Serves 6–8

4 oz (110 g) butter,
   cut into small pieces
4 oz (110 g) soft brown sugar
8 oz (225 g) self-raising flour

3 tsp ground ginger
3 eggs
4 tbsp black treacle
4 pears, peeled, cored and sliced

Preheat the oven to 350°F/180°C/Gas Mk 4. Beat the butter in a bowl, gradually adding in the sugar. In another bowl, mix together the flour and ginger. Beat the eggs in the butter mixture one at a time, alternating with the flour and ginger. Beat in the treacle. Arrange the pears in a buttered ovenproof dish. Spoon the pudding mixture over the pears, smooth over the top and bake in the oven for 35–40 minutes until golden brown.

HAZELNUT PEAR CONDÉ
Serves 4

1 pt (600 ml) milk
3 oz (75 g) pudding rice
4 level tbsp caster sugar
2 oz (50 g) ground hazelnuts
¼pt (150 ml) single cream

2 firm eating pears, peeled,
   cored and sliced
water
a strip of thinly pared lemon rind
whole hazelnuts to decorate

Bring the milk to the boil with the rice and 2 level tablespoons of the caster sugar. Lower the heat, partially cover the pan and simmer very gently, stirring occasionally, until the rice is tender and almost all the liquid has been absorbed. This should be about 30 minutes. Allow to cool, stir in the ground hazelnuts and cream. Turn into 4 stemmed glasses. Place the pears in a pan with the remaining sugar, water to cover and lemon rind. Simmer gently until tender. Remove the pears, drain, arrange over the rice. Discard the lemon rind and simmer the juice rapidly to reduce to about 4 tablespoons. Spoon over the pear slices. Chill. Serve decorated with whole hazelnuts.

GOOSEBERRY MACAROON CRUNCH
Serves 6

1 lb (450 g) gooseberries, topped and tailed
2 tbsp water
4 oz (110 g) caster sugar
2 tbsp Kirsch
4 oz (110 g) French almond macaroons (ratafias), crumbled
¼ pt (150 ml) whipping cream
3 macaroons or 6 ratafias, to decorate

Cook the gooseberries with the water and sugar for 10–15 minutes until the fruit is soft and well reduced. Push through a sieve. Stir in the Kirsch. Chill for 30 minutes. Arrange the macaroon crumbs and gooseberry purée in alternate layers in 6 tall glasses. Chill in the refrigerator for several hours for the flavours to mellow. Whip the cream until it just holds its shape. Spoon some of the soft cream over each glass and top each with a halved macaroon or whole ratafias. Serve immediately.

BAKED PEACHES
Serves 6

6 large peaches, peeled,
  halved and stoned
½ oz (10 g) butter
1 oz (25 g) caster sugar

1 egg yolk
2 oz (50 g) macaroons, crushed
1 tbsp ground almonds
pinch of ground cinnamon

Preheat the oven to 350°F/180°C/Gas Mk 4. Arrange the peach halves cut-side up in buttered ovenproof dish. In a bowl, mix together the sugar, egg yolk, macaroons, almonds and cinnamon. Divide the mixture equally and pile on top of each peach half. Bake in the oven for 25 minutes.

BLUEBERRY OAT CRUMBLE
Serves 8

2 lb (900 g) blueberries
4 oz (110 g) light soft brown sugar,
  plus 3 tbsp
4 oz (110 g) plain flour, plus 2 tbsp
2 tbsp lemon juice

4 oz (110 g) butter
3 oz (75 g) rolled oats
2 oz (50 g) walnut halves,
  chopped and toasted

Preheat the oven to 375°F/190°C/Gas Mk 5. Place the blueberries,
3 tablespoons of the sugar, 2 tablespoons of the flour and the lemon
juice in a bowl and mix well. Arrange in a 2½ pint (1.5 ltr) pie dish.
For the topping, place the butter and remaining flour in a bowl and
rub in. Mix in the remaining sugar, oats and nuts. Evenly arrange on
top of the blueberries and lightly press down with the back of a
spoon. Bake in the oven for 30–35 minutes until the crumble is golden
brown. Can be served hot or cold.

APPLE AND WALNUT SURPRISE
Serves 6

4 oz (110 g) self-raising flour
2 oz (50 g) butter, melted
1 egg
1 tsp vanilla essence
2 tsp lemon rind, grated

2 oz (50 g) caster sugar
6 oz (175 g) stoned dates, chopped
2 tbsp chopped walnuts
4 medium cooking apples,
  cored and diced

Preheat the oven to 400°F/200°C/Gas Mk 6. Place the flour in a bowl.
Make a well in the centre and pour in the butter, egg, vanilla essence
and lemon rind. Mix thoroughly using a wooden spoon. Add in the
sugar, dates, walnuts and apples and mix well. Arrange the mixture in
a greased shallow ovenproof dish and bake in oven for 50–60 minutes
until risen and deep golden brown in colour. Cut into squares
and serve.

BAKED FIG AND ORANGE PUDDING
Serves 4–5

4 oz (110 g) margarine,
  cut into small pieces
4 oz (110 g) soft brown sugar
2 large eggs

1 orange, grated rind and juice
4 oz (110 g) self-raising flour
4 oz (110 g) figs, chopped
1 tbsp demerara sugar

Preheat the oven to 350°F/180°C/Gas Mk 4. Cream the margarine and brown sugar together until soft and fluffy. Add the eggs one at a time and beat well after each addition. Beat in the orange rind. Fold in the flour together with the figs and orange juice. Turn the mixture into a 1½ pt (900 ml) greased ovenproof dish. Leave the top uncovered and bake just above the centre of the oven for 1 hour until firm and springy to the touch. Remove from the oven and sprinkle over the demerara sugar. Serve with cream.

SPICED DRIED FRUIT COMPOTE
Serves 4

1 tbsp jasmine tea
½ tsp ground cinnamon
¼ tsp ground cloves
½ pt (300 ml) boiling water
4 oz (110 g) dried apricots, soaked
  overnight, drained

4 oz (110 g) dried prunes, soaked
  overnight, drained and stoned
4 oz (110 g) dried apple rings
¼ pt (150 ml) dry white wine
2 oz (50 g) sugar
toasted flaked almonds, to decorate

Put the tea, cinnamon and cloves in a bowl, pour in the boiling water and leave for 20 minutes. Put the dried fruit in a saucepan, then strain in the tea and spice liquid. Add the wine and sugar. Heat gently until the sugar has dissolved. Simmer for 20 minutes until tender, then cover and leave for 1–2 hours until cold. Turn the compote into a serving bowl and chill for at least 2 hours. Sprinkle with almonds just before serving.

PINEAPPLE ROMANOFF
Serves 6–8

1 large pineapple, skinned,
  cored and cut into segments
6 tbsp icing sugar
3 tbsp Cointreau

3 tbsp rum
½ pt (300 ml) double cream
3 tbsp Kirsch
grated rind of 1 orange

Toss the pineapple segments with 4 tablespoons of the icing sugar. Arrange the segments in a bowl suitable for serving, and pour over them a mixture of Cointreau and rum. Chill in the refrigerator. One hour before serving, whip the cream, add the remaining icing sugar and flavour with Kirsch. Spoon whipped cream onto the marinated pineapple pieces, tossing until every piece is coated with the creamy liqueur mixture. Top with finely grated orange rind and keep cold until time to serve.

BLACKCURRANT SHORTCAKE
Serves 3–4

8 oz (225 g) fresh blackcurrants
1 tbsp caster sugar
4 oz (110 g) plain flour
½ tsp baking powder

1½ oz (35 g) butter
cut into small pieces
2½ oz (60 g) soft brown sugar

Preheat the oven to 350°F/180°C/Gas Mk 4. Arrange the blackcurrants all over the base of an 8 in (20 cm) lightly-buttered sandwich tin, approximately 1¼ in (3 cm) deep. Sprinkle the caster sugar over them. Measure the flour and baking powder into a mixing bowl, then rub the butter into the flour until the mixture is crumbly. Next add the brown sugar and stir it evenly into the mixture. Now spread the whole amount over the fruit in the tin, use a fork to even it out and press down. Bake in the oven for 25–30 minutes. This is delicious served with ice cream or whipped cream

PLUM DOWDY
Serves 4

6 slices, white or brown bread
3 oz (75 g) butter
1½ lb (675 g) purple cooking plums,
washed, halved and stoned

2 tbsp golden syrup
2 tbsp water
2 oz (50 g) brown sugar

Preheat the oven to 375°F/190°C/Gas Mk 5. Grease a deep baking dish. Butter the bread slices on one side only. Line the base and sides of the dish with half the slices, butter side upwards. Place the plums in the centre of the dish, cut sides upwards. Place the water and syrup in a pan over a low heat, stirring constantly until smooth and runny. Pour the syrup over the fruit. Cover with the remaining bread slices, butter side up and sprinkle over the sugar. Bake in the centre of the oven for 1½ hours. Serve warm or cold.

PLUM AND SULTANA BAKE
Serves 6–8

2 x 1¼ lb (560 g) cans of
  red plums in syrup
9 oz (250 ml) self–raising flour
1 tsp salt
¼ tsp grated nutmeg

2 oz (50 g) lard
2 oz (50 g) caster sugar
3 oz (75 g) sultanas
7 fl oz (200 ml) natural yoghurt

Preheat the oven to 400°F/200°C/Gas Mk 6. Drain the plums and reserve the syrup. Stone the plums and place in a 2½ pint (1.5 ltr) pie dish. Pour in enough syrup to cover the fruit. Place the flour, salt and nutmeg in a bowl and rub in the lard. Stir in the sugar and sultanas. After making a well in the centre of the mixture, pour in the yoghurt and mix to a soft dough. Divide the dough into 8 small thick rounds and arrange on top of the plums. Bake in the oven for 35 minutes. Serve hot.

FRESH PEACHES MARSALA
Serves 6

2 lemons, grated rind and juice
3 tbsp light brown sugar
4 tbsp Marsala or sweet sherry

6 fresh peaches
¼ pt (150 ml) double cream

Preheat the oven to 170°C/325°F/Gas Mk 3. Put the lemon rind and juice, sugar and Marsala in the base of an ovenproof dish which is large enough to hold the peaches in a single layer. Make a small cross on the top of each peach and arrange in the dish. Cover and bake for 15–25 minutes until just tender. Check after 15 minutes because very ripe peaches will become too soft if cooked for longer. Cool in the dish. Carefully peel away the skins and place on a serving dish. Spoon over the juice and chill. If liked, reserve half the juice and whip with the cream to make a Marsala syllabub to accompany them.

STUFFED APRICOTS
Makes 10

10 large dried apricots
2 oz (50 g) low-fat soft cheese
2 oz (50 g) desiccated coconut

Wash the apricots and remove the stones leaving the pocket in the fruit. Mix together the cheese and coconut and spoon into the apricot pockets. Place apricots in petit four paper cases or arrange on a serving dish.

BAKED SPICED PEARS
Serves 6

6 pears, Conference or
hard cooking variety
water
½ lemon, rind and juice

4 cloves
4 whole allspice
1 tbsp demerara sugar
1 tbsp pear liqueur (optional)

Preheat the oven to 300°F/150°C/Gas Mk 1. Wash the pears leaving the stalks attached. Do not peel but remove the cores. If the pears are very large, then halve them. Place the pears in an ovenproof dish and almost cover with water. Add the rind of the lemon and the juice of half a lemon. Add the spices, sugar and liqueur (if required) and cook in oven for 1½ to 2 hours.

CHERRIES JUBILEE
Serves 4

1 lb (450 g) can of stoned dark cherries
2 level tbsp sugar
1 stick cinnamon
½ orange, juice and grated rind

1 tsp cornflour
4 tbsp cognac
4 tbsp cherry brandy
vanilla ice cream

Drain the cherries and measure out ½ pint (300 ml) of the juice. Combine the sugar, cinnamon, orange juice, grated orange rind, cornflour and cherry juice and bring slowly to a boil in a saucepan. Allow to bubble for 5 minutes stirring occasionally. Add the cherries and heat through. Heat the cognac and cherry brandy and pour over the cherries. Ignite and ,when the flames die down, pour the hot mixture over individual portions of vanilla ice cream.

SUGARED BRANDY PEACHES
Serves 4

4 fresh peaches, skinned and halved
10 tbsp brandy
2 tbsp demerara sugar

Put the peach halves in a flameproof dish cut side down and spoon over the brandy. Leave for 2 hours, turning once or twice. Just before serving make sure each peach is cut side down and sprinkle with demerara sugar. Remove the apricots from the dish. Cook under a preheated grill for 10 minutes. Return to the dish. Serve immediately with whipped cream. The peaches may also be served in individual dishes if preferred.

FRUIT BERRY SALAD
Serves 6

4 passion fruits
2 mangoes, peeled and sliced
8 oz (225 g) blueberries
8 oz (225 g) loganberries

8 oz (225 g) raspberries
2 tbsp sugar
1 lime, juice and grated zest
1 tsp angostura bitters

Cut the passion fruit in half and scoop out the flesh. Place in a sieve over a large bowl. Push the flesh through the sieve discarding the seeds. Combine the flesh with the mangoes and berries, sprinkle with sugar, add the lime juice and zest, and bitters and toss well. Chill for at least 2 hours before serving.

PLUM BANANA PUDDING
Serves 4

2 tbsp plum jam
2 bananas, peeled and sliced
4 oz (110 g) butter, cut into
* small pieces*

4 oz (110 g) sugar
4 oz (110 g) flour
2 beaten eggs

Preheat the oven to 375°F/190°C/Gas Mk 5. Place the jam in the bottom of a greased pudding basin and cover with the bananas. Cream the butter and sugar together in a bowl. Blend in the flour and add the eggs. Beat well and pile on top of the bananas. Cover and bake in the oven for 1¼–1½ hours. Turn out onto a warm dish and serve.

FRUIT COMPOTE
Serves 4

1½ lb (675 g) mixed fresh
  redcurrants and blackcurrants
10 oz (300 g) sugar
1 tbsp water

2 tbsp brandy
whipped cream
sponge finger biscuits

In a saucepan, place the fruit, sugar and water and gently heat until the sugar has dissolved. Turn off the heat, pour in the brandy and stir well. Leave to cool and pour into individual serving dishes. Chill in the refrigerator for about 3 hours. Decorate with whipped cream and serve accompanied with sponge finger biscuits.

BANANAS RIO
Serves 6

6 medium ripe bananas
4 fl oz (125 ml) orange juice
1 tbsp lemon juice
1½ oz (35 g) brown sugar
pinch of salt
2 oz (50 g) butter
3 oz (75 g) coconut, freshly grated, or desiccated coconut

Preheat the oven to 400°F/200°C/Gas Mk 6. Place the bananas in a buttered shallow casserole dish. In a bowl, mix together the orange and lemon juices, brown sugar and salt and pour over the bananas. Place small knobs of butter over the top and bake in the oven for 10–15 minutes. Sprinkle with coconut and serve.

STRAWBERRY SNOW
Serves 4

1 lb (450 g) ripe strawberries
2 egg whites
4 oz (110 g) sugar
4 fl oz (120 ml) thick double cream
few drops of vanilla essence

Purée the strawberries, then place in a bowl together with the egg whites and sugar. Beat well until stiff and glossy. Stiffly whisk the cream and vanilla essence together and fold into the strawberry mixture. Pile into individual glass dishes, chill and serve.

CHOCOLATE BANANAS
Serves 4

8 oz (225 g) plain chocolate, broken into pieces
4 bananas, peeled and halved
8 oz (225 g) unsalted peanuts, chopped

Place the chocolate in a basin over a saucepan of hot water and leave until melted. Remove the melted chocolate from the heat, cool slightly, then dip in each banana half. Place the peanuts on a shallow plate and roll in the chocolate bananas. Line a tray with greaseproof paper, place on the bananas and chill until firm.

DANISH APPLE DELIGHT
Serves 4

1 lb (450 g) cooking apples, peeled, cored and sliced
¼ pt (150 ml) apple juice
1½ oz (35 g) macaroon biscuits
½ pt (300 ml) double cream

Place the apples and apple juice in a saucepan and cook gently until tender. Leave to cool and pile into four individual glass dishes. Crumble the biscuits and arrange on top of the apples. Chill until cold. Whip the cream until it reaches soft peak stage. Spoon into each dish. Chill well before serving.

FRUIT KEBABS
Serves 8

8 fl oz (225 ml) clear honey
6 tbsp lemon juice
4 oz (110 g) butter
4 dessert apples, cored and diced

4 pears, cored and diced
2 small melons, cored and diced
24 cherries

In a saucepan stir the honey, lemon juice and butter over low heat until well blended. Remove from the heat and dip the fruit into the sauce. Thread fruit alternately on to long metal skewers and cook under grill the on a low heat until the fruit is glazed and heated through. Brush with the sauce from time to time and turn often.

BANANA FLAMBÉ
Serves 6

6 bananas
2 oz (50 g) butter
3 oz (75 g) soft brown sugar
juice of 1 orange
toasted almonds
rum

Peel and halve the bananas. Put the butter and sugar in a large frying pan and heat slowly until golden brown. Add the orange juice. Add the bananas and simmer for 2–3 minutes, turning over once, until golden brown. Sprinkle with rum. Allow the rum to get warm for a few moments and flame it with a match. Serve sprinkled with toasted almonds and with whipped cream.

PINEAPPLE AMBROSIA
Serves 4

3 oz (75 g) marshmallows
1 fresh pineapple (or 12 oz (350 g) can of pineapple, drained)
¼ pt (150 ml) double cream
2 level tsp caster sugar
8 maraschino cherries, chopped
sugar-frosted mint leaves, for decoration

Scissor-snip the marshmallows into quarters (dip the scissors in hot water to prevent sticking). Remove the peel and core from the pineapple. Chop the flesh finely and combine with the marshmallows. Chill. Just before serving, whip the cream with the sugar and fold into the pineapple with the chopped cherries. Pile into 4 glasses. To decorate, lightly brush the mint leaves with egg white and sprinkle with caster sugar. Leave to dry for a short time and use to decorate the dishes.

MOUSSES AND JELLIES

APRICOT CHIFFON
Serves 4-6

4¼ oz (125 g) packet lemon jelly
¼ pt (150 ml) boiling water
15 oz (425 g) can apricot halves

½ pt (300 ml) double cream
16 langue de chat biscuits

Dissolve the jelly in the boiling water. Drain the apricots and add the syrup to the jelly to make it up to ¾ pint (450 ml). Chill until it starts to set. Reserve 5 apricot halves and chop the rest into quarters. Whip the cream until it stands in soft peaks. Whisk the setting jelly until it is foamy, then whisk in the cream. Fold in the chopped apricots and turn into a 1 lb (450 g) loaf tin. Chill until set. To serve, turn the apricot chiffon out onto a serving dish. Decorate the sides of the chiffon with langue de chat biscuits and top with the reserved apricots.

CITRUS HONEYCOMB MOULD
Serves 4-6

1 orange
1 small lemon
¾ pt (450 ml) milk

2 eggs
2½ oz (60 g) caster sugar
½ oz (10 g) gelatine

Scrub the orange and the lemon and remove the rind from both very carefully taking care not to include the white pith. Place the rinds in a small saucepan, add the milk and bring to the boil slowly. Remove from the heat and leave to infuse for 15 minutes. Separate the eggs, placing the whites in a very clean bowl and beating the yolks with the sugar in a separate bowl until thick and creamy. Strain the milk onto the egg yolks, return to the saucepan and stir over a low heat. Cook for 2 minutes, when the mixture should have separated. Squeeze the juice from the orange and lemon and sprinkle the gelatine onto the juice. Leave to soften and then pour the milk over and stir until the gelatine has dissolved. Whisk the egg whites until stiff and add to the milk mixture. Fold in with a metal spoon when the whites will float to the surface. Pour into a 1½ pint (900 ml) mould, which has been rinsed out with cold water, and leave to set. To turn out the mousse, dip the mould in a bowl of hot water briefly and invert onto a serving dish. Chill in the refrigerator until ready to serve.

STRAWBERRY FOAM
Serves 8

1 oz (25 g) powdered gelatine
½pt (300 ml) water
1 pt (600 ml) strawberry purée made
  from 2 lb (900 g) strawberries

2 egg whites
6 tbsp evaporated milk
4 oz (110 g) small whole
  strawberries

Put the water in a small bowl and sprinkle the gelatine on top. Place over a saucepan of simmering water and stir to dissolve. When it has dissolved stir the gelatine into the puréed strawberries. Put in a cool place, stirring frequently, until the mixture begins to thicken. When it is just starting to set, add the egg whites and evaporated milk and beat until foamy with an electric mixer, if possible, or a rotary whisk. Divide the mixture between eight glass serving dishes and leave to set. Just before serving put a swirl of whipped cream on top of each dish and decorate with the whole strawberries.

SCOTTISH CREAMS
Serves 6

6 tbsp thin-shred marmalade
1 oz (25 g) caster sugar
4 tbsp whisky

juice of 1 lemon
½pt (300 ml) double cream

Put the marmalade, sugar, whisky and lemon juice in a bowl and mix well. Whip the cream until fairly stiff and gradually whisk it into the marmalade mixture. Divide the mixture between six small serving glasses.

SYLLABUB
Serves 6

1 small lemon
3 oz (75 g) caster sugar
¼pt (150 ml) white wine
2 tbsp sweet sherry
10 fl oz (300 ml) carton of double cream

Wash and scrub the lemon. Squeeze out all the juice and grate the rind of half the lemon. Place the rind, lemon juice, sugar, white wine and sherry in a bowl. Stir well and leave in a cool place for 2 hours. Add the cream to the bowl and whisk until thick. Place spoonfuls of syllabub into 6 small glass serving dishes. Leave in a cool place for several hours before serving. The syllabub should have a creamy foam layer on top and a liquid layer below.

ST CLEMENT'S FOOL
Serves 6

4 large oranges
3 level tsp powdered gelatine
1½ tsp lemon juice
½ pt (300 ml) apple purée made
  from 1 lb (450 g) cooking apples

½ level tsp ground ginger
caster sugar
7 fl oz (210 ml) buttermilk
2 egg whites

Cut three oranges in half with a sharp, serrated knife and carefully remove the orange flesh. Cut the flesh into small pieces, removing all skin and pith. Clean out the orange halves. Sprinkle the gelatine on top of the lemon juice in a small bowl and place the bowl over a saucepan of simmering water until the gelatine dissolves. Mix together the apple purée, which should be quite firm and free from juice, lemon juice and gelatine and ginger, and add sugar to taste. Add the orange pieces and buttermilk and stir well. Leave in a cool place, stirring frequently, until it starts to thicken. Whisk the egg whites until stiff and fold into the apple mixture when it is on the point of setting. Spoon into the orange cases and decorate with twists of fresh orange cut from the fourth orange.

RHUBARB AND ORANGE FOOL
Serves 6

1 lb (450 g) rhubarb,
  washed and chopped
1 orange, grated rind and juice
pinch of cinnamon
1–2 oz (25–50 g) sugar

½ pt (300 ml) whipping cream
1 tsp orangeflower water
shredded orange rind for decoration
sponge fingers to serve

Put the rhubarb, orange rind, orange juice, cinnamon and sugar in a saucepan. Cover and heat gently for 15 minutes. Remove the lid and boil quickly for 10 minutes, stirring frequently until the mixture is thick. Remove from the heat and leave to cool for 1 hour. Stiffly whip the cream and fold into the mixture together with the orangeflower water. Pile into individual serving dishes and chill for 1–2 hours. Decorate with orange rind and serve with sponge fingers.

GOOSEBERRY CUSTARD FOOL
Serves 6

1 lb (450 g) gooseberries,
topped and tailed
4 oz (110 g) granulated sugar
3½ level tbsp custard powder

2 level tbsp caster sugar
1 pt (600 ml) milk
whipped cream for decoration

Wash the gooseberries and place in a medium-sized saucepan with 2 tbsp water. Bring to the boil, cover and simmer for 8–10 minutes until the gooseberries are tender. Stir in the sugar. Put the gooseberries in a sieve set over a bowl. Make a purée by pressing the gooseberries through the sieve with the back of a spoon. Alternatively, liquidise in an electric blender and strain. Make 1 pint (600 ml) of custard, as directed on the package, using the custard powder, caster sugar and milk. Beat the gooseberry purée into the custard, leave to cool slightly, then divide the mixture between six individual serving dishes. Leave to cool. Just before serving, top each glass with some whipped cream.

MOCHA MOUSSE
Serves 6

2 large eggs
2 oz (50 g) caster sugar
2 oz (50 g) custard powder
1 pt (600 ml) milk
2 level tbsp instant coffee powder
3 oz (75 g) grated plain chocolate

Separate the eggs and put the yolks and the whites into separate bowls. Beat the sugar into the egg yolks. Blend the custard powder with a little of the milk to make a smooth paste, then stir it into the sugar and egg yolk mixture. Heat the remaining milk with the coffee powder and, when it is just below boiling point, pour it onto the custard mixture, stirring all the time. Return the liquid to the pan and, stirring continuously over low heat, bring the custard to the boil. Leave the mixture to cool, stirring it occasionally to prevent a skin from forming. When the custard is cold, whisk the egg whites until they form stiff peaks. Using a metal spoon, fold them into the mixture with two-thirds of the grated chocolate. Divide the mousse between four small glass serving dishes and sprinkle each with a little of the remaining chocolate.

HONEY MOUSSE
Serves 6

3 eggs, separated
4 oz (110 g) caster sugar
finely grated rind of 2 lemons
6 tbsp lemon juice
2 tsp powdered gelatine

½ pt (300 ml) whipping cream
2 tbsp clear honey
chopped nuts and grated
chocolate to decorate

Put the egg yolks, sugar and lemon rind in a bowl and whisk thoroughly until thick. Stir in 3 tbsp of the lemon juice and set the bowl over a saucepan of simmering water until the mousse thickens. Remove the bowl from the saucepan and set aside to cool, whisking occasionally. Put the gelatine and remaining lemon juice in a bowl and set over a saucepan of simmering water, stirring until the gelatine has dissolved. Whip the cream and whisk the egg whites until stiff. Fold half the cream into the mousse together with the gelatine liquid, honey and egg whites. Pile into a 2 pint (1.2 ltr) glass bowl and decorate with the remaining cream, nuts and chocolate.

COFFEE CREAM MOUSSE
Serves 4

1 oz (25 g) cornflour
1 tbsp cocoa powder
2 tbsp instant coffee powder
3 oz (75 g) caster sugar
¾ pt (450 ml) milk

2 eggs, separated
½ oz (10 g) gelatine
3 tbsp hot water
¼ pt (150 ml) thick cream

Put the cornflour, cocoa, powder coffee powder and 1 oz (25 g) of the sugar in a bowl and mix well. Blend together with 5 tbsp of the milk. Heat the remaining milk in a saucepan, then pour onto the cornflour mixture. Stir, then return the mixture to the saucepan. Bring to the boil and cook for 3 minutes, stirring continuously. Lower the heat, beat the egg yolks and add to the mixture. Cook for several minutes but do not boil. Dissolve the gelatine in the hot water and then stir into the milk mixture. Remove from the heat and set aside to cool. Whisk the egg whites and remaining sugar in a bowl until stiff. Fold the cream and egg whites into the milk mixture and pour into a dampened 2 pint (1.2 ltr) mould. Leave to set before turning out onto a serving dish.

CITRUS WHIP
Serves 6

¼ pt (150 ml) water
1 packet lemon jelly
grated rind of 1 lemon
juice of 2 lemons

3 large eggs
6 oz (175 g) caster sugar
4 slices of lemon to decorate

Dissolve the jelly in the water over a medium heat. Stir in the lemon rind and juice and put to one side. Separate the eggs, putting the whites and yolks in separate bowls. Add the sugar to the yolks and beat them until light in colour and creamy in consistency. Stir in the melted jelly. Whisk the egg whites until they form stiff peaks, then, using a metal spoon, fold them into the lemon mixture. Turn the dessert into a serving dish and leave it in a cool place overnight to set. Decorate with lemon slices before serving.

SYRUP AND ORANGE MOUSSE
Serves 4

3 eggs, separated
1 large orange
6 oz (175 g) maple syrup
½ oz (10 g) gelatine
1 pt (600 ml) natural yoghurt

Put the egg yolks in a small bowl set over a saucepan of simmering water and add the grated rind of half the orange. Stir over a low heat until thickened, then remove from the heat. Stir in the syrup. Squeeze the juice from the orange, and melt the gelatine in the orange juice in a small saucepan over low heat. Do not boil. Stir this mixture into the egg yolks and leave until it is just starting to set. Whisk the egg whites until stiff. Stir the yoghurt into the yolks and syrup, then fold in the egg whites. Pour the mixture into a serving dish and leave to set in a cool place for 2 hours.

BLACKCURRANT CROWN MOUSSE
Serves 4–6

1 packet blackcurrant jelly
¼ pt (150 ml) boiling water
10 oz (300 g) can of blackcurrants

1 small can evaporated milk, chilled
¼ pt (150 ml) double cream

Break the jelly into pieces and dissolve it in the boiling water. Drain the blackcurrants, reserving the juice, and, when the jelly has melted, stir the juice into the jelly and make it up to ¾ pt (450 ml) with cold water. Reserve a few whole blackcurrants for decoration and rub the rest through a sieve to make a purée. Whisk the evaporated milk until it is thick and leaves a trail when the whisk is lifted out. Lightly whip the cream. Mix the purée into the cold jelly, then fold in the evaporated milk and cream. Pour the mousse mixture into a 1½ pint (900 ml) greased jelly mould and leave it in a cool place to set overnight if possible. Dip the mould into hot water briefly, then turn the mouse out onto a serving dish and decorate it with the reserved blackcurrants.

APRICOT FOOL
Serves 6

2 lb (900 g) fresh ripe apricots
4 tbsp water
5 oz (150 g) caster sugar

2 tbsp Curacao liqueur
½ pt (300 ml) soured cream

Stone the apricots and stew them gently with the water and sugar until tender. Purée through a sieve or in a blender until smooth. Cool. Stir the Curacao into the cold apricot purée and adjust the sweetening if necessary. Layer alternative spoonfuls of apricot mixture and soured cream into a large glass dish or six individual serving glasses. Chill before serving.

CARIBBEAN MOUSSE
Serves 4

1 packet lime jelly
¼ pt (150 ml) water
juice of 2 lemons

rind of 1 lemon
4 large eggs, separated
6 oz (175 g) caster sugar

Melt the jelly in a saucepan with the water over gentle heat. Remove the pan from the heat and stir in the lemon juice and rind. Leave to cool slightly. Beat the egg yolks and sugar together until creamy in colour and texture and then stir into the cooling jelly. Leave until almost set. Whisk the egg whites until they are very stiff and fold carefully into the mixture with a metal spoon as lightly and evenly as possible. Turn the mousse into a glass bowl and leave until set.

GOOSEBERRY AND HAZELNUT FOOL
Serves 10

1½ lb (675 g) gooseberries
2 elderflower heads
4 oz (110 g) low-fat cream cheese
1 oz (25 g) clear honey
1 pt (600 ml) thick set
  natural yoghurt

½ oz (10 g) gelatine
6 tbsp hot water
4 oz (110 g) toasted hazelnuts,
  finely chopped

Wash, top and tail the gooseberries and place in a saucepan with enough water to cover. Add the elderflower heads. Cover and cook until soft – about 20 minutes. Discard the elderflower heads. Drain the gooseberries, and liquidise in a blender or press the fruit through a sieve. Pour the purée into a bowl and mix with the cheese and honey. Add the yoghurt. Dissolve the gelatine in the hot water and when it has cooled, stir it into the purée. Fold in the nuts, reserving a few for decoration.

LEMON ISLAND RING
Serves 6

2 packets lemon jelly
½ level tsp cinnamon
½ level tsp grated nutmeg
rind and juice of 1 lemon

4 oz (110 g) caster sugar
¼ pt (150 ml) double cream
¼ pt (150 ml) single cream
1 x 10 oz (300 g) tin apple purée

Make the jelly using slightly less than the amount of water directed on the packets. Stir in the spices, grated rind and juice of the lemon and the caster sugar, and leave to set. Brush a 3 pint (1.8 ltr) ring mould with a little oil. Mix the creams together and whip until firm. Using a metal spoon fold in the setting jelly, together with the apple purée. Pour into the ring mould and leave until set. Turn out onto a serving plate.

APPLE-BERRY FOOL
Serves 4

2 eating apples, peeled and cored
lemon juice
1 lb (450 g) raspberries, hulled
3 level tbsp granulated sugar

1 level tbsp custard powder
¼ pt (150 ml) milk
¼ pt (150 ml) double cream
cream to decorate

Cut four thin slices of apple for decoration and sprinkle with lemon juice to prevent browning. Reserve four whole raspberries for decoration. Roughly chop the remaining apple and place in a pan with the raspberries and sugar. Cook gently to a pulp, then sieve to remove pips. Blend the custard powder with a little milk and heat the rest of the milk in a saucepan. Pour the hot milk onto the blended custard powder, stirring, then return to the pan and stir over a gentle heat until the custard thickens. Beat the custard into the fruit pulp and cool. Whip the cream until 'floppy' and fold it into the fruit mixture. Spoon into four serving glasses and chill. Decorate each glass with a spoonful of whipped cream, an apple slice and a whole raspberry.

LEMON MOUSSE
Serves 4

6 oz (175 g) caster sugar
3 eggs, separated
grated rind of 5 lemons

½ oz (10 g) gelatine
2 tbsp warm water

Put the grated lemon rind in a bowl together with the egg yolks and sugar. Beat well until stiff. In another bowl, whisk the egg whites until they form stiff peaks. Dissolve the gelatine in the water, then mix into the egg yolk mixture. Beat well until the mixture is nearly set, then fold in the egg whites. Pile into individual glass serving dishes and chill before serving.

STRAWBERRY AND BANANA FOOL
Serves 4

12 oz (350 g) strawberries
1 banana
juice of 1 orange
½ packet orange jelly
¼ pt (150 ml) double cream

Sieve the strawberries. Mash the banana and add it to the strawberries. Pour the orange juice into a pan, break up the jelly squares and add them to the pan. Heat gently until dissolved. Cool slightly, then stir into the strawberry mixture. Whip the cream, and stir it into the mixture. Pour into four small glass serving dishes. Leave to set.

GOOSEBERRY FOAM
Serves 6

1 lb (450 g) gooseberries,
  topped and tailed
4 oz (110 g) granulated sugar
1 packet lime jelly

1 small can evaporated milk, chilled
¼ pt (150 ml) double cream, whipped
chopped walnuts to decorate
6 walnut halves

Put the gooseberries in a saucepan with 2 tbsp water. Bring to the boil, cover, lower the heat and simmer gently for 10 minutes. Liquidise in a blender or purée through a sieve. Add the sugar and jelly to the gooseberries and stir until they have both dissolved. Leave the mixture in a cool place until it starts to set. Put the evaporated milk in a bowl and whisk until thick; then whisk in the gooseberry mixture, a little at a time. Pour the mixture into six individual glass dishes and leave to set. Pipe a cream rosette on top of each and sprinkle the top with chopped walnuts. Place half a walnut on each swirl of cream.

PEACH MOUSSE
Serves 4

6 fresh ripe peaches
½ packet lemon jelly
¼ pt (150 ml) boiling water
¼ pt (150 ml) thick cream
extra cream to decorate

Skin four of the peaches and purée the flesh. Slice the remaining two peaches. Make the jelly using the boiling water and whisk when chilled. Whisk the cream until fairly stiff, then add the jelly and beat the combined mixture well. Fold in the peach purée. Pile the mixture into four serving dishes and leave to set. Decorate with the sliced peaches and whipped cream. Serve chilled.

CHOCOLATE AND ORANGE MOUSSE
Serves 4

3 oz (75 g) plain chocolate
3 eggs
1 orange, rind and juice
3 oz (75 g) caster sugar

2 level tsp powdered gelatine
¼ pt (150 ml) double cream
whipped cream
grated chocolate

Melt the chocolate in a small bowl set over a pan of simmering water. Separate the eggs. Beat the yolks, orange rind and sugar to a thick cream, then stir in the melted chocolate. Mix the gelatine with the orange juice in a small bowl and dissolve it over a pan of simmering water. Cool slightly. Whip the cream until it just holds it shape and fold it into the mixture. Whip the egg whites until they form stiff peaks and fold these in. Spoon into four small serving dishes. Leave to set. Decorate with cream and chocolate.

ORANGE FOOL
Serves 6

4–6 trifle sponge cakes, cut into ½ in (1.25 cm) slices
grated rind and juice of 2 oranges
grated rind and juice of 1 lemon
1–2 oz (25–50 g) sugar
½ pt (300 ml) double cream
orange slices to decorate

Line six individual serving dishes with the sponge slices, covering the base and half-way up the sides. Place the orange rind and juice and the lemon rind and juice in a bowl and stir in the sugar until it dissolves. Put the cream in a bowl and whip until it starts to thicken. Gradually stir in the fruit juice. Continue to whip until the cream is thick and the juice has been absorbed. Divide the mixture between the six dishes and chill in the refrigerator for 2 hours. Decorate with orange slices before serving.

AVOCADO AND LIME DESSERT
Serves 4

2 large ripe avocado pears, peeled and stoned
4 limes
3 oz (75 g) icing sugar
mint leaves

Remove all the flesh from the avocados. Mash with a fork then pass through a sieve to obtain a smooth purée. Strain the juice of three limes and mix this into the avocado purée. Stir in the icing sugar and mix thoroughly. Pile the mixture into four serving dishes and serve immediately, garnished with slices of the remaining lime and mint leaves.

MANGO SYLLABUB
Serves 4

1 large ripe mango	*3 egg whites*
1 glass of white wine	*4 oz (110 g) caster sugar*
juice of 1 small lemon	*½ pt (300 ml) double cream*

Peel the mango and remove the stone. Place the mango flesh in a blender with the wine and lemon juice and blend to a purée, or pass the mango flesh through a sieve and then mix well with the wine and lemon juice. Place the egg whites in a bowl and whisk until they form stiff peaks, then gradually whisk in the sugar. In another bowl whisk the cream until it forms soft peaks and fold it into the purée. Fold the egg whites into the purée. Pour into a serving dish and chill before serving.

LEMON BLANCMANGE
Serves 4

4 tbsp cornflour
1 pt (600 ml) milk
strip of lemon rind
3 tbsp sugar

Put the cornflour in a bowl and mix to a smooth paste with 2 tbsp of the milk. Pour the remaining milk into a saucepan, add the lemon rind and bring to the boil. Strain the milk into the cornflour, stirring constantly, then return the mixture to the saucepan. Bring to the boil, stirring until it thickens, lower the heat and cook for 3 minutes. Stir in the sugar to taste. Pour into a 1 pint (600 ml) dampened jelly mould and leave to set. Turn out onto a serving dish.

CHOCOLATE AND COFFEE APPLE WHIP
Serves 4

1 lb (450 g) cooking apples, peeled, cored and chopped
2½ oz (60 g) fresh white breadcrumbs
3 tbsp caster sugar
2 tbsp drinking chocolate powder
1 tbsp instant coffee powder
¼ pt (150 ml) whipping cream, whipped
chopped mixed nuts to decorate

Put the apples in a saucepan over low heat and cook until tender. Purée in a blender or pass through a sieve. Put the breadcrumbs, sugar, chocolate and coffee powders in a bowl and mix well. Arrange alternating layers of the apples and the breadcrumb mixture in individual glass dishes finishing with a layer of breadcrumbs on top. Chill in the refrigerator overnight. Decorate with whipped cream and chopped nuts and serve.

GOOSEBERRY FOOL
Serves 6

18 oz (500 g) green gooseberries
2 oz (50 g) Barbados sugar
½ tsp ground cinnamon

pinch of ground cloves
½ pt (300 ml) thick cream
mint leaves

Top and tail the fruit. Place in a large saucepan with the sugar, cinnamon and cloves and 4 tbsp of water. Cover and cook over low heat for 20 minutes until the fruit is very soft. Transfer the fruit to a bowl and break up with a fork, but do not reduce to a purée. Whip the cream until it forms soft peaks, then gently fold into the gooseberries with a metal spoon. Pile the mixture into a serving bowl, chill for 1 hour and serve garnished with mint leaves.

RUM CHOCOLATE MOUSSE
Serves 6

1½ oz (40 g) drinking
   chocolate powder
½ oz (10 g) gelatine
¼ pt (150 ml) water
6 oz (175 g) marshmallows
3 eggs, separated

2 oz (50 g) caster sugar
¼ pt (150 ml) evaporated milk
1 tbsp rum
whipped thick cream to decorate
chopped walnuts to decorate

Put the chocolate powder, gelatine, water and 2 oz (50 g) of the marshmallows in a saucepan over very low heat and cook until the marshmallows and gelatine have dissolved. Remove from the heat and set aside until lukewarm. Put the egg yolks and sugar in a bowl and beat together until thick. Stir in the chocolate and marshmallow mixture from the saucepan. Lightly stir in the evaporated milk and rum. Cut the remaining marshmallows into small pieces and stir into the mixture. Whisk the egg whites and fold in. Pile the mixture into a 1½ pint (900 ml) soufflé dish and chill until set. Decorate with whipped cream and walnuts.

CHESTNUT AND CHOCOLATE PARFAIT
Serves 6

8 oz (225 g) dark chocolate,
broken into small pieces
1 tbsp brandy or rum
1 tbsp strong coffee
1 tbsp water

4 oz (110 g) margarine
4 oz (110 g) caster sugar
1 lb (450 g) tin chestnut purée
toasted almond flakes

Melt the chocolate, brandy or rum, coffee and water in a small, heatproof bowl set over a saucepan of simmering water. Cream the margarine and sugar together until light and fluffy. Beat the chestnut purée well and stir into the creamed mixture. Add the chocolate mixture a little at a time and fold in thoroughly. Line a 2 lb (900 g) loaf tin with oiled greaseproof paper and pour in the mixture, levelling the top. Chill in the refrigerator until set. Just before serving, decorate with flaked toasted almonds.

CHOCOLATE BLANCMANGE
Serves 4

4 tbsp cornflour
1 pt (600 ml) milk
2 oz (50 g) melted plain chocolate
3 tbsp sugar

Put the cornflour in a bowl and mix to a smooth paste with 2 tbsp of the milk. Pour the remaining milk into a saucepan, stir in the chocolate and bring to the boil. Strain the milk into the cornflour, stirring constantly, then return the mixture to the pan. Bring to the boil, stirring, until it thickens, then lower the heat and cook for 3 minutes. Stir in sugar to taste. Pour into a 1 pint (600 ml) dampened jelly mould and leave to set. Turn out onto a dish and serve.

GINGER CREAMS
Serves 6

6 level tbsp ginger marmalade
4 level tsp soft brown sugar
2 tsp lemon juice
2 tbsp double cream, whipped
½ pt (300 g) soured cream
2 egg whites, whisked

Mix the marmalade, sugar and lemon juice together. Fold in the soured cream, whipped double cream and whisked egg whites. Spoon into individual glasses and chill.

CHESTNUT DREAM
Serves 6

4 oz (110 g) plain chocolate, broken into small pieces
3 oz (75 g) caster sugar
2 tbsp water
1 lb (450 g) tinned chestnut purée
2 eggs
6 oz (175 g) softened butter
whipped double cream and grated chocolate to decorate

Put the chocolate, sugar and water in a saucepan and melt, stirring, over gentle heat. When the mixture has cooled slightly, mix into the chestnut purée. Separate the eggs and beat the yolks into the mixture one at a time. Cut the butter into pieces and also beat in. Whisk the egg whites until they form stiff peaks, then fold into the mixture using a metal spoon. Spoon this mixture into a buttered 1¾ pint (1 ltr) mould, cover and leave in the refrigerator overnight. To serve, turn out and decorate with whipped cream and chocolate shavings.

STRAWBERRY SYLLABUB
Serves 4

8 oz (225 g) strawberries
4 level tbsp icing sugar
2 tbsp sherry or 3 tbsp white wine
5 fl oz (150 ml) double cream
5 fl oz (150 ml) single cream

Wash the strawberries and dry. Reserve four whole strawberries for decoration. Hull and quarter the remainder and place in a bowl, with the icing sugar and sherry or wine. Mix together gently, cover and leave for 30 minutes. Strain the syrup from the strawberries into a bowl, add the double and single creams and whisk until the mixture forms soft peaks. Carefully fold in the quartered strawberries. Divide the mixture between four small serving dishes and top each dish with one of the whole strawberries. Leave in a cool place for several hours before serving. The syllabub should have a creamy foam layer on top and a liquid layer below.

SUMMER JELLY
Serves 6

2 oz (50 g) redcurrants
4 oz (110 g) cherries, stoned
2 oz (50 g) sugar
4¼ oz (125 g) packet of
  strawberry-flavoured jelly

8 oz (225 g) raspberries, hulled
4 oz (110 g) strawberries, halved
8 sponge fingers

Gently cook the redcurrants and cherries with the sugar until soft. Strain, reserving the juice. Make the juice up to ½ pint (300 ml) with water, add the jelly and stir over low heat until the jelly dissolves. Make up to 1 pint (600 ml) with cold water. Add all the fruit to the jelly. Pour about a quarter of the jelly into a 2 pint (1.2 ltr) ring mould or pudding basin. Chill until it starts to set. Press the sponge fingers into the jelly at intervals around the edge. Pour in another quarter of the fruit jelly and chill until set. Add another quarter of jelly and chill. When it has set add the remaining jelly and chill. To serve, dip the mould in hot water briefly and then turn out onto a plate.

AVOCADO LEMON CREAMS
Serves 4

2 ripe avocado pears, peeled, stoned and chopped
juice of 2 lemons and some grated lemon rind
1 oz (25 g) icing sugar
3½ fl oz (100 ml) whipping cream, whipped

Purée the avocado flesh, the juice of the lemons and the icing sugar in a blender. Divide the mixture between 4 small serving dishes. Spread the whipped cream over the top of each dish and decorate with a little grated lemon rind. Serve chilled.

DAIRY DESSERTS

CREME CARAMEL
Serves 4

2 oz (50 g) granulated sugar
2 tbsp cold water
2 tbsp boiling water
½ pt (300 ml) milk

4 eggs, beaten
1 oz (25 g) caster sugar
½ tsp vanilla essence

Preheat the oven to 325°F/170°C/Gas Mk 3. Lightly grease a 1 pint (600 ml) ovenproof dish. Place the sugar in a heavy-based saucepan with the cold water. Slowly bring to the boil to dissolve the sugar, then boil quickly so that the sugar caramelises and turns a deep golden colour. Immediately add the boiling water, taking care as the caramel will tend to spit, and pour into the prepared dish. Swirl the caramel around the base of the dish to coat. Scald the milk in a saucepan and pour over the eggs, whisking continuously. Add the caster sugar and vanilla. Strain through a fine nylon sieve over the caramel. Bake in a bain-marie or a dish with water to come halfway up the sides of the caramel dish, in the oven for about 50 minutes or until set. Remove from the oven and allow to cool in the dish. Turn out to serve. Crème caramel is best served slightly chilled.

RASBERRY SOUFFLÉ
Serves 4

8 oz (225 g) raspberries, fresh or frozen
2 tbsp lemon juice
2 large egg whites
pinch of salt
2 oz (50 g) caster sugar

Preheat the oven to 350°F/180°C/Gas Mk 4. Grease four individual ramekin dishes. Purée the raspberries in an electric blender and sieve. Stir in the lemon juice. Whisk the salt with the egg whites until soft peaks form. Whisk in the sugar, 1 tbsp at a time until the mixture is stiff and glossy. Fold the raspberry purée into the egg whites using a metal spoon. Divide into the ramekin dishes. Place the dishes on a baking tray and bake for 10 minutes in the oven. Serve at once.

CARAMEL RICE
Serves 4–6

1 pt (600 ml) milk
5 oz (150 g) pudding rice
2 oz (50 g) granulated sugar
1 oz (25 g) butter
4 kiwi fruits, peeled and sliced
4 small red plums,
    stoned and quartered

3 oz (75 g) red seedless grapes
¼pt (150 ml) single cream
2 oz (50 g) demerara sugar
caster sugar and fresh mint
    leaves to decorate

Bring the milk to boiling point in a large saucepan, then stir in the rice and granulated sugar. Bring back to the boil, cover the pan and simmer gently, stirring occasionally, until all the milk is absorbed. This will take about 30–40 minutes. Remove from the heat, stir in the butter, and leave to cool. Arrange the fruits in the bases of 4 individual glass dishes, fold the cream into the rice and spoon over the fruit. Sprinkle on demerara sugar and place under a preheated grill for 2–3 minutes until the sugar melts and begins to caramelise. Serve immediately decorated with caster sugar and mint leaves.

CHOCOLATE SOUFFLÉ
Serves 4–6.

½oz (10 g) butter
3 tbsp caster sugar
4 oz (110 g) plain chocolate, broken into pieces
3 tbsp brandy
4 large eggs, separated
pinch of salt or cream of tartar
icing sugar

Preheat the oven to 400°F/200°C/Gas Mk 6. Place a baking sheet in the centre of the oven. Grease a 2½ pint (1.5 ltr) soufflé dish with the butter and coat with 1 tbsp of the sugar. Shake out any excess. Place the chocolate and brandy in a heatproof bowl over a pan of hot water. Put on a very low heat until the chocolate has melted, then take the pan from the heat. Beat the remaining sugar into the egg yolks and stir into the chocolate. Whisk the egg whites for about 30 seconds, add the salt or cream of tartar. Whisk until stiff peaks are formed. Add 2 spoonfuls of egg whites to the chocolate base, then fold into the remaining egg white. Place the mixture into the prepared soufflé dish and bake for 20–25 minutes. Dust the soufflé with a little icing sugar and serve at once.

COFFEE CUSTARDS
Serves 4

1 small can of evaporated milk
water
3 oz (75 g) caster sugar, plus
  1 level tbsp

2 level tbsp instant coffee granules
2 large eggs
⅛ level tsp mixed spice

Preheat the oven to 375°F/190°C/Gas Mk 5. Make the evaporated milk up to ¾ pint (450 ml) with water, add 3 oz (75 g) of the sugar and the coffee and slowly heat in a saucepan to dissolve the sugar. Beat the eggs in a basin and slowly pour onto the coffee flavoured milk. Strain into a jug and pour equally into 4 individual ramekins. Place the dishes in a roasting tin and pour hot water into the tin to come half way up the dishes. Bake for 40–45 minutes or until set. To serve, mix the remaining sugar and the spice together and sprinkle over the top of each custard. Serve with langue du chat biscuits.

APRICOT SOUFFLÉ
Serves 6

6 oz (175 g) dried apricots
½ oz (10 g) butter
4 tbsp caster sugar
2 large eggs, separated

1 tbsp apricot brandy
2 tbsp double cream
1 large extra egg white
pinch of salt or cream of tartar

Put the apricots in a saucepan, add enough water to cover and bring to the boil over a low heat. Cover and simmer for 40 minutes or until the fruit is soft. Preheat the oven to 375°F/190°C/Gas Mk 5. Place a baking sheet in the centre of the oven. Grease a 2½ pint (1.5 ltr) soufflé dish with the butter and coat with 1 tbsp of the sugar. Shake out any excess. Drain the apricots and blend in a food processor or rub through a sieve. Cool until just warm. Lightly beat the remaining sugar into the egg yolks. Stir the mixture into the fruit purée, adding the brandy. Stir in the cream and set aside. Whisk the egg whites for 30 seconds. Add the salt or cream of tartar and whisk until stiff peaks are formed. Add 2 spoonfuls of the egg whites to the purée base, then fold this into the remaining egg whites. Place the mixture into the prepared soufflé dish and bake for 25–30 minutes. Serve at once.

SOUFFLÉ ROTHSCHILD
Serves 6

2 tbsp Kirsch
6 oz (175 g) glacé fruit,
* finely chopped*
2 oz (50 g) butter
3 oz (75 g) caster sugar
8 fl oz (250 ml) milk

1 oz (25 g) plain flour
4 large eggs, separated
1 large egg white
pinch of salt or cream of tartar
icing sugar

Sprinkle Kirsch over the glacé fruit and set aside for 30 minutes. Preheat the oven to 375°F/190°C/Gas Mk 5 and place a baking sheet in the centre of oven. Grease six individual ramekin dishes with ½ oz (10 g) of the butter and coat with 1 oz (25 g) of the sugar, shaking out any excess. Place the remaining sugar and milk in a small saucepan over a low heat and bring to just below boiling point. Remove the pan and set aside. Melt the remaining butter over a low heat, stir in the flour and cook, stirring constantly, for 30 seconds. Remove the pan from the heat and slowly stir in the milk. Return to the heat and bring to the boil continually stirring. Simmer for 5 minutes, stirring from time to time. Remove from the heat and cool to just warm. Lightly beat the egg yolks and stir into the cooled sauce adding the glacé fruit and Kirsch. Whisk the egg whites briskly for 30 seconds. Add the salt or cream of tartar and continue to whisk until stiff peaks are formed. Add 2 spoonfuls of the egg whites to the sauce then fold the mixture into the remaining egg whites. Divide the mixture between the ramekins and place on the baking sheet. Bake for 15–20 minutes. Dust with icing sugar and serve at once.

ZABAGLIONE
Serves 4–6

6 egg yolks
6 tbsp caster sugar
2 tsp finely grated orange or lemon rind
6 tbsp Marsala or sweet white wine

Whisk the egg yolks, sugar, and rind together in a bowl until frothy. Stir in the Marsala or white wine and place the bowl over a saucepan of barely simmering water. Whisk until the mixture thickens and rises. Pour into stemmed glasses and serve at once. Decorate with a little extra grated rind, if liked.

APPLE AND GINGER CLOUD
Serves 4

3 cooking apples, peeled, cored and chopped
1 tbsp water
2 oz (50 g) sugar
2 oz (50 g) preserved ginger, sliced
2 egg whites
pinch of salt
2 tbsp caster sugar

Place the apples, sugar and water in a pan over low heat and simmer for 10 minutes, or until soft. Remove from the heat and rub the mixture through a sieve, making a purée. Stir the ginger into the purée and transfer to a flameproof serving dish. Set aside to cool. Preheat the grill to a high temperature. Whisk the salt and egg whites together until softly peaked, then gradually whisk in the caster sugar. Place the meringue mixture in a pile in the centre of the apple purée and grill for 1 minute, or until the meringue is a pale golden colour. Serve at once.

CHOCOLATE QUEEN OF PUDDINGS
Serves 4

2 oz (50 g) butter
4 oz (110 g) fresh white breadcrumbs
1 pt (600 ml) milk
2 oz (50 g) drinking chocolate
3 eggs, separated
2 tbsp apricot jam
6 oz (150 g) caster sugar

Grease a 1½ pint (900 ml) pie dish and tip in the breadcrumbs. Gently heat the milk with the butter and drinking chocolate. Leave to cool for about 2 minutes and then beat in the egg yolks. Carefully pour over the breadcrumbs and leave to stand for 30 minutes. Preheat the oven to 350°F/180°C/Gas Mk 4. Bake for about 40 minutes until set. Remove from the oven and increase the oven temperature to 450°F/230°C/Gas Mk 8. Spread the top with the apricot jam. Whisk the egg whites very stiffly, fold in half the sugar and whisk again. Fold in the remaining sugar and pile the meringue on top of the pudding. Put the pudding back in the oven and cook for about 5 minutes until the meringue peaks are golden brown. Serve with single cream.

CREME DE RICE
Serves

3 oz (75 g) short grain rice
1 pt (600 ml) milk
1 oz (25 g) sugar
1 egg, separated

½ oz (10 g) butter
1 packet orange jelly
¼ pt (150 ml) boiling water
glacé cherries to decorate

Place the rice, milk and sugar into a large saucepan. Stir and bring to the boil, reduce the heat, cover and simmer for 30 minutes, stirring occasionally. Lightly beat the egg yolk and stir into the mixture together with the butter. Remove from the heat. Dissolve the jelly in the boiling water. When cool, stir into the rice. Whisk the egg white until stiff then fold into the rice mixture. Lightly oil a ring mould and press in the mixture. Chill until well set. To serve, turn out onto a dish and decorate with the glacé cherries cut into halves.

SEMOLINA APRICOT RING
Serves 4

1 pt (600 ml) milk
1 oz (25 g) semolina
2 level tbsp caster sugar
15 oz (425 g) can of apricot halves
2 level tsp powdered gelatine

Put the milk into a wet saucepan and bring the milk to the boil. When it is almost boiling sprinkle in the semolina. Boil, and cook gently until thick and creamy, stirring often. Add the sugar and when dissolved take off the heat and leave to cool. Place a circle of wet greaseproof paper on top of the semolina to prevent a skin forming while it is cooling. Strain the apricots and make the juice up to ½ pint (300 ml) with water if necessary. Measure the gelatine into a small saucepan and add 2 tbsp of the juice. Leave to soften for about 5 minutes then add the remaining juice and heat very gently until the gelatine is dissolved. Pour a little of this into the base of a 1½ pint (900 ml) wetted ring mould and put in the refrigerator to set firm. Arrange the apricot halves on the jelly and pour over a little more of the liquid gelatine in juice and leave to set firm again. Pour over the cooled semolina and leave to a few hours until quite cold and set firm. Loosen the sides and turn out onto a serving plate.

APRICOT RICE CREAM
Serves 6

3 oz (75 g) pudding rice
1¼ pt (750 ml) milk
2–3 drops vanilla essence
1 egg white
¼ pt (150 ml) double cream,
*   whipped into soft peak*

3 oz (75 g) caster sugar
15 oz (425 g) can of
*   apricots in natural juice*
2 tbsp Kirsch
2 oz (50 g) flaked almonds,
*   slightly toasted*

Preheat the oven to 325°F/170°C/Gas Mk 3. In a saucepan, place the rice, milk and vanilla essence and bring to the boil, stirring constantly. Lower heat and simmer for 40–45 minutes until the rice is soft and most of the liquid has been absorbed. Remove from the heat and leave to cool slightly. Whisk the egg white to form soft peaks and fold into the rice. Fold in the whipped cream together with 2 oz (50 g) of the sugar. Pile the rice mixture into an ovenproof dish. Make a purée of the apricots in a blender, then stir in the remaining sugar and the Kirsch. Spoon the purée over the top of the rice and sprinkle on the almonds. Cook in the oven for 15 minutes and serve.

SCANDINAVIAN CREAM
Serves 6

butter for greasing
6 oz (175 g) apricot jam
3 large eggs, 1 separated
1 level tbsp caster sugar

few drops vanilla essence
¾ pt (450 ml) milk
4 oz (110 g) dark chocolate
½ pt (300 ml) double cream

Preheat the oven to 325°F/170°C/Gas Mk 3. Grease a 2 pint (1.2 ltr) soufflé dish and spread the base with a good layer of apricot jam. Beat lightly together 2 whole eggs, 1 egg yolk, the sugar and vanilla essence. Heat the milk but do not boil, and pour onto the egg mixture, stirring until well incorporated. Strain onto the jam and cover with foil. Stand the dish in a roasting tin half filled with cold water and cook in the oven for 1¾ hours, until the custard is set. Remove from the tin and leave to get cold. Grate half the chocolate over the top of the cold custard. Whip the cream until it holds shape. Whisk the remaining egg white until stiff and fold into a third of the whipped cream. Spoon onto the top of the chocolate and gently level off. Pipe the remaining whipped cream around the edge of the dish. Shave the remaining chocolate with a potato peeler into curls and pile in the centre of the dish.

MERINGUE BREAD PUDDING
Serves 4–5

½pt (300 ml) milk
2 level tbsp marmalade
pinch of salt
6 oz (175 g) bread, without
  crusts and cubed

2 large eggs, separated
2 oz (50 g) sugar
few drops of vanilla essence
4 oz (110 g) mixed dried fruit

Preheat the oven to 350°F/180°C/Gas Mk 4. Put the milk, marmalade and a pinch of salt in a pan and bring to the boil. Put the bread in a basin and pour the boiling milk over it. Stir and leave to stand for 10 minutes. Beat the bread to a paste with a wooden spoon, then stir in the egg yolks, sugar, vanilla essence and mixed dried fruit. Whisk the egg whites until stiff then fold them into the bread mixture. Spoon into a 1½ pint (900 ml) greased ovenproof dish. Stand the dish in a roasting tin and place in the centre of the oven. Pour hot water into the tin to a depth of about 1 in (2.5 cm). Bake for about 1¼ hours or until risen and firm to the touch. Serve with thin cream.

CARDINAL CREAMS
Serves 4

2 oz (50 g) pudding rice
2 oz (50 g) granulated sugar
1 pt (600 ml) milk
8 oz (225 g) strawberries
1 tbsp caster sugar

½oz (10 g) gelatine
3 tbsp water
1 tsp vanilla essence
5 fluid oz (150 ml) double cream

Place the rice, sugar and milk in a saucepan. Bring to boil, stirring, partly cover and simmer for 30 minutes until the rice is tender, just giving an occasional stir. Wash the strawberries, reserve 4 for decoration, remove hulls and slice the remainder. Spread the strawberries on a plate. Sprinkle with sugar. Place the water in a basin, add the gelatine and stir. Place the basin in a saucepan of water over a low heat and stir until the gelatine is dissolved. Add 2 tbsp of the gelatine and the vanilla essence to the rice and leave to cool. Whisk the cream until just thick, add three-quarters to the cooled rice and pour into 4 glasses. Place in a refrigerator to set. Add the sliced strawberries to the remaining gelatine (melt in warm water if necessary). Divide between the glasses and leave to set. Top each with the remaining cream and a strawberry.

CREMA FRITTA
Serves 4–6

3 eggs
2 oz (50 g) caster sugar
2 oz (50 g) plain flour
8 fl oz (250 ml) milk
10 fl oz (300 ml) single cream

finely grated rind of ½ lemon
4 oz (110 g) dry white breadcrumbs
vegetable oil, for frying
caster sugar, to serve

Preheat the oven to 350°F/180°C/Gas Mk 4. In a large bowl, beat two eggs and the sugar together until the mixture is pale. Add the flour, beating all the time, then very slowly beat in the milk and cream. Add the lemon rind. Pour the mixture into a buttered 7 in (18 cm) shallow square cake tin. Bake in the oven for about 1 hour until a skewer inserted in the middle comes out clean. Leave to cool for 2–3 hours, preferably overnight. When completely cold, cut into sixteen cubes and remove from the cake tin. Beat the remaining egg in a bowl. Dip the cubes in the egg and then in the breadcrumbs until well coated. Heat the oil in a frying pan and, when hot, slide in the cubes. Fry for 2–3 minutes until golden brown and a crust is formed. Turn and fry the second side. Drain well on absorbent kitchen paper. Serve immediately, sprinkled with caster sugar.

SEMOLINA CHERRY PUDDING
Serves 4

1 oz (25 g) semolina
1 pt (600 ml) milk
2 tbsp sugar
1 egg yolk, beaten
2–3 drops almond essence

14 oz (400 g) can of morello
  cherries, stoned
2 tsp arrowroot
1 tbsp caster sugar

Place the semolina in a bowl and mix in a little of the milk. Heat the remaining milk until almost boiling and pour over the semolina, stirring constantly. Return the mixture to the saucepan. Stir in the sugar and bring to the boil. Lower the heat and simmer for 10–15 minutes stirring from time to time, until the mixture has thickened. Remove from the heat and stir in the egg yolk and almond essence. Meanwhile, place the cherries in a small saucepan and add the arrowroot and caster sugar. Bring to the boil, stirring constantly. Arrange the semolina in a serving dish and pour over the cherry sauce.

RUM AND COFFEE JUNKET
Serves 4

1 pt (600 ml) milk,
  plus an extra 4 tbsp
2 tbsp caster sugar
2 tsp rennet essence

2 tsp rum
¼ pt (150 ml) soured cream
2 tsp coffee and chicory essence
chocolate flakes, for decoration

Heat 1 pint (600 ml) of the milk in a saucepan until just warm. Stir in the rennet and rum, and the sugar and stir until sugar is dissolved. Pour the mixture at once into four individual dishes and leave in a warm place for 4 hours until set. Place the soured cream in a bowl and lightly whisk. Gradually whisk in the 4 tbsp of milk and the coffee and chicory essence until smooth. Carefully pour a thin layer of the mixture over the junket and decorate with chocolate flakes. Chill for about 1 hour before serving.

LEMON RICE PUDDING
Serves 6

3 oz (75 g) pudding rice
3 oz (75 g) caster sugar
grated rind of 1 lemon
2 pt (1.2 ltr) full cream milk
2 oz (50 g) butter

Preheat the oven to 350°F/180°C/Gas Mk 4. Place the rice, sugar and lemon rind in a well buttered ovenproof dish and pour over the milk. Bake for 1 hour, stirring occasionally. Then reduce the oven temperature to 325°F/170°C/Gas Mk 3, and bake for about another 1 hour. Place dots of butter on top to serve.

AMBROSIA
Serves 4

4 tsp gelatine
4 tbsp cold water
12 fl oz (350 ml) sour cream
3 oz (75 g) brown sugar
1 tbsp vanilla essence
juice of ½ lemon

4 tsp rum
2 egg whites
4 fl oz (120 ml) double
  thick cream, whipped
6 macaroon biscuits

Place the cold water in a small bowl, sprinkle on the gelatine and leave for about 5 minutes until spongy. Place the bowl over a pan of hot water and stir to dissolve. Place the sour cream and sugar in a bowl and beat well. Add in the vanilla essence, lemon juice and rum. Mix in the gelatine. Place the mixture in a refrigerator and leave to chill until it begins to thicken. Whisk the egg whites until stiff, then fold into the chilled mixture. Pile into individual glass dishes and chill again until set. Top with the whipped cream and crumbled macaroon biscuits and serve.

LEMON SOUFFLÉ
Serves 6

3 large eggs, separated
3 oz (75 g) caster sugar
2 lemons, rind and juice
½ oz (10 g) gelatine
3 tbsp cold water
½ pt (300 ml) double cream, whipped

Whisk the egg yolks together with the caster sugar and the rind and juice of the lemons in a bowl over a pan of gently simmering water until really thick and creamy. Melt the gelatine in the cold water. Stand the bowl in a pan of hot water until the gelatine is completely liquid, then blend well into the whisked eggs. Fold the whipped cream lightly into the mixture with a metal spoon and leave until just beginning to set. Whisk the egg whites until fairly stiff and fold in. Pour into a wetted mould and leave to set.

VARIATIONS:

ORANGE: Use the rind and juice of 1 large orange and add a little Cointreau.
CHOCOLATE: Use 4 oz (110 g) plain chocolate, melted over hot water together with 1 tbsp of rum or brandy.
STRAWBERRY: Pass 8 oz (225 g) fresh ripe strawberries through a sieve. Melt 2 oz (50 g) sugar in ¼ pint (150 ml) water to a syrup. Add to the strawberries after melting the gelatine in the sugar syrup, then stir into the whisked egg yolks.
RASPBERRY: As for strawberry soufflé.
An oiled jam jar may be set in the middle of the mould, or a ring mould used if available. The centre hole may then be filled with fresh fruit.

CHOCOLATE VANILLA PUDDINGS
Serves 8

5 oz (150 g) plain chocolate
5 fl oz (150 ml) double cream
4 eggs
3 oz (75 g) caster sugar
4 oz (110 g) butter, cut into small pieces

2 tsp vanilla essence
3 oz (75 g) fresh white breadcrumbs
single cream to serve
chocolate curls to decorate

Preheat the oven to 350°F/180°C/Gas Mk 4. Lightly butter eight 5 fl oz (150 ml) ramekin dishes. Finely chop the chocolate in a food processor. Bring the double cream to simmering point in a small saucepan, pour onto the chocolate and process until smooth. Cool for 2–3 minutes only. Add 2 whole eggs and 2 yolks, reserving the 2 whites, processing after each addition. Add the sugar, butter and vanilla essence and blend thoroughly. Pour into a bowl and stir in the breadcrumbs. Whisk the reserved egg whites until stiff and fold into the chocolate mixture. Pour into the ramekins. Place in a roasting tin and pour in hot water to come half way up the outsides of the dishes. Bake for about 30–35 minutes or until lightly set. Cool, cover and refrigerate overnight. Leave at room temperature for at least 30 minutes before serving. Serve with single cream and chocolate curls.

ORANGE POSSET
Serves 4

1 pt (600 ml) double cream
1 tbsp grated orange rind
1 tsp grated lemon rind
¼ pt (150 ml) dry white wine
4 tbsp orange juice
1 tbsp lemon juice
4 oz (110 g) icing sugar

3 egg whites
2 tbsp caster sugar
¼ pt (150 ml) whipped
  whipping cream
1 oz (25 g) ratafia biscuits
1 orange, sliced

Place in the cream in a bowl and whip until stiff. Stir in the lemon and orange rinds. Gradually pour in the wine, beating well all the time. Very slowly stir in the lemon and orange juices. Beat in the icing sugar. In another bowl, whisk the egg whites, then add the caster sugar beating so that the mixture remains stiff. Fold this mixture into the meringue mixture and arrange in a serving dish. Chill for about 4 hours. When just ready to serve, decorate with whipped cream, orange slices and ratafia biscuits.

FLOATING ISLANDS
Serves 4

5 egg yolks, beaten
¾ pt (450 ml) milk
2 oz (50 g) caster sugar, plus 5 tbsp
½ tsp vanilla flavouring
1 egg white

Put the egg yolks, milk and 2 oz (50 g) of the sugar in the top of a double boiler or in a heavy-based saucepan over low heat. Cook gently for about 15 minutes, stirring constantly, until the mixture thickens and coats the back of the stirring spoon. Stir in the vanilla flavouring. Divide the custard between four stemmed glasses or dessert dishes. Cover and refrigerate for one hour. Meanwhile, whisk the egg white until it will stand in stiff peaks. Add 2 tbsp of the remaining sugar and whisk again until the sugar is dissolved. Put some cold water into a shallow tin. Bring to a gentle simmer and spoon on the meringue in four even mounds. Poach for about 5 minutes until set, turning once. Remove the meringues with a slotted spoon, drain for a minute on absorbent kitchen paper and spoon on to the custard in the glasses. Put the remaining sugar into a heavy-based saucepan and cook, stirring constantly, for about 3 minutes or until it forms a golden syrup. Remove from the heat and leave for 2 minutes to cool slightly, then drizzle a little of the warm syrup over the top of each meringue. Serve immediately.

LOVELY RICH RICE PUDDING
Serves 4

1½ oz (35 g) butter or margarine
4 oz (110 g) round grain rice,
washed and drained
grated rind of 1 lemon
2 oz (50 g) sugar
1 large egg

1 pt (600 ml) milk
2 oz (50 g) sultanas
1 oz (25 g) glacé cherries, chopped
1 oz (25 g) angelica, chopped
1 tsp nutmeg

Preheat the oven to 325°F/170°C/Gas Mk 3. Rub ½ oz (10 g) of the butter around the rim of a 2 pint (1.2 ltr) ovenproof dish. Mix the rice, lemon rind and sugar together and place in the dish. Beat the egg with milk and strain on to the rice. Stir in the sultanas, glacé cherries and angelica. Sprinkle nutmeg on top and dot with the rest of the butter. Bake in the centre of the oven for 2 hours until the middle of the pudding is soft but firm and the skin golden brown.

PINEAPPLE PUDDING
Serves 6

12 oz (350 g) curd cheese
grated rind of a lemon
2 oz (50 g) caster sugar
14 oz (400 g) can of crushed
  pineapple

3 tbsp water
½ oz (10 g) gelatine
2 eggs, separated
1 packet trifle sponges
¼ pt (150 ml) double cream

Beat the curd cheese with half the caster sugar and lemon rind until smooth and creamy. Drain the crushed pineapple, reserving the juice. Mix the pineapple into the curd cheese and mix well. Put the water into a cup and sprinkle the gelatine over. Leave to soften. Add the remaining caster sugar to the egg yolks and beat until creamy and pale in colour. If necessary, make the reserved pineapple juice up to 5 fl oz (150 ml) with water, and bring to the boil. Take off the heat and stir in the creamed yolks. Pour back into a clean saucepan and cook very gently until the custard is slightly thickened. Remove from the heat, add the dissolved gelatine and stir to dissolve. Stir the custard into the curd cheese and blend. Cool until the mixture is beginning to set. Slice the trifle sponges in half lengthways and open them out. Trim and use to line the base and sides of a 3 pint (1.8 ltr) pudding basin, putting the sugared side outwards. Beat the whites until stiff and the cream to soft peaks. Fold the cream into the curd mixture, followed by the whites. Pour into the sponge lined basin and top with any remaining sponge cakes. Cover with clingfilm and chill in the refrigerator until set. When ready to serve turn out onto a serving plate and dredge with icing sugar. Decorate with glacé cherries and angelica leaves.

CHOCOLATE AND COFFEE JUNKET
Serves 2

10 fl oz (300 ml) milk
½ oz (10 g) dark chocolate, grated
½ tsp instant coffee granules

1 tsp caster sugar
2 tsp rennet

In a saucepan, pour the milk together with the chocolate and coffee granules. Gently heat until the chocolate starts to melt and the coffee dissolves, stirring from time to time. Remove from the heat and add the sugar and rennet. Stir well. Pour into two serving dishes and leave to cool. Place in a refrigerator for a few hours to set before serving.

GINGER BAVAROIS
Serves 6

3 egg yolks
2 oz (50 g) caster sugar
¾ pt (450 ml) milk
2 level tbsp powdered gelatine
4 tbsp stem ginger syrup

½ pt (300 ml) double cream
3 oz (75 g) stem ginger
 finely chopped
chopped stem ginger to decorate

Beat the egg yolks with the sugar until pale and fluffy. Heat the milk gently without boiling, and whisk into the egg mixture. Return to the pan and stir over a gentle heat until it thickens enough to coat the back of the spoon. Sprinkle the gelatine over the stem ginger syrup. When it swells stir into the hot custard until dissolved. Cool until it begins to set. Lightly whip the cream and fold into the custard with the measured stem ginger. Turn into a wetted 2½ pint (1.5 ltr) ring mould and chill until set. Turn out onto a flat serving plate and decorate the top with chopped ginger.

CREME BRULEE
Serves 6

6 egg yolks
2 oz (50 g) caster sugar
1½ tbsp cornflour
1 pt (600 ml) double cream
1 vanilla pod or a few drops vanilla essence
6 oz (175 g) granulated sugar

Beat the egg yolks together with the caster sugar and cornflour until creamy. Bring the cream to the boil very slowly with the vanilla pod, or vanilla essence, and pour over the egg yolks. Return to a clean saucepan and bring back almost to boiling point again. Pour into a shallow ovenproof dish and put in a slow oven until set. When cold put in the refrigerator overnight. About an hour before serving put the granulated sugar in a heavy based saucepan and heat gently until the sugar has dissolved and is caramelised. Do not stir. When the syrup is clear and golden brown remove from the heat and pour over the egg custard. Leave to harden and then tap with a metal spoon to break the caramel up before serving.

BAKED RICE PUDDING
Serves 4

1 pt (600 ml) milk
1½ oz (35 g) pudding rice
1 oz (25 g) caster sugar
few drops of vanilla essence

½ oz (10 g) butter, cut into small
  pieces
2–3 tbsp single cream or top of milk
grated nutmeg to taste

Preheat the oven to 300°F/150°C/Gas Mk 2. Generously grease a
1½ pint (900 ml) pie dish. Heat the milk just to the boiling point in a
saucepan. While the milk is heating, sprinkle the rice over the base of
the prepared dish and add the sugar, vanilla essence and butter. Pour
the hot milk over the rice and mix well together. Place the dish in the
bottom half of the oven and bake for about 2 hours or until the rice is
tender and creamy and the top is brown. Stir the pudding every
15 minutes during the first hour of baking to mix in the skin that
will form. Then stir in the cream and sprinkle the top with grated
nutmeg. Leave the pudding undisturbed until baked.

LEMON & CHOCOLATE DREAMS
Serves 4

¼ pt (150 ml) double cream
7 fl oz (200 ml) can of condensed milk
1 lemon, finely grated rind and juice
4 oz (110 g) plain chocolate digestive biscuits
finely grated rind of 1 orange
grated chocolate

Whip the cream until it forms soft peaks. Slowly and gently fold the
condensed milk into the whipped cream. Stir in the finely grated
lemon rind and juice until the mixture thickens slightly. Crush the
digestive biscuits with a rolling pin. The best way to do this is to put
them in a polythene bag and tie the end, then crush them. Stir the
grated orange rind into the bag of crumbs. Spoon a layer of the cream
mixture in the bottom of four individual glass dishes. Cover this with
biscuit crumbs, followed by the rest of the cream mixture. Chill in the
refrigerator for 1 hour and then decorate with a swirl of whipped
cream and grated chocolate curls.

CALYPSO CHOCOLATE PUDDING
Serves 4–6

2 oz (50 g) semolina
2 level tbsp cocoa
2 oz (50 g) caster sugar

1 pt (600 ml) milk
3 bananas
1 tbsp lemon juice

Mix together the semolina, cocoa, sugar and a little of the measured milk in a basin. Pour the remaining milk into a saucepan and bring to the boil. Stir into the ingredients in the basin, return mixture to the saucepan. Bring to the boil, stirring continuously. Cook over a gentle heat for 5 minutes, stirring occasionally. Remove from the heat. Peel and slice 2 bananas, add to the semolina mixture and stir gently. Pour the mixture into a 1½ pint (900 ml) oval pie dish. Leave to set in a cool place. Slice the remaining banana and toss in the lemon juice to prevent browning. Loosen the edge of the pudding and invert onto a serving dish. Dry the banana slices lightly on kitchen paper. Arrange in a ring on top of the pudding.

BAKED CUSTARD PUDDING
Serves 4

4 egg yolks
2 egg whites
2 tbsp caster sugar
pinch of salt

½ tsp vanilla extract
1 pt (600 ml) milk
butter

Preheat the oven to 350°F/180°C/Gas Mk 4. Beat the egg yolks and whites in a bowl with the caster sugar, salt and vanilla extract. Heat the milk without allowing it to boil and pour it slowly on to the beaten eggs, stirring constantly. Strain the mixture into a well buttered soufflé dish. Place the dish in a baking tin with a little cold water around it and cook in the oven for 50 to 60 minutes, until the custard sets and the top is golden brown. The water in the tin will prevent the custard from becoming too hot and curdling. Sprinkle the custard with a little caster sugar before serving.

YOGHURT BRULEE
Serves 4

2 eggs
½ oz (10 g) cornflour
2 level tbsp caster sugar
½ pt (300 ml) milk

3 tsp vanilla essence
¼ pt (150 ml) natural yoghurt
4 level tbsp demerara sugar

Make a paste with the eggs, cornflour, caster sugar and half the milk. Mix together until smooth, then beat in the remaining milk, vanilla essence and yoghurt. Place in a saucepan and bring to the boil stirring constantly until thickened. Pour into 4 oiled ramekins and leave until cold. Chill overnight in a refrigerator. Just before serving, spoon the demerara sugar on top of each ramekin and then place under a hot grill until the sugar bubbles and melts. Serve immediately.

SWEET PASTA PUDDING
Serves 4–5

3 oz (75 g) macaroni or pasta rings
1 pt (600 ml) milk
small can evaporated milk
2 oz (50 g) sugar

Preheat the oven to 325°F/170°C/Gas Mk 3. Put the milk, evaporated milk, sugar and pasta in a saucepan. Bring to the boil then reduce the heat and simmer for 20 minutes, stirring occasionally. Transfer the pasta mixture to a 2 pint (1.2 ltr) ovenproof dish and bake in the centre of oven for 20–30 minutes.

CREAMY GINGER ROLL
Serves 4

5 oz (150 ml) carton single cream
5 oz (150 ml) carton double cream
8 oz (225 g) ginger biscuits
2 tbsp cooking sherry
mandarin oranges to decorate
strip of angelica cut diagonally

Chill the creams and whip them together until fairly stiff. Dip each biscuit quickly into the cooking sherry and sandwich all of them together with the whipped cream. When the log shape is complete cover the exterior with whipped cream. Lay a row of mandarin oranges with angelica leaves along the top of the roll to decorate.

BAKED BREAD AND BUTTER PUDDING
Serves 4

2–4 slices of bread
butter, for spreading
2 eggs
1 pt (600 ml) milk

1 tbsp caster sugar
few drops of vanilla extract
2 tbsp currants or sultanas

Preheat the oven to 350°F/180°C/Gas Mk 4. Remove crusts from the bread, butter slices and cut into thin strips. Lay bread strips in a well-buttered Pyrex loaf dish. The dish should be about half full. Whisk the eggs in a mixing bowl, add the milk, sugar and vanilla extract. Mix well together and strain over bread strips. Allow the pudding to stand until the bread is well soaked. Sprinkle with the currants or sultanas. Bake for 45 to 60 minutes until golden brown and firm to the touch. Sprinkle with sugar and serve hot.

RICH CUSTARD SPONGE
Serves 6

¾ pt (450 ml) milk
4 eggs, beaten
¼ pt (150 ml) double cream
2 oz (50 g) caster sugar
½ tsp vanilla essence

4 oz (110 g) trifle sponges
1 level tbsp currants
1 level tbsp sultanas
1 level tbsp stoned raisins
½ level tsp freshly grated nutmeg

Preheat the oven to 300°F/150°C/Gas Mk 2. Heat the milk in a saucepan and when it is on the verge of boiling pour on to the beaten eggs, cream, sugar and vanilla essence. Dip the sponges into the custard and use to line the sides only of a 2 pint (1.2 ltr) ovenproof dish. Place the dried fruit in the bottom of the dish and pour the rest of the custard over. Sprinkle with nutmeg and bake for about 1 hour until lightly set. Serve warm with pouring cream.

CHEESECAKES

EASY CREAMY LEMON CHEESCAKE
Serves 6–8

6 oz (175 g) digestive biscuits,
  crumbed
1½ lb (675 g) curd cheese or
  sieved cottage cheese
6 oz (175 g) caster sugar

2 level tbsp cornflour
3 eggs
¼ pt (150 ml) double cream
1 tsp vanilla essence
1 lemon, finely grated peel and juice

Preheat the oven to 300°F/150°C/Gas Mk 2. Grease an 8 in (20 cm) springform pan and spread the biscuit crumbs evenly over the base of the pan. Thoroughly beat together all the other ingredients until the mixture is very smooth. Pour into the tin and bake for 1¼ hours. Switch off the oven and open door. Leave the cheesecake to cool in the oven for 30 minutes. Remove from the oven and cool completely before removing from pan.

JELLIED CHEESECAKE
Serves 6

8 oz (225 g) digestive biscuits,
  crushed
4 oz (110 g) butter, melted
½ oz (10 g) gelatine
4 tbsp cold water
3 eggs

4 oz (110 g) plus 2 tbsp sugar
2 fl oz (60 ml) milk
1 lemon, juice and grated rind
12 oz (350 g) cottage cheese
5 fl oz (150 ml) double cream,
  stiffly whipped

Mix the butter and biscuits and line the base of an 8 in (20 cm) springform cake tin. Sprinkle the gelatine over the water in a small saucepan and set aside for 5 minutes to soften. Dissolve over a low heat. Separate 2 of the eggs and beat the yolks with the whole egg, 4 oz (110 g) of the sugar and the milk. Gently heat the mixture, stirring continuously, for 3–4 minutes until it thickens. Do not let the mixture boil. Remove the pan from the heat and stir in the dissolved gelatine. Set aside to cool to room temperature. Mix in the lemon juice and rind, the cottage cheese and the remaining sugar. Fold in the cream. Whisk the egg whites until they form stiff peaks, then fold them into the cheese mixture. Spoon into the tin. Chill for 2 hours or until set.

RICOTTA CHEESECAKE
Serves 6

8 oz (225 g) digestive biscuits,
  crumbled
4 oz (110 g) butter
1½ oz (35 g) sugar
1 lb (450 g) Ricotta cheese
pinch of salt
1 tbsp plain flour
4 oz (110 g) soft brown sugar

2 eggs, separated
½ tsp saffron
1 tsp finely grated orange rind
1 oz (25 g) raisins
1 oz (25 g) candied orange peel,
  chopped
½ tsp ground cinnamon
2 tbsp icing sugar

Preheat the oven to 350°F/180°C/Gas Mk 4. Lightly grease the sides
and base of a plain sided, loose-bottomed flan tin. In a plastic bag
crush the biscuits with a rolling pin. Sieve the crushed biscuits
through a coarse sieve. Melt the butter in a pan and stir in the sugar.
Stir in the biscuit crumbs. Use this mixture to line the bottom and
sides of the tin. Bake in the oven for 10 minutes. Remove and leave to
cool. Increase the oven temperature to 375°F/190°C/Gas Mk 5. Beat
the cheese until smooth, then stir in the salt, flour, brown sugar, egg
yolks, saffron and grated orange rind. Stir in the raisins and orange
peel. Whisk the egg whites until they form stiff peaks. Fold them
into the cheese mixture. Spoon over the flan base and bake for
30–35 minutes, or until firm. Set aside to cool and sprinkle with the
cinnamon and icing sugar before serving.

BOOZY RAISIN CHEESECAKE
Serves 6

4 oz (110 g) raisins
4 fl oz (125 ml) port
6 oz (175 g) digestive biscuits,
  crushed
3 oz (75 g) butter, melted

1 tsp mixed spice
8 oz (225 g) cottage cheese
½ pt (300 ml) plain yoghurt
2 tbsp double cream

Soak the raisins in the port overnight. Mix together the biscuits,
butter and mixed spice and line the base and sides of a 7 in (18 cm)
loose-bottomed cake tin. Chill. Sieve the cottage cheese, then
gradually beat in the yoghurt and cream. Drain the raisins and fold
them into the cheese mixture. Spoon the mixture into the tin and
smooth the surface. Chill for at least an hour before serving.

ALMOND AND BLACKCURRANT CHEESECAKE
Serves 6

10 oz (300 g) pkt Jamaica ginger cake
2 tsp gelatine
4 tbsp orange juice
3 oz (75 g) ground almonds with honey
2 oz (50 g) icing sugar, sifted

14 oz (400 g) full fat soft cheese
4 oz (110 g) curd cheese
4 fl oz (125 ml) carton Greek
 yoghurt

For the topping:
1 lb (450 g) can of blackcurrants
 in syrup
3 oz (75 g) caster sugar

4 tsp arrowroot
2 tsp water
orange rind

Cut the ginger cake to fit an 8 in (20 cm) greased and base-lined springform cake tin. Press well into the base. Dissolve the gelatine in the orange juice over a pan of simmering water. Toast the ground almonds until golden and mix with the icing sugar. Beat the cheeses together until smooth, then gradually beat in the Greek yoghurt, gelatine and almond mixtures until smooth. Spoon into the cake tin, level the surface and chill in the refrigerator for 3 hours or until set. Drain the blackcurrants and strain the juice into a small pan. Add the caster sugar and heat gently until the sugar is dissolved. Blend arrowroot with the water, stir into the juice and bring to the boil, stirring all the time. Stir in the blackcurrants and cook gently for one minute. Leave to cool. Carefully remove the cheesecake from the tin and just before serving spoon the blackcurrants over the top of the cheesecake and garnish with thin curls of orange rind.

APPLE AND RHUBARB STREUSEL CHEESECAKE
Serves 8

4 oz (110 g) rhubarb, trimmed and
 roughly chopped
11 oz (325 g) caster sugar
2 oz (50 g) self-raising flour, sifted
½ tsp baking powder
2 oz (50 g) butter, softened

1 egg, beaten
4 eggs, separated
1 lb (450 g) curd cheese
1 oz (25 g) plain flour, sifted
6 oz (175 g) apple purée
¼ pt (150 ml) low-fat fromage frais

For the topping:
1 oz (25 g) plain flour, sifted
¾ oz (20 g) butter
¾ oz (20 g) demerara sugar

pinch of ground nutmeg
pinch of ground cloves
apple slices tossed in lemon juice, to decorate

Preheat the oven to 325°F/170°C/Gas Mk 3. Heat the chopped rhubarb in a small pan with 1 oz (25 g) of the caster sugar and enough water to prevent burning. Simmer gently for 1–2 minutes or until the rhubarb is softened. Beat the sifted self-raising flour and baking powder in a bowl with the butter, 2 oz (50 g) of the caster sugar and the beaten egg. Spread the mixture over the bottom of an 8 in (20 cm) lightly greased and base-lined springform cake tin. Whisk the remaining egg yolks and sugar together until thick and pale. Soften the cheese by beating in a bowl and then beat into the egg mixture. Stir in the apple purée, the plain flour and the fromage frais. Then stir in the rhubarb purée. Place the egg whites in a clean bowl and whisk until stiff. Fold into the fruit mixture and then pour into the cake tin and smooth the top. Bake for 1¼ hours. While the cheesecake is cooking mix together the topping ingredients and rub together until it resembles breadcrumbs. Remove the cheesecake from the oven, sprinkle on the topping and return to the oven for a further 15 minutes. Leave in the tin until cool. Decorate with the apple slices and grated lemon rind.

HONEY AND CINNAMON CHEESECAKE
Serves 8

4 oz (110 g) butter, cut into pieces
7 oz (200 g) plain flour, sifted
2–3 tbsp water
4 oz (110 g) dried dates or apricots
8 oz (225 g) cottage cheese

7 oz (200 g) cream cheese
3 eggs
1 tbsp flour
4 tbsp clear honey
¼ tsp ground cinnamon

For the topping: 3 oranges, sliced
3 tbsp demerara sugar
¼ tsp ground cinnamon

Preheat the oven to 350°F/180°C/Gas Mk 4. Rub the butter into the flour until the mixture resembles breadcrumbs. Mix in enough water to make a stiff dough and knead lightly on a floured board. Roll out and carefully line a 10 in (25 cm) flan dish. Chop the dates or apricots and place evenly over the base. Beat all the remaining ingredients together then pour over the fruit. Bake for 45 minutes. Cool completely. Arrange the orange slices on the top of the cheesecake and sprinkle generously with the cinnamon and demerara sugar mixed together.

CHOCOMINT DREAM CHEESECAKE
Serves 6–8

4 oz (110 g) butter, gently melted
8 oz (225 g) chocolate digestive
  biscuits, crushed
4 oz (110 g) plain chocolate,
  broken into small pieces
8 tbsp milk
14 oz (400 g) Philadelphia cream
  cheese

4 oz (110 g) caster sugar
1 tsp peppermint essence
1 tsp vanilla essence
2 tbsp water
½ oz (10 g) powdered gelatine
¼ pt (150 ml) double cream
box of mints, to decorate

Stir the biscuit crumbs into the melted butter, mix well and press into the base of an 8 in (20 cm) lightly greased base-lined springform cake tin. Smooth over and keep chilled in the refrigerator until required. Melt the chocolate in a bowl placed on a pan of simmering water. Stir in the milk. Stir until well combined, remove from the heat and leave to cool. Place the cheese in a bowl and beat until softened. Stir in the sugar, peppermint and vanilla essences and lastly the melted chocolate mixture. Sprinkle the gelatine over the water in a small bowl. Place the bowl over simmering water for 1–2 minutes or until the gelatine has dissolved. Leave to cool slightly and then pour into the cheese mixture, stirring all the time. Whisk the double cream in a clean bowl until firm. Carefully fold into the chocolate mixture, then spoon into the biscuit base. Grate some plain chocolate on top and refrigerate until set. Carefully remove from the tin and decorate with mints around the outside edge.

APPLE CHEESECAKE
Serves 6–8

8 oz (225 g) digestive biscuits
1 tsp ground cinnamon
4 oz (110 g) butter, melted

For the topping:
1 lb (450 g) cooking apples, peeled,
  cored and chopped (alternatively,
  1 lb (450 g) can of apple pie filling)
1 tsp ground cinnamon
2 oz (50 g) demerara sugar (or honey)
1 lemon, grated rind and juice

2 tsp gelatine
12 oz (350 g) cream cheese
½ pt (300 ml) double cream, whipped
1 eating apple, thinly sliced
sprig of mint

Place the biscuits in a large plastic bag and crush with a rolling pin. Tip the crumbs into a large mixing bowl and stir in the cinnamon and melted butter. Press over the base of an 8 in (20 cm) loose-bottomed flan tin. Chill until quite firm. Gently cook the apples, ground cinnamon, demerara sugar and grated lemon rind until pulpy. Stir frequently and add a little water if necessary to prevent the apples from sticking. Warm the lemon juice and dissolve the gelatine in it. Cool, and then put into a blender with the cream cheese and the apple purée. Blend until well mixed and smooth. Tip into a bowl and fold in the whipped cream. Spoon over the base and level the top. Chill for at least 2 hours. Arrange the apple slices in a fan shaped ring on the top. Brush with lemon juice. Decorate with a sprig of mint in the centre.

ALMOND AND BLACK CHERRY CHEESECAKE
Serves 8

6 oz (175 g) sweet shortcrust pastry	2–3 drops almond essence
2 oz (50 g) butter	1 oz (25 g) semolina
3 oz (75 g) caster sugar	8 oz (225 g) can of black
2 large eggs, separated	cherries in syrup
8 oz (225 g) curd cheese	2 tsp arrowroot
2 oz (50 g) ground almonds	whipped cream to decorate

Preheat the oven to 400°F/200°C/Gas Mark 6. Roll the pastry and use to line an 8 in (20 cm) springform tin. Trim the edges, prick the base with a fork and bake for 15 minutes. Cream together the butter and sugar until light and fluffy, and then beat in the egg yolks, one at a time. Gradually beat in the cheese, almonds, almond essence and semolina. Whisk the egg whites until they form soft peaks, then fold into the mixture. Pour the mixture into the pastry case and level the surface. Bake for 45 minutes, turn off the heat and leave the cheesecake in the oven until cold. Remove from the tin. Drain the cherries and reserve 5 fl oz (150 ml) of the syrup. Arrange the cherries over the top of the cake, depipping if necessary. Stir a little of the reserved syrup into the arrowroot to blend and then stir into the remaining reserved syrup. Bring to the boil over a low heat, stirring all the time. Boil for 1 minute until it thickens and then cool thoroughly. Spoon over the cherries and leave to set. Alternatively spread the cheesecake evenly with cherry pie filling. Decorate with whipped cream

CHOCOLATE CARAMEL CHEESECAKE
Serves

4 oz (110 g) butter
8 oz (225 g) plain chocolate
  digestives, crushed
3 oz (75 g) butter
6 oz (175 g) soft brown sugar

6 oz (175 g) can of evaporated milk
7 oz (200 g) cream cheese
2 tsp gelatine powder
2 tbsp water
½ pt (300 ml) double cream

For the topping:
6 oz (175 g) plain chocolate
2 oz (50 g) butter
whipped cream and chocolate shapes to decorate

Melt the 4 oz (110 g) of butter gently and stir into the crushed biscuits mixing well. Press into the base of an 8 in (20 cm) lightly greased and base-lined springform cake tin. Chill until needed. Gently heat the 3 oz (75 g) of butter, the sugar and the evaporated milk together until the sugar dissolves. Raise the heat and boil the mixture rapidly for 4 minutes until the soft ball stage (240°F/115°C on a sugar thermometer or when a small drop of the mixture in cold water forms a soft ball). Let the mixture cool a little and then beat into the cream cheese. Dissolve the gelatine in the water in a bowl over a pan of simmering water. Cool slightly and then fold into the cheese mixture. Chill until it starts to set. Whip the cream until it holds its shape and then fold in. Spoon over the base and level the top. Chill until firm. For the topping, melt the chocolate and then beat in the butter a little at a time. Cool until it begins to thicken. Remove the cheesecake from the tin when set and spread with the topping. Pipe cream round the edges and decorate with chocolate shapes.

ST CLEMENT'S CHEESECAKE
Serves 6

1 egg, beaten
2 oz (50 g) caster sugar
1 oz (25 g) self-raising flour, sifted
few drops vanilla essence
1 lb (450 g) cottage cheese, drained
3 eggs, separated

¼ pt (150 ml) natural yoghurt
1 lemon, finely grated rind and juice
1 orange, finely grated rind and juice
2 tbsp Cointreau (optional)
2 tbsp water
½ oz (10 g) powdered gelatine

To decorate:
orange segments
halved lemon slices

Preheat the oven to 375°F/190°C/Gas Mk 5. Whisk 1 oz (25 g) caster sugar with the egg until thick and pale. Gently fold in the sifted flour and vanilla essence. Spoon the mixture into an 8 in (20 cm) lightly greased and base-lined springform cake tin. Smooth the surface. Bake for 5 minutes or until well risen. Remove from the oven and leave to cool completely. Blend the cheese until smooth and combine with the egg yolks, yoghurt, remaining sugar, fruit rind and juice and the Cointreau, if used. Sprinkle the gelatine over the water in a bowl. Place the bowl over a pan of simmering water and stir until dissolved. Cool slightly. When cooled a little pour into the cheese mixture, mixing well. Whisk the egg whites until stiff in a clean bowl. Carefully fold into the cheese mixture and then spoon into the tin. Refrigerate until set. Carefully remove from the cake tin and decorate with orange segments and lemon slices.

JACK HORNER CHEESECAKE
Serves 8

2 oz (50 g) butter, melted	½ tsp almond essence
8 oz (225 g) digestive biscuits, crushed	¼ pt (150 ml) soured cream
8 oz (225 g) cottage cheese, sieved	2 oz (50 g) ground almonds
8 oz (225 g) full fat cream cheese	3–4 red plums, stoned
4 oz (110 g) caster sugar	1 oz (25 g) toasted flaked almonds
3 eggs separated	icing sugar to dredge
1 oz (25 g) cornflour	cream to serve

Preheat the oven to 300°F/150°C/Gas Mk 2. Mix the melted butter and crushed biscuits together until well blended and press into the base of an 8 in (20 cm) greased, base-lined springform or loose bottomed cake tin. Chill until needed. Place both cheeses in a large bowl, add the sugar, egg yolks, cornflour, almond essence, soured cream and ground almonds and blend all well together. A food processor is a great help in this direction, otherwise it means plenty of elbow grease! Whisk the egg whites until stiff in a clean bowl and fold into the cheese mixture. Pour over the biscuit base and cook in a preheated oven for 1½ hours until golden. Turn off the heat and leave the door ajar until the cheesecake is completely cold. Carefully remove from the tin and slide onto a serving plate. Slice each plum into six and arrange around the edge. Sprinkle with flaked almonds and dredge with icing sugar. Serve with cream.

BLACKCURRANT CHEESECAKE
Serves 4–5

6 oz (175 g) digestive biscuits, crushed
2 oz (50 g) butter, melted
¼ tsp vanilla essence
juice of ½ lemon
2 tbsp water
½ oz (10 g) gelatine
6 oz (175 g) soft cream cheese

2 large eggs, separated
2 oz (50 g) caster sugar
7 fl oz (200 ml) double cream
12 oz (350 g) can of blackcurrants,
    drained – reserve the syrup
2 tsp arrowroot

Preheat the oven to 400°F/200°C/Gas Mk 6. Lightly grease a 7 in (18 cm) loose-bottomed cake tin. Mix together the biscuit crumbs, vanilla and the melted butter. Press the mixture into the base of the tin and bake for 15 minutes. Remove and cool completely, then line the sides of the tin with greaseproof paper oiled on both sides. Mix the lemon juice and water together and sprinkle over the gelatine in a small pan. Set aside. Beat together the cream cheese, egg yolks and sugar until smooth and creamy. Gradually stir in the cream and 4 tbsp of the reserved syrup. Fold in half of the blackcurrants. Whisk the egg whites until they form stiff peaks. Fold them into the cheese and cream mixture. Set the lemon juice and gelatine over a low heat until the gelatine has dissolved. Stir it into the cheese and cream mixture and pour into the prepared tin. Chill in the refrigerator until set. Mix the arrowroot with 2 tbsp of the remaining syrup. Put the rest of the syrup in a pan over a moderate heat and bring to the boil. Add the arrowroot and cook, stirring constantly, until the syrup is thick and transparent. Remove from the heat and stir in the remaining blackcurrants. Set aside to cool. Carefully remove the cheesecake from the tin and pour over the thickened blackcurrant mixture. Chill until required, but take out of the refrigerator about 30 minutes before serving.

CHERRY CHEESECAKE
Serves 6

2 oz (50 g) Weetabix
1 tbsp soft brown sugar
4 tbsp margarine, melted

For the filling:
8 oz (225 g) low-fat cottage cheese
½ oz (10 g) gelatine
3 tbsp water
5 oz (150 g) low-fat yoghurt

4 oz (110 g) cream
1 lb (450 g) tin of black cherry pie
    filling
½ oz (10 g) cornflour

Crumble the Weetabix into a large bowl and mix in the melted margarine and the sugar. Press into the base of a 8 in (20 cm) loose bottomed flan tin. Blend the cottage cheese in a blender until very smooth. Sprinkle the gelatine over the water in a bowl. Place the bowl over a pan of simmering water and stir until dissolved. Mix the cottage cheese, yoghurt, gelatine and cream together and whisk for 1 minute. Pour the mixture into the flan tin and leave in the refrigerator for at least 2 hours. Put the cornflour in a saucepan and mix in 1 tbsp of the cherry pie filling. Cook over a low heat for a few seconds and then add the rest of the tin. Bring to the boil and simmer for 1 minute. Cool thoroughly. When cold spread over the chilled cheesecake. This recipe is low in calories.

ORANGE CHEESECAKE
Serves 6–8

3 oranges
juice of 1 lemon
2 tbsp powdered gelatine
2 eggs, separated
½ pt (300 ml) milk

3 oz (75 g) caster sugar
1 lb 4 oz (560 g) plain cottage cheese
¼ pt (150 ml) double cream, whipped
extra whipped cream for decoration

Crumb base:
4 oz (110 g) digestive biscuits
2 oz (50 g) caster sugar

2 oz (50 g) butter, melted
3 oranges, peeled and segmented

Finely grate the rind of 2 oranges and squeeze the juice from all of them. Add the lemon juice. Put 4 tbsp of the juices into a small bowl and sprinkle the gelatine over. Whisk together the egg yolks, milk and 2 oz (50 g) sugar. Turn into a pan and cook without boiling for a few minutes. Add the soaked gelatine and stir continuously until dissolved. Leave to cool until just starting to set and then add the grated orange rind and an additional 6 tbsp of the mixed juices. Blend the cheese until smooth and add the jelly mixture to the blender. Whisk the egg whites stiffly, add 1 oz (25 g) sugar and whisk again until stiff. Fold gently into the almost set cheese mixture, followed by the whipped cream. Turn into a 10 in (25 cm) spring form cake tin base lined with greaseproof paper. Crush the biscuits and stir in the sugar and melted butter. Spread over the cheese mixture and press lightly with a spatula. Chill thoroughly. To serve, turn out and decorate with overlapping segments of orange and swirls of whipped cream.

ALMOND CHEESECAKE
Serves 6

3 oz (75 g) digestive biscuits, crushed
2 oz (50 g) ground almonds

4 oz (110 g) butter, melted
3 tbsp caster sugar

For the filling:
1 lb (450 g) cream cheese
7 oz (200 g) caster sugar
3 large eggs
2 oz (50 g) ground almonds

1½ tsp almond essence
pinch salt
8 fl oz (250 ml) soured cream
½ tsp vanilla essence

Preheat the oven to 350°F/180°C/Gas Mk 4. Combine all the ingredients for the crumb crust and press onto the bottom and halfway up the sides of a 9 in (23 cm) springform cake tin. Chill. Beat the cheese with 5 oz (150 g) of the sugar, add the eggs one at a time, beating in. Add the almonds, 1 tsp of the almond essence and salt. Pour into the crust and bake in a preheated oven for 45 minutes. Cool in the tin on a wire rack for 20 minutes. Combine the remaining sugar and almond essence with the salt, cream and vanilla essence. Spread over the cake. Return to the oven and bake for 10 minutes. Cool, then chill for at least 2 hours.

SLIMMERS' PINEAPPLE CHEESECAKE
Serves 6

2 oz (50 g) Weetabix
4 tbsp margarine, melted
2 eggs, separated
1 large tin of sweetened skimmed
   condensed milk
1 lemon, grated rind and juice

8 oz (225 g) tin of crushed pineapple
8 oz (225 g) low-fat cottage cheese
5 oz (150 g) low-fat yoghurt
1 oz (25 g) powdered gelatine
sprig of mint

Crumble the Weetabix and stir in the melted margarine. Press into the base of an 10 in (25 cm) loose-bottomed flan tin. Chill. Separate the eggs and whisk the yolks with the condensed milk. Whisk in the grated rind of the lemon, the lemon juice and the yoghurt. Over a gentle heat dissolve the gelatine in the juice from the crushed pineapple, cool a little and then stir into the mixture. Put the cottage cheese into a blender and beat until smooth. Add the crushed pineapple and blend again. Add the cheese and pineapple to the egg mixture and whisk for a further thirty seconds. Whisk the egg whites until very stiff and fold into the mixture. Pour over the prepared base, smooth the top and put in the refrigerator for at least three hours. Decorate with mint leaves.

BAKED CHEESECAKE
Serves 6

8 oz (225 g) digestive biscuits
2 level tsp caster sugar
4 oz (110 g) butter, melted

For the filling:
½ pt (300 ml) milk
1 tbsp lemon juice
4 eggs
5 oz (150 g) caster sugar

2 level tbsp flour
¼ tsp salt
1 lb (450 g) cottage cheese
icing sugar, for dusting

Preheat the oven to 325°F/170°C/Gas Mk 3. Lightly grease an 8 in
(20 cm) round loose-bottomed springform cake tin. Crumb the
biscuits with the sugar in a blender and mix into the melted butter.
Press half of this mixture into the base of the tin. Put the remaining
ingredients, except the icing sugar and remaining half of crumbs into a
blender and mix well together. Pour over the crumb base. Bake for
1–1¼ hours or until centre is firm. Cool until really firm and then
cover carefully with the remaining crumbs. Cut 6 strips of
greaseproof paper, 1 in (2.5 cm) wide, and place in a lattice fashion
over the crumbs. Dust with icing sugar and then carefully remove the
paper strips.

MANHATTAN CHEESECAKE
Serves

1 lb (450 g) cream cheese
1 lb (450 g) ricotta cheese
12 oz (350 g) caster sugar
4 large eggs
2 oz (50 g) butter, melted
3 tbsp flour

3 tbsp cornflour
2 tsp vanilla essence
2 tsp grated lemon rind
¾ pt (450 ml) soured cream
whipped cream
grated nutmeg

Preheat the oven to 325°F/170°C/Gas Mk 3. Beat the cream cheese
with the ricotta and sugar. Then beat in the eggs one at a time. Add
the butter, flour, cornflour, vanilla and lemon rind, and combine well.
Fold in the soured cream and pour the mixture into a greased 10 in
(25 cm) springform tin. Bake for 1 hour. Turn off the heat but do not
open the oven door. Leave the cake in the closed oven for 2 hours.
Remove the cake to a rack and allow to cool in the tin. Chill for at
least 2 hours. Remove the sides of the tin and transfer the cheesecake
to a serving dish. Top with whipped cream and sprinkle with
grated nutmeg.

RASPBERRY CHEESECAKE
Serves 8

8 oz (225 g) plain flour, sifted
5 oz (150 g) butter, cut into small pieces
¾ oz (20 g) icing sugar, sifted
1 egg yolk
12 oz (350 g) low-fat cream cheese
4 tbsp clear honey
¼ pt (150 ml) half-fat single cream

7 oz (200 g) fresh raspberries
 (plus 1 oz (25 g) for decoration)
1 tbsp raspberry liqueur (optional)
2 tbsp water
½ oz (10 g) powdered gelatine
3 egg whites
4 tbsp raspberry jam

To decorate:
¼ pt (150 ml) half-fat double cream,
 whipped
fresh sprigs of mint

Preheat the oven to 375°F/190°C/Gas Mk 5. Mix the flour, butter, sugar and egg yolk very well together. Turn onto a floured surface and knead lightly. Using your knuckles press into the base and halfway up the sides of an 8 in (20 cm) lightly greased and base-lined springform cake tin. Bake for 15–20 minutes until cooked and golden brown. Remove from the oven and leave to cool completely. Beat together the cream cheese and honey until softened. Beat in the cream. Purée 4 oz (110 g) of the raspberries with the liqueur, if used, in a blender and stir into the cheese mixture. Keep in the refrigerator until needed. Sprinkle the gelatine over the water in a bowl. Place the bowl over a pan of simmering water and stir until dissolved. Remove from the heat and when cooled slightly stir into the cheese mixture. Whisk egg whites in a clean bowl until thick and foamy and then fold lightly into the cheese mixture. Spread the jam over the pastry base, and arrange the remainder of the raspberries on top (reserving 1 oz (25 g) for decoration). Spoon the filling into the tin. Smooth over the top and leave in the refrigerator until set. Carefully remove from the tin and decorate with piped whipped cream around the outside edge, and with the remaining raspberries and mint.

BANANA AND GINGER CHEESECAKE
Serves 6

8 oz (225 g) ginger biscuits,
 crushed finely
4 oz (110 g) unsalted butter, melted
8 oz (225 g) full fat soft cheese
5 fl oz (150 ml) soured cream
3 bananas
2 tbsp clear honey

1 tbsp chopped preserved ginger
 (with syrup)
3 tsp gelatine
4 tbsp lemon juice
banana slices, to decorate
preserved ginger slices to decorate

Stir the crushed ginger biscuits into the melted butter and press firmly into the base of an 8 in (20 cm) springform cake tin. Chill in the refrigerator for at least 30 minutes or until required. Beat the cheese and cream together until light. Peel and mash the bananas and then beat into the cheese mixture with the ginger syrup, chopped ginger and honey. Sprinkle the gelatine over the lemon juice in a small bowl and stand in a saucepan of gently simmering water until dissolved. Stir the dissolved gelatine slowly into the cheese mixture and then pour over the base. Chill in the refrigerator for about 3–4 hours until the mixture is set. To serve, remove carefully from the tin and decorate with slices of banana and preserved ginger. Serve before the banana starts to discolour.

SPONGE BASED LEMON CHEESECAKE
Serves 8

2 eggs
2 oz (50 g) caster sugar
2 oz (50 g) plain flour, sifted

For the filling:

8 oz (225 g) fromage frais	*¼ pt (150 ml) double cream*
8 oz (225 g) cream cheese	*1 egg white*
2 tbsp lemon juice	*pinch of salt*
3 tsp gelatine	*3 tbsp icing sugar*
3 tbsp water	

Preheat the oven to 425°F/220°C/Gas Mk 7. Whisk the eggs and sugar together in a large bowl until light, thick and fluffy. Sift the flour into the eggs and fold in gently using a metal spoon. Pour into an 8 in (20 cm) greased and base-lined springform tin and cook in the oven until well risen and golden. Cool in the tin. When it is cold, turn out onto a board and slice in half horizontally. Place one half back into the cleaned tin. Beat the fromage frais and cream cheese together. Sprinkle the gelatine over the lemon juice and water in a small bowl. Place the bowl in a pan of gently simmering water and stir until it has completely dissolved. Beat into the cheeses. Whisk the cream until it is softly thick and fold into the mixture. Whisk the egg white with a pinch of salt until it is standing in peaks. Fold into the cheesecake mixture. Spread the mixture gently over the sponge base and place the second half on top. Chill until set. Remove from the tin and dust with sifted icing sugar.

BLACK FOREST CHEESECAKE
Serves 8–10

3 oz (75 g) plain chocolate
2½ oz (60 g) butter
9 oz (250 g) plain chocolate
digestive biscuits crumbs
15 oz (425 g) can of stoned
black cherries in syrup
12 oz (350 g) full-fat soft cheese
3 oz (90 g) caster sugar

2 eggs, separated
1 tbsp kirsch
2 tbsp cold water
½ oz (10 g) gelatine
½ pt (300 ml) double cream
1 tbsp arrowroot
kirsch or lemon juice to taste
chocolate curls

Line and grease the base of a 9 in (23 cm) loose-bottomed cake tin. Melt the chocolate and butter together and mix with the biscuit crumbs. Press evenly all over the base of the tin and chill. Drain the cherries and cut in half. Reserve the syrup. Spread one-third of the cherries on the base and set aside. Beat the cheese and sugar together until soft and creamy and then beat in the kirsch and egg yolks. Put the water in a small bowl standing in a saucepan of hot water and sprinkle on the gelatine. Stir until the gelatine dissolves. Leave to cool slightly. Beat the cream until it forms soft peaks, and whisk the egg whites until stiff. Beat the gelatine into the cheese mixture a little at a time until it is well incorporated, then fold in the cream and lastly the egg whites. Turn onto the base and chill until firm. Blend the arrowroot with a little of the reserved syrup. Heat the remaining syrup in a small pan, add the kirsch or lemon juice, and bring to the boil. Gradually stir in the arrowroot and continue stirring until the sauce thickens and clears. Cool under a piece of damp greaseproof paper to prevent a skin forming on top. Remove the tin from the cheesecake. When ready to serve place the remaining cherries on top, leaving about half an inch uncovered around the top, and spoon a little cherry sauce over them. Arrange chocolate curls around the edge. Serve the remaining sauce separately.

SWEDISH CHEESECAKE
Serves 8

1 lb (450 g) Cottage cheese
pinch of salt
1 tbsp plain flour
2 oz (50 g) caster sugar

3 eggs, lightly beaten
15 fl oz (450 ml) single cream
2 oz (50 g) blanched, toasted and
chopped almonds

Preheat the oven to 275°F/140°C/Gas Mk 1. Lightly grease a shallow 4 pint (2.4 ltr) baking dish. Beat the cottage cheese until smooth. Stir in the flour, salt, eggs, sugar, cream and almonds. Pour the mixture into the baking dish and cook for 1 hour, or until a skewer inserted in the centre comes out clean.

ITALIAN CHEESECAKE
Serves 12

8 oz (225 g) plain flour
¼ tsp salt
6 oz (175 g) butter, cut into
  small pieces
4 egg yolks, lightly beaten

2 tbsp caster sugar
5 tbsp Marsala (or light, fortified
  sweet white wine)
grated rind of 1 lemon

For the filling:
2½ lb (1.1 kg) Ricotta or
  curd cheese, sieved
4 oz (110 g) caster sugar
4 egg yolks
2 tbsp plain flour
pinch of salt
½ tsp vanilla essence

whole grated rind of orange
2 lemons, grated rind and juice
3 tbsp raisins
2 tbsp finely chopped candied peel
2 tbsp slivered, blanched almonds
1 egg white, lightly beaten

Preheat the oven to 350°F/180°C/Gas Mk 4. Grease a 10 in (25 cm) springform tin. Sift together the flour and salt and make a well in the centre. Drop in the butter, egg yolks, sugar, Marsala and lemon rind. Blend these into the flour with the fingertips and lightly knead the dough until it is smooth. Roll into a ball, wrap in clingfilm and refrigerate for 1 hour. Take off one quarter of the dough, dust with flour, wrap again and return to the refrigerator. Roll out the remaining dough 2 in (5 cm) larger than the tin. Line the tin, bring the pastry up the sides and neaten the edge. Set aside in a cool place. Beat together the cheese and sugar, adding the egg yolks one at a time. Then beat in the flour, salt, vanilla essence, orange and lemon rind and juice. Stir in the raisins and candied peel. Pour the mixture into the prepared case and smooth the top. Sprinkle with the slivered almonds. Roll out the reserved pastry into a 10 in (25 cm) long rectangle and cut into long strips. Arrange in lattice fashion over the top of the cheesecake. Brush the strips with the egg white. Bake for 1 hour or until golden and firm to the touch. Leave until completely cold.

COOKED STRAWBERRY CHEESECAKE
Serves 5

6 oz (175 g) shortbread biscuits, crushed
finely grated rind of 1 lemon
2 oz (50 g) caster sugar
2 oz (50 g) butter, melted
8 oz (225 g) cottage cheese, sieved

8 oz (225 g) full fat cream cheese
1 egg, lightly beaten
8 oz (225 g) strawberries, halved
2 tbsp redcurrant jelly
1 tbsp hot water

Preheat the oven to 350°F/180°C/Gas Mk 4. Lightly grease a 7 in
(18 cm) loose-bottomed cake tin. Mix together the biscuit crumbs,
1 tablespoon of the sugar, the grated lemon rind and the melted
butter. Press into the base and as far up the sides as the amount will
allow. Bake for 10 minutes. Set on one side to cool. Increase the oven
temperature to 375°F/190°C/Gas 5. Beat together both cheeses, the
egg and remaining sugar until smooth and creamy. Spoon into the
base and level the surface. Bake for 40–45 minutes or until firm to the
touch. Leave to cool. Remove the cheesecake from the tin and arrange
the halved strawberries on top. Dissolve the redcurrant jelly in the
water and glaze the strawberries carefully. Cool before serving.

STRAWBERRY CHEESECAKE
Serves 4–5

6 oz (175 g) shortbread biscuits,
   crushed
2 oz (50 g) butter, melted
finely grated rind of an orange
2 oz (50 g) caster sugar
8 oz (225 g) soft cream cheese

8 oz (225 g) cottage cheese
1 egg, lightly beaten
8 oz (225 g) strawberries, halved
2 tbsp redcurrant jelly
1 tbsp hot water

Preheat the oven to 350°F/180°C/Gas Mk 4. Lightly grease a 7 in
(18 cm) loose-bottomed cake tin. Mix together the biscuit crumbs,
orange rind, a tablespoon of the sugar and the melted butter. Put the
mixture into the base and up the sides of the tin and cook for
10 minutes. Increase the oven temperature to 375°F/190°C/Gas Mk 5.
Beat together the sieved cottage cheese, cream cheese, egg and remaining sugar until smooth and creamy. Pile on top of the crumb base and
bake for 40–45 minutes. Set aside to cool. Remove the cheesecake
from the tin and arrange the strawberries on top. Dissolve the
redcurrant jelly in the water and brush over the strawberries to glaze.

ALMOND MACAROON CHEESECAKE
Serves 6

10 oz (300 g) almond macaroons,
    crushed
3 oz (75 g) butter, melted
8 oz (225 g) curd cheese
5 fl oz (150 ml) yoghurt
2 eggs, lightly beaten

2 tbsp clear honey
½ oz (10 g) gelatine
2 tbsp orange or grapefruit juice
grated zest of 1 orange
1 oz toasted blanched almonds

Lightly grease a 8 in (20 cm) flan ring and stand on a flat, greased serving plate. Mix together 8 oz (225 g) of the crushed macaroons with the melted butter and line the base and sides of the flan ring. Chill. Beat together the cheese and yoghurt until smooth and then beat in the eggs and honey. Sprinkle the gelatine over the fruit juice in a pan and leave for 5 minutes. Dissolve over a very low heat. Cool slightly and then pour into the cheese mixture, beating all the time. Stir in the grated orange zest and the remainder of the crushed macaroons. Pour this into the biscuit case and chill for at least 2 hours. Just prior to serving remove the flan ring very carefully and decorate the top with the toasted almonds.

YORKSHIRE CURD CHEESECAKE
Serves 4

8 oz (225 g) sweet shortcrust pastry
8 oz (225 g) curd cheese
2 oz (50 g) caster sugar
finely grated zest of 1 lemon

2 tbsp currants
½ oz (10 g) melted butter
½ tsp nutmeg, freshly grated
2 eggs, separated, plus 1 extra white

Preheat the oven to 220°C/425°F/Gas Mk 7. Use the pastry to line an 8 in (20 cm) loose-bottomed flan tin. Lightly prick the base all over. Mix together the cheese, sugar, lemon zest, currants, melted butter and half the nutmeg. Beat the yolks into this mixture. Whisk the egg whites until they form stiff peaks and fold these into the cheese mixture. Pour into the flan case and sprinkle the remaining nutmeg over the top. Bake in the centre of the oven for 10 minutes, then lower the heat to 350°F/180°C/Gas Mk 4. Bake for 20 minutes more, until the pastry is crisp and the filling set and golden brown. Cool slightly before removing from the tin. Serve warm or cold.

CHOCOLATE AND LEMON CHEESECAKE
Serves 6

3 oz (75 g) plain chocolate
4 oz (110 g) butter
9 oz (250 g) plain chocolate
  digestive biscuits crumbs
juice of ½ lemon
8 oz (225 g) full-fat soft cheese
2 tbsp clear honey

1 egg, separated
¼ pt (150 ml) cold milk
vanilla essence
½ oz (10 g) gelatine
2 tsp brandy
2 tbsp cold water
½ lemon

Line and grease the base of an 8 in (20 cm) loose-bottomed cake tin. Melt 2 oz (50g) of the chocolate and butter together and mix with the biscuit crumbs. Press evenly all over the base of the tin and chill. Beat the lemon juice into the cheese. Beat the egg yolk, honey and milk together in a heatproof bowl. Stand the bowl in a saucepan of simmering water and whisk with an electric mixer until the custard thickens. Cool for 2 minutes and then gradually beat it into the cheese a little at a time, also incorporating the brandy and a few drops of vanilla essence. Soften the gelatine in the water, then stand the bowl in a saucepan of gently simmering water and stir until dissolved. Cool for about 3 minutes and then stir a little at a time into the cheese mixture. Leave to cool. Whisk the egg white until it forms soft peaks and fold into the cheese mixture when it is just starting to set. Turn the mixture into the base and chill. Slice the half lemon, then cut each slice in half just from the centre to the edge and twist into a curl. Melt the remaining chocolate for the topping and dribble from a fork over the top. Decorate with the lemon curls.

GERMAN CHEESECAKE
Serves 6

1 oz (25 g) unsalted butter, melted
4 oz (110 g) sweet biscuit crumbs
4 oz (110 g) unsalted butter
4 tbsp caster sugar
1 lb (450 g) German quark

½ pt (300 ml) soured cream
4 tsp orange juice
2 tsp grated orange rind
4 large eggs, separated

Preheat the oven to 350°F/180°C/Gas Mk 4. Mix the butter and biscuit crumbs and press into the base of a 9 in (23 cm) loose-bottomed cake tin. Cream the butter and sugar until light and fluffy, beat in the quark, cream, orange juice, rind and egg yolks. Whisk the egg whites until stiff and fold into the mixture. Pour into the cake tin and bake for about 1¼ hours until set and golden brown on top.

EASY UNCOOKED CHEESECAKE
Serves 6

2 layers of 6 in (15 cm) sponge cake
8 oz (225 g) curd cheese
2 oz (50 g) caster sugar
½ lemon, juice and grated rind

½ pt (300 ml) double cream
¼ oz (5 g) powdered gelatine
2 tbsp hot water

Line a deep 6 in (15 cm) cake tin with foil and lay one layer of sponge cake in the bottom. Beat the curd cheese with the sugar, lemon juice and rind until smooth. Stir in the stiffly whipped double cream. Melt the gelatine powder in the hot water and allow to cool slightly. Stir into the cheese mixture, mixing well. Spoon the cheese mixture on top of the sponge cake, level off and place the second layer of sponge cake on top. Sprinkle thickly with caster sugar and chill for at least 2 hours before serving.

EASTER CHEESE GATEAU
Serves 4–6

1 round sponge cake 6 in (15 cm)
wide and 3 in (7.5 cm) high
16 lb (450 g) cottage cheese
4 oz (110 g) caster sugar
1 tbsp double cream
pinch of salt
1 tsp ground cinnamon

2 tbsp sweet sherry
4 tbsp lemon juice
2 oz (50 g) chopped mixed peel
8 oz (225 g) marzipan
4 tbsp apricot jam
2 tbsp water
small sugar Easter eggs to decorate

Split the sponge cake into four equal sized horizontal layers. Put the bottom layer into a 6 in (15 cm) springform cake tin. Sieve the cheese into a bowl and beat in the caster sugar. Add the cream, pinch of salt, cinnamon, sherry and half of the lemon juice and beat together until well blended (or put in a processor). Fold in the peel. Spread one third of the mixture over the sponge base, cover with the second sponge layer and repeat the process finishing with a top layer of sponge cake. Place a circle of greaseproof paper on top with a light weight and leave in a cool place overnight. Roll out 4 oz (110 g) of the marzipan into a strip to fit the sides of the cake. Melt the apricot jam with the remaining lemon juice and the water gently in a saucepan and strain to form a glaze. Paint the sides of the gateau with the glaze and wrap the marzipan strip around it. Seal the join with a little glaze. Paint the top of the gateau with the glaze. Roll the remaining marzipan into 11 small balls and place at even intervals around the top edge of the cake. Pile a few sugar Easter eggs in the centre.

CARIBBEAN CHEESECAKE
Serves 10

4 oz (110 g) digestive biscuits, crushed
4 oz (110 g) desiccated coconut
3 oz (75 g) butter, melted
15 oz (425 g) can of pineapple
   chunks, drained
1 lime, finely grated rind and juice
2 oz (50 g) caster sugar
8 oz (225 g) cream cheese

7 oz (200 g) creme fraiche
½oz (10g) gelatine
¼pt (150 ml) double cream, whipped
12 oz (350 g) mixed tropical fruit
   such as kiwi fruit, pawpaw,
   pineapple and banana: all
   peeled and sliced.

Stir the crushed biscuits and coconut into the melted butter until well mixed. Press into an 8 in (20 cm) lightly greased springform tin. Put in the refrigerator for at least 2 hours to set. Put the pineapple in a food processor and blend until smooth, then beat in the cream cheese, creme fraiche, sugar and grated rind. Sprinkle the gelatine over the lime juice in a cup. Stand the cup in a pan of gently simmering water until the gelatine is dissolved. Allow to cool slightly and then fold into the pineapple mixture together with the whipped cream. Spoon onto the base and chill for 3–4 hours until firm. When ready to serve, remove from the tin and decorate with the fresh tropical fruit.

UNCOOKED CHEESECAKE
Serves 6

4 oz (110 g) digestive biscuits, crushed
1 oz (25 g) butter

For the filling:
3 eggs, separated
3 oz (75 g) caster sugar
2 lemons, grated rind and juice
½ oz (10 g) powdered gelatine

3 tbsp water
12 oz (350 g) cream cheese
¼ pt (150 ml) double cream
   or evaporated milk

Butter a tin or flan dish lavishly and sprinkle over the biscuit crumbs. Beat the yolks with the sugar and grated lemon rind until creamy in colour and fluffy. Dissolve the gelatine in the water and add to 3 tbsp of the lemon juice. Add to the egg mixture, and then stir in the cream cheese, a little at a time, and the lightly whipped cream (or evaporated milk). Whisk the egg whites until stiff and fold in gently. Pour into the biscuit lined dish and chill for at least 2 hours. Decorate with whipped cream and sprinkle with a little grated lemon rind or lemon rind curls.

AUSTRIAN CURD CAKE
Serves 6

12 oz (350 g) cottage cheese
2½ oz (65 g) butter, cut into small
  pieces
5 oz (150 g) caster sugar
3 oz (75 g) raisins
sifted icing sugar

1 oz (25 g) ground almonds
2 tbsp semolina
1 medium lemon, grated rind and
  juice
2 eggs, separated

Preheat the oven to 375°F/190°C/Gas Mk 5. Sieve the cheese. Cream
the butter with the sugar; gradually beat in the cheese and egg yolks.
Blend in the raisins, almonds, semolina, lemon rind and juice. Beat the
egg whites until stiff, then lightly fold into the creamed mixture.
Spoon into a 7 in (18 cm) greased and lined sandwich tin. Bake for
1 hour or until golden brown. Cool in the tin, then remove and dust
with the sifted icing sugar.

APRICOT YOGHURT CHEESECAKE
Serves 8

8 digestive biscuits, crushed
2 oz (50 g) butter, melted
8 oz (225g) tin of apricot halves

For the filling:
2 oz (50 g) butter, cut into small pieces
2 oz (50 g) caster sugar
2 level tbsp plain flour
1 lb (450 g) curd cheese
2 eggs

½ tsp vanilla essence
¼ pt (150 ml) soured cream
¼ pt (150 ml) Greek yoghurt
2 oz (50 g) caster sugar

Preheat the oven to 325°F/170°C/Gas Mk 3. Stir the biscuit crumbs
into the melted butter until well mixed and press firmly over the base
of an 8 in (20 cm) lightly greased springform tin. Drain the
apricot halves and place over the base. Chill. Cream the butter, sugar
and flour until light and fluffy. Add the cheese and beat well. Beat in
the eggs one at a time and gently stir the vanilla essence and soured
cream into the mixture. Pour over the apricot base. Bake in the oven
for 50 minutes until firm to the touch. Lower the oven temperature to
300°F/150°C/ Gas Mk 2. Blend the yoghurt and sugar together and
spread over the top of the cheesecake. Return to the oven for a further
15 minutes until the yoghurt is set. Remove from oven and run a
knife around the edge of the tin to loosen, and then leave to get completely cold before removing. Chill overnight if possible.

SNOWY RASPBERRY CHEESECAKE
Serves 6

6 oz (175 g) digestive biscuits,
  finely crushed
2 oz (50 g) butter, melted
8 oz (225 g) low-fat soft cheese
¼ pt (150 ml) soured cream
1 tsp grated lemon rind
1 tbsp lemon juice
1 tsp vanilla essence

7 oz (200 g) caster sugar
3 eggs, 2 separated
12 oz (350 g) frozen raspberries,
  thawed
5 tbsp redcurrant jelly
1 tbsp water
pinch of salt

Preheat the oven to 300°F/150°C/Gas Mk 2. Mix the biscuits well with the melted butter and press into the base and up the sides of a 9 in (23 cm) flan dish. Chill in the refrigerator until needed or for at least 30 minutes. Beat together the cheese and soured cream, and then beat in the lemon rind, lemon juice, vanilla and 3 oz (75 g) of the sugar. Beat in the whole egg, followed by the two egg yolks and beat until smooth. Pour onto the biscuit crumb base and bake for about 1 hour or until the filling is firm to the touch. Remove from the oven and leave to cool. At this stage the cheesecake may be left in the refrigerator until ready for the second stage of cooking. To complete, arrange the raspberries on the top of the cheesecake. Melt the redcurrant jelly in a small saucepan with the water over a gentle heat and spoon it over the fruit. Let the jelly cool and set and then cover the cheesecake lightly with foil and chill in the refrigerator for at least 6 hours. Reheat the oven to 350°F/180°C/Gas Mk 4. Whisk the egg whites with a pinch of salt until stiff. Whisk in half the remaining sugar and continue whisking until the meringue is stiff and shiny. Fold the remaining sugar in with a metal spoon. Spread the meringue carefully over the fruit so that it completely covers the redcurrant topping, and tease the meringue into little peaks. Cook in the preheated oven for 10 minutes until the meringue is golden brown. Serve at once.

AUSTRIAN SOUFFLÉ CHEESECAKE

6 chocolate covered mini
  Swiss rolls
2 oz (50 g) plain chocolate,
  broken into small pieces
1 lb (450 g) full-fat soft cream cheese

5 fl oz single cream
3 eggs, separated
6 tbsp water
3 oz (75 g) caster sugar
½ oz (10 g) gelatine

To make the base cut each Swiss roll into 5 slices. Arrange slices against the inside of a deep, round 8 in (20 cm) loose-bottomed cake tin. Place remaining slices on the base of the tin. Melt the chocolate in a bowl over a pan of hot water. Using a teaspoon drizzle half the chocolate over the base. Beat the cream cheese until smooth adding the single cream a little at a time. Place the yolks in a bowl with the sugar and half of the water and whisk them over a saucepan of hot water until thick and creamy. Remove from the heat and whisk until cool. Fold into the cream cheese mixture using a metal spoon. Sprinkle the gelatine over the remaining water. Place the basin in a pan of gently simmering water and stir until the gelatine has dissolved. Remove from the heat and allow to cool slightly before stirring into the cheese mixture. Whisk egg whites in a clean, dry bowl until stiff and fold into the mixture with a metal spoon. Pour into tin. Remelt the chocolate over hot water and drizzle over the top of the cheesecake. Place in refrigerator for at least 3 hours. Remove from the tin onto a serving plate. Serve with whipped cream.

PLUM CHEESECAKE
Serves 6

3 oz (75 g) butter
4½ oz (140 g) digestive biscuit crumbs
8 oz (225 g) fresh, cooked
   or tinned plums
3 tbsp clear honey
8 oz (225 g) cream cheese
¼ pt (150 ml) soured cream
2 eggs, separated
1 lemon, grated rind and juice
¼ pt (150 ml) natural yoghurt
1 tbsp lemon juice

Preheat the oven to 350°F/180°C/Gas Mk 4. Line the base and grease the inside of a 9 in (23 cm) springform cake tin. Melt 1 oz (25 g) of the butter and stir in the biscuit crumbs. Press evenly over the base of the tin. Stone the plums, drain well and place on top of the crumbs. Chill. Cream the remaining butter and 2 tbsp of the honey together until light and fluffy. Gradually beat in the cream cheese, soured cream, egg yolks, lemon rind and juice. Leave 1 tablespoon of juice for later. Whisk the egg whites until stiff and fold into the cheese mixture. Pour onto the prepared base and bake for 1 hour until set and golden. Reduce the oven temperature to 300°F/150°C/Gas Mk 2. Beat together the yoghurt, honey and remaining lemon juice, and pour over the top of the cheesecake. Bake for a further 15 minutes until set. Cool in the turned off oven with the door open for 30 minutes. Remove from the tin when cold.

HOT CHOCOLATE CHEESECAKE
Serves 8–10

4 oz (110 g) unsalted butter, melted
8 oz (225 g) chocolate digestive
  biscuits, crushed

For the filling:
2 eggs, separated
3 oz (75 g) caster sugar
8 oz (225 g) curd cheese
1½ oz (35 g) ground hazelnuts

5 fl oz (150 ml) double cream
1 oz (25 g) cocoa powder
2 tsp dark rum (optional)
sifted icing sugar to decorate

Preheat the oven to 325°F/170°C/Gas Mk 3. Stir the melted butter into the crushed biscuits, and then press into the base and about 1 in up the sides of an 8 in (20 cm) very lightly greased loose-bottomed cake tin. Chill for at least 30 minutes. Whisk the egg yolks and sugar together until thick and holding shape. Beat the cheese, nuts, cream, cocoa powder and rum (if used) together until well mixed and soft, then fold into the egg yolk mixture. Whisk the egg whites until stiff, then fold gently into the cheese mixture. Pour into the biscuit base and bake for 1½ to 1¾ hours until firm to touch. Remove carefully from the tin, sift icing sugar over the top and serve while hot.

REDCURRANT CHEESECAKE
Serves 4–5

6 oz (175 g) shortbread biscuits,
  crushed
2 oz (50 g) butter, melted
finely grated rind of an orange
2 oz (50 g) caster sugar
8 oz (225 g) soft cream cheese
8 oz (225 g) Cottage cheese

4 fl oz (125 ml) single cream
1 egg white, stiffly beaten
1¼ lb (550 g) redcurrants
½ oz (10 g) gelatine
2 tbsp water
½ pt (300 ml) double cream

Lightly grease a 7 in (18 cm) loose-bottomed cake tin. Mix together the biscuit crumbs, orange rind, a tablespoon of the sugar and the melted butter. Put the mixture into the base of the tin. Beat together the cheeses and sugar until smooth and creamy. Stir in the single cream and 1 lb (450 g) of the redcurrants. Dissolve the gelatine in the water and beat it into the cheese mixture. Spoon on top of the crumb base and chill for 30 minutes, or until set. Whisk the double cream until it forms stiff peaks, fold in the egg white and spoon over the cheesecake, making swirling patters with the back of a spoon. Sprinkle over the remaining redcurrants and serve.

BAKED ORANGE CHEESECAKE
Serves 6

6 oz (175 g) Marie biscuits
2 tbsp caster sugar
2½ oz (60 g) butter or margarine, melted

For the filling:

8 oz (225 g) cottage cheese	*½ small orange, pared and skinned*
4 fl oz (125 ml) milk	*1 oz (25 g) caster sugar*
2 eggs	*1 tbsp flour*

Preheat the oven to 325°F/170°C/Gas Mk 3. Crumb the Marie biscuits by placing in a plastic bag and crushing with a rolling pin. Add the sugar and stir in the melted butter. Press three-quarters of the crumbs into a 8 in (20 cm) lightly greased flan tin or pie dish. Chill well. Place rest of the ingredients in a blender and blend until well mixed. Pour into the dish and sprinkle with reserved crumbs. Bake for 1 hour or until cheesecake is firm. Chill.

STRAWBERRY AND RHUBARB CHEESECAKE
Serves 10

8 oz (225 g) ginger biscuits, crushed	*juice of ½ lemon*
4 oz (110 g) butter, melted	*1 oz (25g) gelatine*
10 oz (300 g) fresh rhubarb	*½ pt (300 ml) double cream, whipped*
4 oz (110 g) caster sugar	*fresh strawberries, sliced for decoration*
8 oz (225 g) fresh strawberries	*sprig of mint*
7 oz (200 g) soft cheese	
8 oz (225 g) fromage frais	

Stir the crushed ginger biscuits into the melted butter until well mixed. Press into a 9 in (23 cm) lightly greased springform tin. Put in the refrigerator for at least 2 hours to set. Cook the rhubarb in a saucepan with the caster sugar over a gentle heat until the rhubarb is soft. Put the strawberries, soft cheese and fromage frais in a food processor and add the rhubarb. Blend until smooth. Sprinkle the gelatine over the lemon juice in a cup. Stand the cup in a pan of gently simmering water until the gelatine is dissolved. Allow to cool slightly and then fold into the strawberry mixture together with the whipped cream. Spoon onto the base and chill for 3–4 hours until firm. When ready to serve, carefully remove from the tin and decorate with the fresh strawberries cut into a fan shape, adding a mint leaf for added effect.

GREEK HONEY CHEESECAKE
Serves 8

8 oz (225 g) flour
½ tsp salt
6 oz (175 g) butter, chilled and
  cut into very small pieces
3 tbsp iced water
1 lb (450 g) unsalted curd
  or low fat soft cheese

4 eggs
2 tsp ground cinnamon
4–5 tbsp clear honey
Greek yoghurt

Preheat the oven to 350°F/180°C/Gas Mk 4. Sift together the flour and salt. Lightly rub the butter into the flour with the fingertips. Gradually add sufficient iced water to make a soft dough. Form into a ball, wrap in foil and put into the refrigerator for 30 minutes. The dough will be fairly soft and can be pressed into the base and sides of a 10 in (25 cm) pie dish. Bake for 10 minutes in the oven. Set aside to cool. Increase the oven temperature to 375°F/190°C/Gas Mk 5. Beat the cheese with the eggs, one at a time, then beat in the honey and 1 teaspoon ground cinnamon. Pour into the pastry shell, and bake for 35 minutes or until the top is golden and the filling is firm to the touch. Remove from the oven and sprinkle the top with the remaining ground cinnamon. Serve cold with Greek yoghurt.

GINGER AND LEMON CHEESECAKE
Serves 8

15 oz (425 g) ginger biscuits, crushed
7 oz (200 g) unsalted butter, melted
8 oz (225 g) cream cheese
8 oz (225 g) curd cheese

14 oz (400 g) can of condensed milk
2 large lemons, grated rind and juice
3 tsp gelatine
2 tbsp water

Stir the butter into the biscuit crumbs. Press over the base and up the sides of an 8 in (20 cm) springform cake tin. Chill until set. Beat the two cheeses together and, pouring a little at a time, beat in the condensed milk. Add the grated rind from one lemon. Put 5 tbsp of lemon juice into a small bowl with the water and sprinkle the gelatine over. Place in a pan of gently simmering water and stir until dissolved. Leave to cool slightly and then whisk into the cheese mixture. Pour into the tin and chill until set. Cut the remaining lemon into slices with a sharp knife, and then into quarters. Use to decorate the top of the cheesecake.

WALNUT AND BUTTERSCOTCH CHEESECAKE
Serves 10

6 oz (175 g) shortbread biscuits,
   crushed
2 oz (50 g) walnuts, finely chopped
3 oz (75 g) butter, melted
4 oz (110 g) demerara sugar
6 tbsp water
8 oz (225 g) cream cheese

½ oz (10 g) gelatine
½ pt (300 ml) double cream,
   whipped
¼ pt (150 ml) whipping cream
   whipped
15 halves of walnuts

Stir the shortbread and chopped walnuts into the melted butter until
well mixed. Press into an 8 in (20 cm) lightly greased springform tin.
Put in the refrigerator for at least 2 hours to set. Put the demerara
sugar in a saucepan with 4 tbsp of the water and place over a very low
heat until the sugar has dissolved. Then raise the heat and boil for
2–3 minutes until the caramel thickens to a thin syrup-like
consistency. Cool a little and then beat in the cream cheese. Sprinkle
the gelatine over the remaining water in a cup. Stand the cup in a pan
of gently simmering water until the gelatine is dissolved. Cool slightly
and then fold into the caramel cheese mixture together with the
whipped cream. Spoon onto the base and chill for 3–4 hours until
firm. When ready to serve, carefully remove from the tin and pipe the
whipped cream around the edge. Decorate with the walnut halves.

CHOCOLATE HAZELNUT CHEESECAKE
Serves 12

8 oz (225 g) chocolate digestive
   biscuits
12 oz (350 g) unsalted butter
8 oz (225 g) caster sugar
12 oz (350 g) cream cheese

4 oz (110 g) hazelnuts, toasted
   and chopped
12 oz (350 g) plain chocolate
whipped cream for decoration

Crush the biscuits, melt 4 oz (110 g) of the butter and stir together.
Press over the base of an 8 in (20 cm) springform tin and chill until
set. Beat the remaining butter and sugar together until light and fluffy.
Beat in the cream cheese. Melt the chocolate and mix with the
chopped nuts. Stir in. Spread this mixture over the base and make a
decoration of swirls on the top. Chill for at least 6 hours. Remove
from the tin and decorate with whipped cream and grated pieces
of chocolate.

SUNSHINE CHEESECAKE
Serves 12

8 oz (225 g) caster sugar
7 oz (200 g) butter
12 oz (350 g) plain sweet
  biscuit crumbs
6 large oranges
1 lemon jelly tablet
¼ pt (150 ml) very hot water

2 tsp Cointreau or
  Grand Marnier (optional)
1 lb (450 g) full-fat soft cheese
4 tbsp very hot water
8 oz (225g) jar fine shred
orange marmalade

Lightly grease the inside of a 10 in (25 cm) flan ring and place it on a
flat serving plate. Melt the butter and work 4 oz (110 g) of the caster
sugar and crumbs into it until well mixed. Press evenly all over the
base and sides of the flan ring and chill. Take four of the oranges.
Grate the rind of 1 and squeeze the juice from all 4. Dissolve ¾ of the
jelly tablet in the very hot water. When dissolved strain three-quarters
of the orange juice into it, add the Cointreau or Grand Marnier if
used, and leave to cool. Beat the cheese until softened together with
the remaining sugar and the orange rind. Trickle the jelly into the
cheese mixture a little at a time just when it is on the point of setting.
Beat well. Turn into the chilled case and put back in the refrigerator.
Chop up the remaining jelly tablet and dissolve in a basin with the
4 tbsp hot water. Add the remaining orange juice. Chill until firmly
set. Cut the flesh of the remaining oranges free of all skin, pith and
pips. Arrange around the edge of the cheesecake. Warm the
marmalade just enough to make it liquid and strain. Brush over the
cheesecake and orange segments and chill. Chop up the orange jelly
and pile in the centre of the cheesecake. Remove the flan ring
and serve.

FRESH RASPBERRY CHEESECAKE
Serves 8–10

3 oz (75 g) butter
8 oz (225 g) shortcake biscuit
  crumbs
2 tbsp cold water
½ oz (10 g) gelatine
1 lemon, grated rind and juice

12 oz (350 g) full-fat soft cheese
3 oz (75 g) caster sugar
2 eggs, separated
½ pt (300 ml) double cream
2 tsp kirsch
1 lb (450 g) fresh raspberries

Preheat the oven to 350°F/180°C/Gas Mk 4. Lightly grease the inside of a 9 in (23 cm) loose-bottomed cake tin. Melt the butter and mix in the crumbs. Press evenly over the base of the tin. Bake for 8 minutes, then leave to cool. Sprinkle the gelatine over the water in a small bowl. Place the bowl in a pan of gently simmering water and stir until dissolved. Cool until on the point of setting. Strain the lemon juice and mix it together with the grated rind into the gelatine mixture. Beat the cheese with the sugar until soft and creamy. Beat in the egg yolks one at a time until the mixture is light and fluffy. Gradually beat the gelatine and lemon mixture into the cheese mixture until smooth. Whip the cream with the kirsch until it holds soft peaks and fold into the cheese mixture. Whisk the egg whites until stiff and fold in also. Turn into the baked base and chill until set. Arrange the raspberries on the top of the cheesecake and sprinkle very lightly with caster sugar. Serve with whipped cream.

PARTY PIECE CHEESECAKE
Serves 12

3 oz (75 g) butter, softened
6 oz (175 g) crushed cornflakes
2 oz (50 g) caster sugar
1½ lb (675 g) cream cheese
7 oz (200 g) can of sweetened
    condensed milk

4 eggs, separated
½ pt (300 ml) soured cream
1 tsp vanilla essence
1 tsp grated orange rind
½ tsp salt

Preheat the oven to 300°F/150°C/Gas Mk 2. Line the base and grease the inside of a 10 in (25 cm) springform cake tin. Melt the butter and stir in the cornflakes and sugar. Reserve 1 tablespoon of sugar for later. Press half the cornflake mixture evenly over the base of the tin and put the other half on one side. Beat the cream cheese and condensed milk together until smooth. This is best done with an electric mixer if possible. Add the yolks one at a time, beating well between each addition. Then beat in the cream, the reserved sugar, vanilla essence and orange rind. Whisk the egg whites with the salt until it forms soft peaks. Fold into the cheese mixture and spoon into the cake tin. Sprinkle the reserved crushed cornflake mixture on top and bake for about 2 hours, or until a skewer run through the centre comes out clean. Cool in the turned-off oven with the door open. Leave in the tin until cold. Serve with any fruit sauce topping.

RASPBERRY AND ALMOND CHEESECAKE
Serves 4

3 oz (75 g) butter, cut into
  small pieces
6 oz (175 g) rice flour
1 oz (25 g) soft brown sugar
1 oz (25 g) ground almonds
8 oz (225 g) raspberries

8 oz (225 g) cottage cheese
1 tbsp redcurrant jelly
¼ pt (150 ml) whipping cream
½ oz (10 g) gelatine
2 tbsp hot water

Preheat the oven to 300°F/150°C/Gas Mk 2. Place a 7 in (18 cm) flan
ring on a baking sheet. Cream the butter with the flour and sugar.
Add the nuts, then knead to a smooth dough. Press into the case and
cook for 50 minutes. Cool. Reserve 6 raspberries. Sieve the remainder
with the cottage cheese. Melt the jelly and stir in. Whip the cream.
Dissolve the gelatine in the hot water. Fold the gelatine and then
cream into mixture. Spoon into the case and chill. Decorate with the
reserved raspberries.

APRICOT CHEESECAKE
Serves 8

8 oz (225 g) plain flour
5 oz (125 g) butter
10 oz (300 g) caster sugar
5 eggs
2 tbsp water

1 lb (450 g) cream cheese
8 oz (225 g) curd cheese
grated rind of 1 lemon
2 oz (50 g) ready-to-eat
  dried apricots

Preheat the oven to 375°F/190°C/Gas Mk 5. Rub the butter into the
flour finely and add 2 oz (50 g) of the sugar. Add one egg and enough
water to make a soft dough. Knead lightly and chill for 10 minutes.
Roll out the pastry and line the base and sides of an 8 in (20 cm)
springform tin. Bake blind for 10 minutes, until just set. Beat the two
cheeses together with the remaining sugar. Then beat in the remaining
eggs and lemon rind. Chop the apricots into very small pieces and
sprinkle over the pastry base, pour the cheese mixture over and bake
for 30 minutes. Turn the oven off and leave the cheesecake to cool in
the oven for 15 minutes. Remove from the oven, sprinkle the top
heavily with caster sugar and put under a preheated grill. Grill until
the top turns golden brown. Do not let it burn. Leave until the
cheesecake is completely cold and then remove from the tin.

CHOCOLATE RUM CHEESECAKE
Serves 6

6 oz (150 g) digestive biscuits,
  crushed
1½ oz (35 g) butter
1½ oz (35 g) dark chocolate
3 eggs, separated
3 oz (75 g) caster sugar
grated rind and juice of
  ½ orange and ½ lemon

12 oz (350 g) cottage cheese,
  sieved
4 tsp gelatine
5 fl oz (150 ml) double cream,
  whipped
1 tbsp dark rum
1 oz (25 g) dark chocolate, grated

Melt the butter and chocolate together over a low heat. Remove from the heat, stir in the biscuits and use to line the base of a 7 in (18 cm) loose-bottomed cake tin. Chill for 5 hours, or until firm. Whisk together the egg yolks and sugar until thick and creamy. Stir in the fruit rinds and then the sieved cottage cheese. Place the orange and lemon juice in a pan and sprinkle over the gelatine. Set aside for 5 minutes and then dissolve over a low heat. Pour this mixture into the cheese mixture, stirring constantly. Stir in the rum and the cream. Whisk the egg whites until they are stiff and fold them into the mixture. Place the filling in the tin and chill overnight. Turn out onto a serving plate. Decorate with the grated chocolate and serve.

JAMAICAN PIE
Serves 6

3½ oz (90g) butter
6 oz (175g) sifted flour
1 oz (25g) caster sugar
1 lb (450g) full fat soft cheese

2 oz (50g) icing sugar
ground spices to taste: cardoman,
  ginger, mace, cloves and
  grated nutmeg

Preheat the oven to 350°F/180°C/Gas Mk 4. Line the base and grease the inside of an 8 in (20 cm) loose-bottomed sandwich cake tin. Use the butter, flour and caster sugar to make pastry in the usual way. Chill for 30 minutes. Roll out and use to line the sandwich tin. Bake blind. Beat the cheese and icing sugar well until smooth and creamy. Add a good pinch of all the ground spices, except cloves which are very strong - a small pinch will be sufficient. Mix well and taste, adding more if required. The cheese should take on a golden brown colour. Spoon into the pastry case and bake for 30 minutes. Cool in the tin. Serve when cold with cream, and apple sauce if liked.

APRICOT AND WALNUT CHEESECAKE
Serves 8

2 oz (50 g) butter, softened
6 oz (175 g) sweet oatmeal biscuit crumbs
1 oz (25 g) caster sugar

For the filling:

7 oz (200 g) dried
  ready-to-eat apricots
1¼ lb (550 g) full fat soft cheese
4 oz (110 g) caster sugar
4 tbsp soured cream

2 large eggs
1 lemon, grated rind and juice
2 oz (50 g) walnut pieces,
  finely chopped
1½ tbsp flour

Soak the apricots for 1 hour in cold water. Preheat the oven to 425°F/220°C/Gas Mk 7. Line the base and grease the inside of an 8 in (20 cm) springform cake tin. Melt the butter and stir in the biscuit crumbs and sugar. Press evenly over the base of the tin. Chill. Drain the apricots and reserve the water. Finely chop 3 oz (75 g) of the apricots and set the others aside. Beat the cheese with 3 oz (75 g) of the caster sugar, lemon rind and juice, eggs and cream until very smooth. Stir in the flour, apricots and walnuts, mixing them evenly. Spoon into the prepared base. Bake for 15 minutes, then lower the oven temperature to 350°F/180°C/Gas Mk 4, and cook for another 45 minutes or until set and golden brown. Cool in the oven for 30 minutes with the door open, and then leave to get cold in the tin. Put the reserved apricots in a small saucepan with the remaining sugar. Make up the water from soaking the apricots to 3 fl oz (90 ml) if necessary. Poach the apricots gently in this water until soft and syrupy. Cool. Just before serving pour over the cheesecake.

AMERICAN BLUEBERRY CHEESECAKE
Serves 4

4 oz (110 g) digestive biscuits
2 oz (50 g) margarine
1 oz (25 g) caster sugar

For the filling:

8 oz (225 g) cottage cheese, sieved
8 oz (225 g) cream cheese
4 oz (110 g) caster sugar
3 tbsp lemon juice
3 eggs, beaten
½ tsp vanilla essence

¼ pt (150 ml) soured cream
15 oz (425 g) can of bilberries
  or blueberries in syrup
1½ level tsp arrowroot
4 oz (110 g) caster sugar

Preheat the oven to 375°F/190°C/Gas Mk 5. Put the digestive biscuits into a plastic bag and crush into fine crumbs with a rolling pin. Melt the margarine in a saucepan and stir in the biscuit crumbs and the sugar. Mix together then turn into an 8 in (20 cm) round loose-bottomed tin and press down firmly to form a base. Beat the cottage cheese, cream cheese and caster sugar together until smooth. Then beat in the lemon juice, eggs, vanilla essence and soured cream. Mix together and then pour into the tin over the biscuit base. Bake in centre of oven for 35–45 minutes or until the outside is set but the centre is still moist. Remove from the oven and leave to cool in the tin on a wire rack. The centre will set on cooling and may crack slightly and shrink back. Drain the blueberries, reserving the juice, and when the cheesecake is completely cold arrange the fruit on top. Mix the arrowroot to a paste with 1 tablespoon of the juice then mix this with the remaining juice. Bring to the boil to thicken. Cool slightly, then spoon over the topping to form a glaze.

CINNAMON CHEESECAKE
Serves 8–10

3 oz (90 g) butter
6 oz (175 g) dry white breadcrumbs
6 oz (175 g) caster sugar
1½ tsp ground cinnamon
1 oz (25 g) chopped mixed nuts

14 oz (400 g) full fat soft cheese
3 eggs, separated
1 lemon, grated rind and juice
¼ pt (150 ml) single cream

Preheat the oven to 350°F/180°C/Gas Mk 4. Line the base and grease the inside of an 8 in (20 cm) loose-bottomed sandwich cake tin. Loosen the breadcrumbs by sifting through the fingers and put them in the melted butter in a frying pan. Turn them over and over until golden. Take off the heat and stir in 2 oz (50 g) of the sugar, the nuts and cinnamon. Press about two-thirds of the crumb mixture over the base, but not the sides, of the cake tin. Chill. Beat the egg yolks together with the remaining sugar until light and creamy. Push the cream cheese through a sieve into the egg mixture and mix in gently with a fork. Add the lemon rind and juice and the cream. Whisk the egg whites until they form soft peaks. Stir in 2 tablespoonfuls and then fold in the remainder. Turn the mixture onto the chilled base and bake until just firm. Sprinkle the remaining crumbs and nuts on top and bake for a further 15 minutes. Cool in the tin. When cold, run a sharp knife around the inside of the tin and release the sides of the tin. Loosen the cheesecake from the base of the tin very carefully and slide onto a serving plate.

PINEAPPLE AND GINGER CHEESECAKE
Serves 6

2 oz (50 g) butter, melted
3 oz (75 g) digestive biscuits,
  crushed
3 oz (75 g) ginger biscuits,
  crushed
12 oz (350 g) cream cheese
6 oz (175 g) caster sugar

1 egg, well beaten
1 tbsp chopped stem ginger
1½ tsp ground ginger
12 fl oz (350 ml) soured cream
4 tbsp crushed canned
  pineapple, drained

Preheat the oven to 350°F/180°C/Gas mark 4. Lightly grease a 9 in (23 cm) loose-bottomed cake tin. Mix together the biscuits and butter and line the tin with the crumbs. Beat together the cream cheese, half the sugar and the egg until smooth. Stir in the stem ginger and 1 teaspoon of the ground ginger. Pour the mixture into the lined cake tin and bake for 25 minutes, or until set. Meanwhile beat together the soured cream, the remaining sugar and the remaining ground ginger, until the sugar has dissolved. Turn off the oven and spread the soured cream mixture evenly on top of the cake and return it to the oven for 5 minutes. Cool. Arrange the crushed pineapple on top of the cheesecake and chill for at least an hour before serving.

CAKES AND GATEAUX

PINEAPPLE PECAN SPICED CAKE
Serves 8

7 fl oz (200 ml) sunflower oil
8 oz (225 g) caster sugar
8 oz (225 g) self-raising flour
4 eggs
4 tsp ground cinnamon

1 tbsp vanilla essence
4 oz (110 g) pecan nuts,
  chopped
1 medium-sized pineapple
  skinned and diced

Preheat the oven to 350°F/180°C/ Gas Mk 4. Place the oil and caster sugar in a bowl and beat well. Add the flour, eggs, cinnamon and vanilla essence. Stir in the nuts and pineapple and beat until thoroughly mixed. Grease a 10 in (25 cm) cake tin and pour in the cake mixture. Bake in the oven for 1 hour. Remove the from oven and leave to stand for 15 minutes before serving.

APPLE CAKE
Serves 6–8

4 oz (110 g) unsalted butter
6 oz (175 g) digestive biscuits, crushed
2 apples, peeled, cored and sliced
4 oz (110 g) sultanas
9 oz (250 g) Gouda cheese, finely grated
3 level tbsp plain flour

½ tsp mixed spice
1 lemon, grated rind and juice
3 eggs, separated
4 oz (110 g) caster sugar
4 tbsp single cream

For the topping:
2 red-skinned apples, cored, sliced
  and dipped in lemon juice

2 level tbsp apricot jam, sieved
whipped cream

Preheat the oven to 350°F/180°C/Gas Mk 4. In a saucepan, melt 3 oz (75 g) of the butter and stir in the crushed biscuits. Line the base of an 8 in (20 cm) springform cake tin with the biscuit mixture. Cook the apples gently in the remaining butter until just soft. Spread over the biscuit base and scatter the sultanas on top. Mix together the cheese, flour, spice, lemon rind and juice. Beat the egg yolks and sugar together and add to the cheese mixture together with the cream. Whisk the whites until stiff and fold into the mixture. Pour into the tin on top of the apples and bake for 40–50 minutes. Allow to cool. Decorate with the apple slices and brush with the apricot jam. Chill. Serve with whipped cream.

COFFEE WALNUT DESSERT GATEAU
Serves 6–8

1 level tbsp instant coffee powder
3 tsp boiling water
5 oz (150 g) unsalted butter,
  cut into small pieces
3 oz (75 g) icing sugar
3 egg yolks

24 boudoir (or sponge finger) biscuits
¼ pt (150 ml) cold strong black coffee
coffee liqueur (optional)
1 oz (25 g) walnut halves
whipped cream (optional)

N.B.: This cake must be made a day in advance as it needs 24 hours to set.

Dissolve the instant coffee powder in the boiling water. Cream the butter and icing sugar. Beat the egg yolks, then gradually beat them into the creamed mixture. Stir in the dissolved coffee powder. Place 8 of the biscuits side by side on a plate and sprinkle 3–4 tbsp of the black coffee over them. (If preferred, 1 tbsp of the coffee may be replaced by 1 tbsp of coffee liqueur.) Spread one third of the creamed mixture over the biscuits. On top of the first layer arrange 2 rows of biscuits (4 to each row), at right angles to the lower layer. Sprinkle with 3–4 tbsp of the coffee and then coat the biscuits with another third of the creamed mixture. Arrange a final layer of 8 biscuits side by side on top and sprinkle with coffee as before. Spread the remaining creamed mixture on the top. Place the cake aside for 24 hours; this allows the coffee to soak through and give the gateau the desired texture. Decorate the top with the walnut halves. Add whipped cream (optional).

RUM AND COFFEE CAKE
Serves 6–8

5 eggs, separated
8 oz (225 g) caster sugar
rind of half a lemon, grated
4 oz (110 g) self-raising flour

8 fl oz (250 ml) sweetened
  black coffee
4 tbsp rum
double cream

Preheat the oven to 350°F/180°C/Gas Mk 4. Beat 2 oz of the sugar with the egg yolks and the lemon rind. Whisk the egg whites until stiff and then whisk in the rest of the sugar. Fold the whites into the yolk mixture with a metal spoon, and then fold in lightly the sifted flour. Bake for 50 minutes, or until firm to the touch. Turn out onto a wire tray and leave to cool. Place on a large plate. Pour the warm coffee and then the rum over the cake. Serve with double cream.

AUSTRIAN COFFEE CAKE
Serves 6–8

6 oz (175 g) margarine,
  cut into small pieces
6 oz (175 g) caster sugar
3 eggs
6 oz (175 g) self-raising flour,
  sifted

pinch of salt
4 level tbsp coffee essence
1 level tbsp dark brown sugar
½ pt (300 ml) boiling water
2 tbsp rum, optional

Preheat the oven to 375°F/190°C/Gas Mk 5. Cream the margarine
and caster sugar together until light and fluffy. Add the eggs, one at a
time, beating well after each addition. Fold in the sifted flour and salt.
Spoon the mixture into a greased and floured 1½ pint (900 ml) ring
tin. Level the top with the back of a spoon. Bake for 30 minutes or
until springy to the touch and cooked through. Leave to cool in the
tin for five minutes then turn out onto a wire rack to cool. Blend the
coffee essence with the brown sugar, water and rum (if used) and
leave to cool. Stand the cake on a large plate and slowly pour over the
coffee liquid, making sure the entire cake surface is covered. Leave for
two hours to allow the cake to soak up the coffee.

VANILLA SPONGE WITH CHOCOLATE SAUCE
Serves 6

4 oz (110 g) butter, cut into
  small pieces
4 oz (110 g) caster sugar
4 eggs
8 oz (225 g) self-raising flour

2 tsp vanilla essence
icing sugar, for dusting
4 oz (110 g) dark chocolate,
  broken up into small pieces
10 fl oz (300 ml) single cream

Preheat the oven to 350°F/180°C/Gas Mk 4. Use a little of the butter
to grease an 8 in (20 cm) round cake tin which has a disc of baking
paper on the base. Place the remaining butter and the sugar together
in a bowl and beat until light and fluffy. Beat in the eggs, one by one,
alternately beating in the flour. Add in 1 teaspoon of the vanilla
essence. Pile the mixture into the tin. Smooth out the mixture and
bake in the oven for 20–25 minutes until golden brown. Leave to cool
slightly, then remove the cake from the tin. Dust with icing sugar.
Meanwhile, make the sauce by melting the chocolate and cream in a
saucepan over a low heat. Stir in the remaining vanilla essence. Pour
the warm sauce over the cake. Serve.

CHOCOLATE ROULADE
Serves 6–8

4 eggs, separated
5 oz (150 g) caster sugar
1½ oz (35 g) cocoa powder, sifted
½ tsp vanilla essence
¼ pt double cream
1 oz (25 g) plain chocolate, grated
icing sugar, to dust

Preheat the oven to 400°F/200°C/Gas Mk 6. Whisk the egg yolks, sugar, cocoa and vanilla essence together until light and creamy. Whisk the egg whites until stiff. Stir 1 tbsp of the whites into the cocoa mixture, then fold in the remaining whites gently using a metal spoon. Spread this mixture in a lined and greased 13 x 9 in Swiss roll tin. Bake in the upper half of the oven for 15 minutes. Wring a clean tea towel out in cold water, then use to cover the roulade. Allow roulade to cool. Turn the roulade out onto a piece of greaseproof paper and remove the lining paper gently. Mix the cream with the chocolate to make the filling. Score one end of the roulade about half an inch from the end, spread the filling onto the roulade. Roll up the roulade using the paper to assist you. The cake will probably crack, but this is how it is supposed to be. Dust with icing sugar and leave for at least 1 hour for the cream to soak through.

LOVER'S CHOCOLATE GATEAU
Serves 6

4 oz (110 g) plain chocolate, broken into small pieces
4 eggs, separated
4 oz (110 g) caster sugar
4 oz (110 g) softened unsalted butter, cut into small pieces
1 oz (25 g) plain flour
1 oz (25 g) fresh white breadcrumbs
2 oz (50 g) ground almonds

Preheat the oven to 350°F/180°C/Gas Mk 4. Melt the chocolate in a basin over hot water. Remove from the heat and leave to cool. Whisk the egg yolks and sugar in a basin over hot water until thick. Whisk in the melted chocolate and butter. Fold in the dry ingredients with a metal spoon and pour into a greased and lined 7 in (18 cm) cake tin. Bake in the centre of the oven for 1¼–1½ hours or until well risen and firm to the touch. Cool in the tin for 25 minutes, then turn out onto a wire tray.

CRUMB CAKE MOCHA
Serves 6–8

*4 oz (110 g) butter or soft margarine,
  cut into small pieces*
2 level tsp instant coffee powder
1 oz (25 g) caster sugar
1 rounded tbsp golden syrup
2 oz (50 g) walnuts, chopped
1 level tbsp ground coffee

2 oz (50 g) raisins, chopped
2 oz (50 g) glacé cherries, chopped
8 oz (225 g) crushed digestive biscuits
4 oz (110 g) icing sugar, sifted
1 tsp coffee essence
3 tsp water
8 walnut halves to decorate

Cream the butter, coffee powder, sugar and syrup together until soft
and fluffy. Stir in the walnuts, ground coffee, raisins and glacé
cherries. Work in the biscuit crumbs. Press the crumbly mixture into
a well greased 7 in (18 cm) sandwich tin, smooth the top and leave in
the refrigerator until set. Mix the icing sugar, coffee essence and water
together until smooth. Turn the cake out onto a plate and cover the
top with the coffee icing. Decorate with the walnut halves.

PINEAPPLE AND LEMON GATEAU
Serves 6

*5 oz (150 g) butter, cut into
  small pieces*
3 oz (75 g) icing sugar, sifted
2 egg yolks

1 lemon, finely grated rind and juice
12 oz (350 g) can pineapple rings
24 boudoir (or sponge finger) biscuits

Cream the butter with the icing sugar until it is light and fluffy. Beat
in the egg yolks. Stir in the grated lemon rind. Drain, and keep, the
juice from the pineapple rings and finely chop half of the rings. Stir
the chopped pieces into one half of the creamed mixture. Measure
¼ pint (150 ml) pineapple juice and add to the lemon juice. Place 8 of
the boudoir biscuits side by side on a plate and sprinkle with one-
third of the mixed juices. Spread half of the pineapple creamed
mixture over the biscuits. On top of the first layer, arrange 2 rows
(4 to each row) at right angles to the lower layer. Sprinkle these
biscuits with another third of the juice and spread with the remaining
pineapple creamed mixture. Arrange a final layer of biscuits on top
similar to the bottom layer. Sprinkle with the remaining juice and
then spread with half of the remaining plain lemon cream. Cover the
cake and place in the refrigerator for 24 hours. The next day trim the
sides of the gateau with a sharp knife and decorate by piping the
remaining plain lemon butter cream down the centre of the gateau and
along the sides. Decorate with the remaining pineapple slices.

ALMOND GATEAU
Serves 6–8

4 trifle sponge cakes
10 maraschino cherries
1 oz (25 g) walnuts, roughly chopped
1 oz (25 g) plain chocolate, roughly
 chopped
6 oz (175 g) butter, cut into small pieces

6 oz (175 g) caster sugar
6 oz (175 g) ground almonds
1 small can evaporated milk
1 tbsp maraschino-flavoured syrup
2½ fl oz (75 ml) double cream
1 tbsp milk

Cut the sponges in half and press each half, cut-side outwards, around the inside of a 6 in (15 cm) round, loose-bottomed cake tin. Roughly chop six of the cherries. Mix with the walnuts and chocolate. Blend the butter and sugar together in a bowl until light and fluffy. Add the ground almonds, evaporated milk and maraschino syrup and mix well together. Spread half the mixture in the bottom of the cake tin and sprinkle with the chopped cherries, walnuts and chocolate. Spread remaining almond mixture on top and place in the refrigerator overnight. When ready to serve, remove the tin and invert the pudding onto a serving plate. Whisk the cream and milk together until it holds its shape. Then pipe round the top and base of the cake. Decorate the cake with the remaining cherries, each cut into four.

STRAWBERRY TORTE
Serves 6–8

1 pkt Boudoir (or sponge finger)
 biscuits
4 oz (110 g) unsalted butter,
 cut into small pieces
3 oz (75 g) caster sugar
2 egg yolks

4 tbsp hot milk
2 oz (50 g) freshly ground hazelnuts
½ pt (300 ml) strawberry purée
½ pt (300 ml) double cream
icing sugar

Butter a 7½ in (19 cm) loose-bottomed cake tin and line with the Boudoir biscuits. Beat the butter, gradually adding the sugar, until it becomes light and fluffy. Beat in the egg yolks one at a time and then the hot milk a few drops at a time to prevent the butter from melting. Fold in half the strawberry purée. Stir in the nuts. Whip the cream until soft peaks are formed. Gently fold in the cream with a metal spoon. Pour into the biscuit lined cake tin. Cover with foil and leave overnight in the refrigerator. When ready to eat turn out onto a plate and serve with the remaining strawberry purée, sweetened with a little icing sugar, as a sauce.

CHOCOLATE TORTE
Serves 8

2 pkt Boudoir (or sponge finger)
 biscuits
8 oz (225 g) unsalted butter,
 cut into small pieces
8 oz (225 g) soft brown sugar
8 oz (225 g) plain chocolate,
 broken into small pieces

¼ pt (150 ml) hot strong black coffee
4 egg yolks
½ pt (300 ml) double cream
2 tbsp brandy
whipped cream and
 chocolate curls, to decorate

Butter a 9 in (23 cm) springform mould and line with Boudoir biscuits. Cream the butter and sugar together until very light and fluffy. Melt the chocolate in the hot coffee and beat in the egg yolks one at a time. Leave to cool and then beat into the butter and sugar mixture. Whip the cream and fold into the chocolate mixture with the brandy. Pour into the prepared tin, sprinkling the biscuits in the tin with a little brandy. Cover with foil and chill in the refrigerator overnight. Turn out and decorate with swirls of whipped cream and grated chocolate curls.

SEMOLINA SPONGE GATEAU
Serves 6

3 eggs, separated
4 oz (110 g) caster sugar
grated rind of ½ lemon

1 tbsp lemon juice
2 oz (50 g) ground semolina
1 oz (25 g) ground almonds

For the filling:
grated rind of ½ lemon
3 tbsp icing sugar
½ pt (300 ml) whipped whipping cream

3 tbsp whisky
6 oz (175 g) lemon curd

Preheat the oven to 350°F/180°C/Gas Mk 4. Place the egg yolks and sugar in a bowl over a saucepan of simmering water and beat until thick. Add the lemon rind and juice, semolina and almonds and beat well. Whisk the egg whites until stiff and fold into the mixture. Place the mixture in a greased and floured sandwich tin and bake for 30 minutes. Leave to cool for a few minutes, then turn out onto a wire rack. For the filling, mix together the cream, lemon rind and sugar and gradually add the whisky. Cut the cake into two layers and spread the lemon curd over the bottom layer. Then spread half of the filling mixture on top of the lemon curd. Press the top layer of the cake on top of the bottom layer and spread the remaining filling on top.

GERMAN APPLE CAKE
Serves 6–8

4 oz (110 g) butter
4 oz (110 g) caster sugar
8 oz (225 g) self-raising flour

a pinch of salt
1 large egg, beaten

For the filling:
12 oz (350 g) cooking apples,
  peeled and chopped
2 oz (50 g) sultanas

1 oz (25 g) chopped walnuts
½ level tsp ground cinnamon
2 oz (50 g) demerara sugar

Preheat the oven to 350°F/180°C/Gas Mk 4. Melt the butter gently in a pan over a low heat. Do not let it brown. Remove the pan from the heat and stir in the caster sugar, beaten egg and sifted flour and salt. Beat to a fairly stiff consistency. Turn two-thirds into a base-lined and greased deep 7 in (18 cm) round cake tin with a loose base. Spread the mixture to the sides, making the surface level. Mix the apples, sultanas, chopped walnuts and cinnamon together and spoon over the cake base. Sprinkle with the sugar. Dot the remaining cake mixture on top. Bake in the centre of the oven for 50–60 minutes, or until the cake is a light golden brown colour and is cooked through. Leave the cake in the tin for 15 minutes before turning out. This cake is good served as a dessert, warm, with cream or custard or cold as a cake for tea.

STRAWBERRY MOUSSE GATEAUX
Serves 8–10

2 small eggs
3½ oz (90 g) self-raising flour

3½ oz (90 g) soft margarine
3½ oz (90 g) caster sugar

For the mousse:
1 envelope gelatine
4 tbsp water
3 small eggs, separated
  (discarding 1 white)
3 oz (75 g) caster sugar

½ pt (300 ml) strawberry purée,
  made from 12 oz (350 g) fresh
  strawberries
1 tsp lemon juice
¼ pt (150 ml) double cream

Decoration:
12 oz (350 g) fresh strawberries
¼ pt (150 ml) double cream

Preheat the oven to 375°F/190°C/Gas Mk 5. Grease a 8½ inch (22 cm) springform cake tin and the line base with greased greaseproof paper. Beat the eggs, flour, margarine and sugar until fluffy. Turn into the tin, and spread evenly. Bake for 20–25 minutes in the centre of the oven until firm in the centre. Cool for a few minutes, then turn out onto a wire rack. Clean the tin and line with cling film. To make the mousse, put the gelatine in a cup with the water. Place the cup in hot water. Stir until the gelatine dissolves. Cool. Place the yolks and sugar in mixing bowl. Whisk until fluffy and the whisk leaves a trail. Stir in the strawberry puree, lemon juice and gelatine. Whisk the cream until softly stiff and fold into the mixture. Whisk the egg whites until fairly stiff. Fold into strawberry mixture. Cut the sponge into two layers and place the top half in the base of cake tin. Cut 8 oz (225 g) of the strawberries in half lengthways and arrange cut side facing outwards around edge of tin. Pour the strawberry mousse into the tin and place the remaining sponge half on top. Chill until set. Carefully remove from the tin to a serving plate. Whisk the cream until softly stiff. Pipe around the top edge of the gateau, and use the remaining strawberries for decoration.

GERMAN CHOCOLATE TORTE
Serves 6–8

½ oz (10 g) butter
2 tbsp dry breadcrumbs
8 oz (225 g) plain chocolate,
  broken into pieces
1 tbsp instant coffee granules
4 tbsp water

8 eggs, separated
6 oz (175 g) caster sugar
1 tsp vanilla essence
whipping cream and grated
  chocolate for decoration

Preheat the oven to 350°F/180°C/Gas Mk 4. Butter a 9 in (23 cm), 2 lb capacity ovenproof dish or cake tin and sprinkle with the dry breadcrumbs. Melt the chocolate together with the instant coffee and water in a basin over hot water, stirring gently. Remove from the heat and leave to cool slightly. Whisk the egg yolks and sugar in a large bowl until they are thick and creamy, then gradually beat in the cooled chocolate and the vanilla essence. Whisk the egg whites until they are stiff and fold into the mixture with a metal spoon. Fill the tin with about three-quarters of the mixture. Bake in the centre of the oven for 25 minutes. Turn off the oven and leave the torte in the oven for another 5 minutes. Remove from the oven and leave to cool for two hours, when the mixture will have sunk in the middle. Fill this cavity with the remaining mixture and chill for 30 minutes. Whip the cream and spread over the top, then sprinkle with grated chocolate.

STRAWBERRY DECKER CAKE
Serves 4–6

3 oz (75 g) self-raising flour
pinch of salt
3 eggs
4 oz (110 g) caster sugar

For the filling:
½pt (300 ml) whipping cream
1 oz (25 g) icing sugar, sifted

1 lb (450 g) frozen strawberries,
thawed but still cold

Preheat the oven to 375°F/190°C/Gas Mk 5. Sift the flour and salt into a bowl. Beat the eggs in a basin, placed over a pan half full of boiling water. Gradually beat in the sugar. Remove the pan from the heat but leave the bowl in place. Whisk the egg mixture until it has the consistency of a mousse. Remove the bowl from the pan. Continue whisking until cool. Using a metal spoon, fold in the flour, then turn into a 9 x 13 in (23 x 33 cm) Swiss roll tin, lined with oil and floured greaseproof paper. Bake for 20 minutes. Cool slightly, then turn out onto a wire rack. Stiffly whip the cream, gradually adding the icing sugar. Cut the sponge cake width-ways in 3 equal pieces. Spread two-thirds of the cream equally over 2 pieces of the cake, then cover with strawberries (halved or quartered if large). Reserve a few strawberries for decoration. Place one strawberry-topped cake on top of the other, and the remaining cake on top. Spread with the rest of the cream, smoothing over evenly. Top with the reserved strawberries.

BLACKBERRY AND APPLE CAKE
Serves 8

1 lb (450 g) cooking apples
lemon juice
water
4 oz (110 g) frozen blackberries
3½ oz (90 g) softened butter, cut into small pieces
2 eggs
6 oz (175 g) caster sugar
1 tsp almond essence
4 oz (110 g) self-raising flour
1 tsp baking powder
2 oz (50 g) ground almonds
1 oz (25 g) flaked almonds
icing sugar for decoration

Preheat the oven to 350°F/180°C/Gas Mk 4. Peel, core and slice the apples and keep them in cold water into which you have squeezed some lemon juice. Wash and pick over the blackberries. Keep on one side. Beat the butter, eggs, sugar and almond essence until pale and fluffy. Sift the flour and baking powder together and fold into the creamed mixture alternately with the ground almonds using a metal spoon. Spread two-thirds of this mixture into a greased 8 in (20 cm) loose-bottomed cake tin. Pat dry the sliced apples and layer together with the blackberries on top of the cake mix. Place spoonfuls of the remaining cake mixture on top of the fruit and sprinkle the flaked almonds on top. Bake for 30 minutes in the centre of the oven, then turn the heat down to 325°F/170°C/Gas Mk 3 for a further 30 minutes. Serve well dusted with icing sugar.

CHOCOLATE MARBLE LOAF
Serves 4–6

2–3 oz (50–75 g) plain chocolate,
   broken into pieces
4 oz (110 g) margarine, cut
   into small pieces
4 oz (110 g) sugar

2 eggs
5 oz (150 g) self-raising flour
2 tbsp water
1 macaroon

For the sauce:
2 oz (50 g) sugar
½ pt (300 ml) water
1 oz (25 g) cocoa powder

Preheat the oven to 350°F/180°C/Gas Mk 4. Melt the chocolate in the oven for 5 minutes, then remove. Cream the margarine and sugar until soft and fluffy. Add the eggs, one at a time, beating well after each addition. Fold in the flour and water. Spoon half the mixture into another basin and mix in the cooled chocolate. Arrange two layers of chocolate and plain mixture in a greased and base-lined 1½ pint (900 ml) loaf tin, alternating the flavours. With a knife, cut through the mixture in a criss-cross fashion to give the pudding its marble effect. Cut the macaroon into cubes and sprinkle over the top. Bake in the top half of the oven for 40–50 minutes until firm and springy to the touch. Serve with chocolate sauce made by boiling the sugar, water and cocoa powder together for 5 minutes, stirring all the time, until smooth.

GATEAUX AU MARRONS
Serves 6

1 lb (450 g) can of whole chestnuts
4 oz (110 g) caster sugar
3–4 tbsp water

2½ oz (60 g) softened
unsalted butter
a little oil

For the topping:
4 oz (110 g) plain chocolate,
broken into pieces
1 tbsp caster sugar

1 oz (25 g) softened unsalted
butter, cut into small pieces
1 tbsp water

Drain the liquid from the chestnuts and either push through a sieve or liquidise. Make a syrup of the water and sugar by boiling for about 5 minutes, but do not let the syrup colour. Add the softened butter and mix well. Stir into the chestnut purée and when well blended turn into a lightly oiled 9 in (22 cm) flat sandwich tin. Cover loosely and refrigerate overnight. To turn out, run a thin knife around the mould, put a serving plate on top and unmould quickly. If the cake loses its shape pat it together with a knife. For the topping, melt the chocolate with the sugar in a basin over simmering water, stirring until smooth. Beat in the butter. Cool a little and then cover the cake using a spatula, smoothing down with a knife dipped in hot water. Leave to set completely in the refrigerator before cutting into wedges.

GINGER AND LEMON CREAM CAKE
Serves 6

12 oz (350 g) ginger biscuits
½ pt (300 ml) double cream
4 level tbsp icing sugar, sifted

1 lemon, finely grated rind and juice
thin slices of lemon to decorate

In a polythene bag crush half of the ginger biscuits into crumbs. Break the remaining ginger biscuits into small pieces. Whip the cream until soft but stiff and put aside one-third for decoration. Stir the icing sugar, lemon rind and juice, half the crumbs and all the biscuit pieces into the cream. Line an 8 in (20 cm) sandwich tin with enough foil to come up the sides and over the top of the tin. Spoon the ginger and lemon cream into the tin, smoothing the top, and folding down the excess foil to cover it. Chill in the refrigerator overnight until the cake is firm. Carefully turn out onto a plate, smooth the surface and press the remaining biscuit crumbs over the top and sides of the cake. Pipe the remainder of the cream in swirls around the cake and decorate with quarter lemon slices. Chill until required.

APPLE BUTTERSCOTCH ROLL
Serves 4

6 oz (175 g) self-raising flour
pinch of salt
1½ oz (35 g) lard, cut into
   small pieces
1½ oz (35 g) margarine,
   cut into small pieces
3 tbsp milk
2 small cooking apples, peeled,
   cored, and thinly sliced

1 tbsp sugar
4 oz (110 g) demerara sugar
¼ pt (150 ml) water
2 oz (50 g) butter
1 level tsp ground cinnamon
whipped cream

Preheat the oven to 375°F/190°C/Gas Mk 5. Sift the flour with the salt into a bowl and rub in the fats until a fine crumb-like texture is obtained. Add the milk and mix to a soft dough. Knead lightly, roll out on a floured surface to a 6 x 12 in (15 x 30 cm) oblong. Arrange the apple slices so they overlap on the pastry. Sprinkle with the sugar. Roll up like a Swiss roll. Cut into 8 slices and place in an ovenproof dish. Put a small pat of butter on each slice. Dissolve the sugar in the water in a pan over a gentle heat. Boil for 5 minutes. Pour over the slices, and sprinkle with cinnamon. Bake for 30 minutes. Serve hot with the whipped cream.

MOCHA GATEAU
Serves 8

40 Boudoir (or sponge finger)
   biscuits
8 oz (225 g) plain chocolate,
   broken into small pieces
3 tbsp water

2 eggs, separated
2 level tbsp instant coffee
1 pt (600 ml) double cream
chocolate sprinkles

Line a 6 in (15 cm) round cake tin with greaseproof paper. Arrange a layer of sponge fingers around the sides and over the base of the tin, trimming them to fit. Melt the chocolate in a bowl over a pan of gently simmering water. Add the water, beaten egg yolks and the instant coffee. Beat until smooth. Whip half the double cream and fold into the mixture. Whisk the egg whites until stiff and fold in with a metal spoon. Pour half of this mixture into the prepared tin, then put a layer of sponge fingers, another layer of the chocolate mixture and ending with a layer of sponge fingers on top. Chill overnight. Remove the cake from the tin and place on a serving plate. Whip the remaining cream until thick and use to decorate. Scatter with the chocolate sprinkles.

GATEAU ELISABET
Serves 6

4 oz (110 g) plain chocolate,
  cut into pieces
6 oz (175 g) butter
6 oz (175 g) caster sugar
1 tsp almond essence
4 oz (110 g) ground almonds
4 oz (110 g) cake crumbs
  (trifle sponge or Madeira cake)

½ pt (300 ml) double cream
12 boudoir (or sponge finger) biscuits
1 chocolate flake bar
split almonds, to garnish
whipped cream, to garnish

Melt the chocolate in a basin standing over hot water, then remove from the heat and allow to cool slightly. Cream the butter and the sugar until soft and fluffy. Mix in the almond essence, softened chocolate, ground almonds and cake crumbs. Mix thoroughly. Whip the double cream until softly stiff and fold half into the chocolate mixture. Turn into a greased loose-based 6 in (15 cm) cake tin. Smooth the top and tap the tin sharply to release any trapped air. Press a piece of foil over the top and leave in the refrigerator overnight until firm. Loosen the edge of the cake with a knife and turn out onto a plate. Cut the boudoir biscuits in half and press firmly round the sides of the cake, sugared sides on the outside. Decorate the top with the whipped cream, crumbled chocolate flakes and split almonds.

PIES AND TARTS

CHEDDAR APPLE PIE
Serves 6

6 oz (175 g) plain flour
5 oz (150 g) mature Cheddar cheese,
  grated
2 oz (50 g) margarine
6–8 tbsp cold water
8 oz (225 g) cooking apples,
  peeled, cored and sliced

8 oz (225 g) dessert apples,
  peeled, cored and sliced
5 tbsp sweet cider
2 tbsp milk

Preheat the oven to 375°F/190°C/Gas Mk 5. Sift the flour into a bowl and add 2 oz (50 g) grated cheese. Add the margarine and rub in until the mixture resembles fine breadcrumbs. Add sufficient water to make a soft dough. Chill in the refrigerator for 30 minutes. Place the dough on a flat floured surface and roll out half the amount to line a greased 9 in (23 cm) round, deep pie dish. Mix together the apples and remaining cheese in a bowl. Arrange this mixture evenly in the pie dish and pour over the cider. Roll out the remaining half of the pastry to cover the dish. Seal the edges and make a hole in the centre. Brush over some milk and bake in the oven for 45 minutes until the pastry is golden and the apples are soft.

BAKEWELL PUDDING
Serves 4

1 x 7½ oz (210g) packet of frozen puff pastry, thawed
2 eggs
2 egg yolks
4 oz (110 g) butter, melted
4 oz (110 g) caster sugar
2 oz (50 g) ground almonds
2 tbsp raspberry jam

Preheat the oven to 400°F/200°C/Gas Mk 6. Place the pastry on a flat floured surface and roll out to line a 7 in (18 cm) pie plate. Place the eggs and egg yolks in a bowl and beat well together. Mix in the melted butter, sugar and almonds. Spread the jam on the pastry and pour the egg mixture over the top. Bake in the oven for 30 minutes until the filling is firm. This can be served hot or cold.

KEY LIME PIE
Serves 8

8 oz (225 g) digestive biscuits,
  crushed
3 oz (75 g) butter, melted
pinch nutmeg
6 eggs, separated
12 oz (350 g) sweetened
  condensed milk

finely grated rind of 2 limes
juice of 4 limes
8 oz (225 g) caster sugar
½ tsp cream of tartar
pinch salt

Preheat the oven to 375°F/190°C/Gas Mk 5. Mix the biscuit crumbs and nutmeg with the melted butter. Press into the base and sides of a 9 in (23 cm) loose-based flan tin and bake in the oven for 10 minutes. Cool on a rack, and reduce the oven heat to 350°F/180°C/Gas Mk 4. Beat the egg yolks lightly. Beat in the condensed milk, the lime juice and rind. Pour into the cooled crust and bake for 15 minutes. Whisk the egg whites until stiff. Beat in half the sugar, the salt and the cream of tartar and continue whisking until the meringue is stiff and shiny. Fold in the remaining sugar gently with a metal spoon. Spread the meringue over the pie, forking it up into peaks. Return to the oven for a further 10–15 minutes until golden. Decorate with a few thin strips of lime rind and cool.

SYRUP TART
Serves 4–6

4 oz (110 g) plain flour
1 oz (25 g) margarine
1 oz (25 g) lard
1 large egg, beaten
5 oz (150 g) golden syrup
3 oz (75 g) fresh white breadcrumbs

Preheat the oven to 375°F/190°C/Gas Mk 5. Rub the fats into the flour until the mixture resembles fine breadcrumbs. Add half the beaten egg and enough water to give a soft, not sticky dough. On a lightly floured surface, knead the pastry then roll out to a round and use to line a 9 in (23 cm) pie plate. Pinch the edges to decorate. Prick the base with a fork. Heat the golden syrup in a small saucepan. Stir in the breadcrumbs and the rest of the egg, then spread the mixture in the pastry lined pie plate. Bake towards the top of the oven for 30–35 minutes or until the pastry is brown and the filling has set.

GLAZED PINEAPPLE AND GINGER FLAN
Serves 6–8

4 oz (110 g) hard margarine
4 oz (110 g) plain flour
2 oz (50 g) rice flour
2 oz (50 g) icing sugar
5 level tbsp ginger marmalade
1½ lb (675 g) fresh pineapple (trimmed and peeled weight)
8 oz (225 g) cream cheese
1 tbsp caster sugar

Rub the margarine into the flours and sifted icing sugar. Bind with
2 level tbsp ginger marmalade and a little water if necessary. Wrap in
clingfilm and chill in the refrigerator for at least 30 minutes. Roll out
on a lightly floured surface and use to line a 9 in (23 cm) fluted flan
dish. Chill again for 10–15 minutes. Line the pastry case with foil and
bake 'blind' until crisp and lightly coloured. Leave to cool completely.
Core and thinly slice the pineapple. Reserve eleven slices for
decoration. Roughly chop the remainder and combine with the cream
cheese and caster sugar. Put this mixture into the cooled pastry case.
Refrigerate for 20 minutes. Decorate the flan with the reserved
pineapple slices. Heat the remaining marmalade with 2 tbsp water.
Bubble for 2–3 minutes until the mixture becomes syrupy. Brush
evenly over the fruit and leave to set before serving

MINCEMEAT AND ALMOND PIE
Serves 6

8 oz (225 g) cooking apples, peeled, cored and sliced
8 oz (225 g) mincemeat
6 oz (175 g) soft brown sugar
4 oz (110 g) soft margarine
4 oz (110 g) ground almonds
2 eggs, beaten

Preheat the oven to 350°F/180°C/Gas Mk 4. In a 2½ pint (1.5 ltr)
ovenproof pie dish, place the apples and mincemeat and add 2 oz (50
g) of the sugar. Mix well. In a bowl beat the margarine, almonds and
eggs until thoroughly mixed. Spread over the fruit mixture and bake in
oven for 45–60 minutes until the top is golden brown. Serve hot.

CHOCOLATE MARSHMALLOW PIE
Serves 6

1 packet of plain chocolate digestive biscuits, crushed
3 oz (75 g) butter, melted
6 oz (175 g) plain chocolate, broken into small pieces
1 packet plain marshmallows
5 fl oz (150 ml) double cream

Preheat the oven to 350°F/180°C/Gas Mk 4. In a bowl, mix together the biscuit crumbs and melted butter, then press this mixture around the base and sides of an 8 in (20 cm) flan dish. Bake in the oven for 10 minutes, then remove and set aside to cool. Put the chocolate in a heatproof bowl and add the marshmallows and cream. Place the bowl over a saucepan of simmering water until the chocolate and marshmallows have melted. Carefully remove the pie crust from the flan dish and place on a serving plate. Pour the mallow mixture into the crust and leave to set before serving.

GOOSEBERRY BISCUIT FLAN
Serves 4

2 oz (50 g) ginger biscuits
3 oz (75 g) digestive biscuits
3 oz (75 g) butter or hard margarine,
* melted*
1 large orange
2 level tsp powdered gelatine

12 oz (350 g) frozen gooseberries,
* thawed*
3–4 oz (75–110g) granulated sugar
1 x 6 oz (175 g) can creamed rice
¼pt (150 ml) double cream

Put all the biscuits in a plastic bag and crush with a rolling pin. Mix with the melted butter and use this mixture to line a 7 in (18 cm) fluted flan dish. Chill in the refrigerator until set. Pare off a few strips of orange rind with a potato peeler and cut into very fine strips. Blanch, drain and reserve. Grate the remaining orange rind. Soak the gelatine in 2 tbsp water. Stew the gooseberries until thick and pulpy with the grated orange rind and 3 tbsp orange juice. Push the gooseberries through a nylon sieve, or purée in an electric blender then sieve to remove the pips. While still warm, stir in the soaked gelatine and sugar to taste. Mix until both have dissolved. Chill to setting point. Spoon the creamed rice into the biscuit crumb crust. Spread the gooseberry mixture over the top. Refrigerate to set. Decorate with whipped cream and orange shreds.

CURD TART
Serves 8

8 oz (225 g) plain flour
pinch of salt
5 oz (150 g) butter
1 egg yolk
2 tbsp cold water

1 lb (450 g) curd cheese
3 eggs, beaten
3 oz (75 g) currants
4 oz (110 g) demerara sugar
finely grated rind of 1 lemon

Preheat the oven to 375°F/190°C/Gas Mk 5. Sift the flour and salt into a bowl, add 4 oz (110 g) of the butter and rub in until the mixture resembles fine breadcrumbs. Gradually beat in the egg yolk with sufficient water to bind together. Form the dough into a ball and place on a floured flat surface. Roll out and use to line an 8 in (20 cm) fluted flan dish. Place in the refrigerator to chill. Meanwhile, mix together the curd cheese and eggs in a bowl and add the currants, sugar and lemon rind. Melt the remaining 1 oz (25 g) butter and stir in until well mixed. Fill the pastry case with the curd cheese mixture and bake in the oven for 45 minutes until the filling is set and golden. This tart can be served hot or cold.

APPLE FLAN WITH CARDAMOM
Serves 10

Pastry: 4 oz (110 g) flour
1 tbsp sugar

3 oz (75 g) margarine, cut into small pieces
1 egg yolk

Filling: 3 apples, peeled and cored
5 oz (150 g) cottage cheese
2 eggs

3 oz (75 g) sugar
1 tsp grated cardamom

Sauce: 10 fl oz (300 ml) redcurrant jam

Preheat the oven to 400°F/200°C/Gas Mk 6. Make the dough by hand or in a food processor. Mix the flour, sugar, margarine, and egg yolk and work together quickly to form a dough. Leave the dough to rest in the refrigerator for 30 minutes. Roll out or press the dough into a 9 in (23 cm) mould with removable base. Bake blind the dough for 10 minutes. Cut the apples into thin wedges, and arrange these in the mould. Mix together the cottage cheese, eggs, sugar, and cardamom. Pour the mixture over the apples. Bake in the lower part of the oven for 25 minutes. Serve the flan cool or cold. Purée the redcurrant jam in a food processor and serve as a sauce.

PEAR AND ALMOND TART
Serves 6

3 oz (75 g) hard margarine
6 oz (175 g) plain flour

2 oz (50 g) caster sugar
1½–2 tbsp milk

Filling:
3 oz (75 g) butter, softened
3 oz (75 g) caster sugar
1 large egg
3 level tbsp self-raising flour

3 oz (75 g) ground almonds
1 x 14½ oz (410 g) can of
pear halves, drained
½ oz (10 g) flaked almonds

Preheat the oven to 400°F/200°C/Gas Mk 6. Rub the margarine into the flour until the mixture resembles fine breadcrumbs. Add the sugar and mix with as much milk as necessary to bind into a firm dough. Chill in the refrigerator for 30 minutes. Roll out the pastry on a floured surface and use to line a 9 in (23 cm) fluted flan ring. Chill in the refrigerator for 30 minutes. For the filling, cream the butter and sugar until fluffy. Beat in the egg with 1 tbsp flour, then stir in the ground almonds and the rest of the flour. Spread the filling over the pastry. Place the pear halves, hollow side down, in a ring on top of the filling. Sprinkle over the flaked almonds. Bake in the oven for 15 minutes, then reduce the oven to 350°F/180°C/Gas Mk 4 and bake for a further 20–25 minutes until the filling has set. Serve hot or cold with cream.

COCONUT CRUNCH
Serves 4–6

6 oz (175 g) flour
pinch of salt
4 oz (110 g) butter
2 eggs, separated
2 oz (50 g) sugar

¼ pt (150 ml) milk
¼ tsp almond essence
¼ tsp lemon essence
3 oz (75 g) desiccated coconut

Preheat the oven to 350°F/180°C/Gas Mk 4. Sift the flour and salt into a bowl. Rub in the butter and mix to a soft dough with 3–4 tbsp of water. Use the pastry to line an 8 in (20 cm) flan tin. Roll out the pastry trimmings and cut out shapes to decorate. Whisk the egg yolks and sugar, then add the milk, 1 oz (25 g) melted butter and the almond and lemon essences. Whisk the egg whites and fold into the mixture with the coconut. Pour into the pastry case and decorate the top with pastry shapes. Bake for 25–30 minutes until the pastry is golden and the filling has set. Serve hot or cold.

SAVOY PUDDING
Serves 6

6 oz (175 g) shortcrust pastry
2 oz (50 g) butter and extra for
  greasing
2 oz (50 g) caster sugar
2 egg yolks, lightly beaten
few drops of almond essence

3 oz (75 g) sponge cake crumbs
⅓ pt (200 ml) milk
2 oz (50 g) chopped candied peel
2 egg whites
1 tbsp caster sugar

Preheat the oven to 375°F/190°C/Gas Mk 5. Roll out the pastry on a lightly floured board and use to line a greased pie dish. Cream the butter and sugar together, then add the egg yolks, followed by the almond essence and cake crumbs. Stir in the milk gradually, together with the chopped peel. Spoon into the prepared pie shell and bake in the oven for 30 minutes. Whisk the egg whites until stiff, fold in the 1 tbsp of caster sugar and pile this mixture on top of the pudding. Put on the bottom of the oven for 20 minutes to set and brown the meringue.

BUTTERSCOTCH PIE
Serves 6–8

6 oz (175 g) digestive biscuits
3 oz (75 g) margarine or butter
2 oz (50 g) plain flour
6 oz (175 g) brown sugar
8 fl oz (250 ml) milk

1 oz (25 g) butter
4 tbsp cold water
1 tsp vanilla essence
2 large eggs, separated
2 oz (50 g) caster sugar

Preheat the oven to 300°F/150°C/Gas Mk 2. Put the digestive biscuits in a plastic bag and crush with a rolling pin. Melt the margarine or butter in a saucepan, then quickly stir in the biscuit crumbs. Press the mixture evenly into a 9 in (23 cm) pie plate or flan dish, then chill in the refrigerator. For the filling, mix the flour and sugar in a bowl. Heat the milk and add to the mixture with the butter and cold water. Pour into a saucepan and heat very slowly until the mixture thickens, then add the vanilla essence and egg yolks. Cook until very thick and glossy, beating well with a wooden spoon to prevent lumps from forming. Cool slightly and then pour into the biscuit base. Make a swirl on top with a palette knife. Beat the egg whites until they form stiff peaks, then fold in the caster sugar. Pipe or spoon this meringue mixture on top of the flan and bake for 10–15 minutes until lightly browned.

PLUM HAZELNUT LATTICE
Serves 4–6

7 oz (200 g) plain flour
3½ oz (90 g) block margarine
2 oz (50 g) caster sugar
2 oz (50 g) ground hazelnuts
3 egg yolks, lightly beaten
1 lb (450 g) fresh golden plums, halved and stoned
icing sugar for dusting

Preheat the oven to 375°F/190°C/Gas Mk 5. Sift the flour and rub in the margarine until the mixture resembles fine breadcrumbs. Stir in the sugar and hazelnuts. Add the beaten egg yolks and a little cold water, if necessary, to bind to a dough. Roll out two-thirds of the dough and use to line an 8 in (20 cm) fluted flan ring placed on a baking sheet. Arrange the plums in the flan case. Sprinkle over 2 level tbsp sifted icing sugar. Roll out the remaining pastry and use to make a lattice over the plums. Bake in the oven for about 30 minutes. Dredge with icing sugar. Serve warm or cold with thick pouring cream.

RASPBERRY TART
Serves 4

4 oz (110 g) margarine
1 oz (25 g) caster sugar
1 oz (25 g) ground almonds
grated rind of 1 lemon
1 egg yolk

6 oz (175 g) plain flour, sifted
1 tsp ground cinnamon
1 lb (450 g) frozen raspberries, thawed
2 oz (50 g) icing sugar for dredging
double cream to serve (optional)

Preheat the oven to 350°F/180°C/Gas Mk 4. Cream the margarine with the sugar until light and fluffy. Add the ground almonds, grated lemon rind, egg yolk and 2 tbsp flour. Mix well. Add the remaining flour and the ground cinnamon. Mix to form a firm dough and knead on a floured board until smooth. Wrap in foil and chill in the refrigerator for 30 minutes. Use two-thirds of the dough to line an 8 in (20 cm) flan dish, pressing down gently with your fingers. Roll out the remaining pastry and cut into strips approximately 8½ x ½ in (21.5 x 1.25 cm). Drain any excess water from the thawed raspberries and then fill the flan with the raspberries. Arrange strips of pastry on top in a lattice pattern. Bake just above the centre of the oven for approximately 30 minutes. Dust with sifted icing sugar before serving. Serve with whipped double cream if desired.

GINGER CREAM FLAN
Serves

1 x 8 oz (225 g) packet ginger biscuits, crushed
2 oz (50 g) butter
½ pt (300 ml) whipping cream
1 small tin condensed milk
juice of 1 large lemon

Melt the butter and stir into the crushed ginger biscuits. Line a flan dish with the crumb mixture and chill. Mix the condensed milk and lemon juice together. Whip half the cream until stiff and fold in the condensed milk and lemon juice mixture. Pour into the case and chill again. Decorate with the remaining whipped cream and grated chocolate curls.

BLACK CHERRY SPONGE TART
Serves 6

5 oz (150 g) butter or
hard margarine
1 oz (25 g) caster sugar
3 egg yolks
6 oz (175 g) plain flour
2 oz (50 g) soft dark brown sugar

juice and finely grated rind of 1 lemon
1 large egg, beaten
2 oz (50 g) self-raising flour
1 x 15 oz (425 g) can pitted
black cherries, drained
icing sugar for dredging

Preheat the oven to 350°F/180°C/Gas Mk 4. Cream 3 oz (75 g) of the butter or margarine until soft and gradually beat in the caster sugar, followed by the egg yolks. Cut and fold the plain flour through the creamed ingredients, then knead lightly until smooth. Wrap in clingfilm and chill in the refrigerator for 15 minutes. Roll out the dough and use to line a 9 in (23 cm) loose-based fluted flan tin. Chill for 10 minutes. Line the pastry case with foil and bake 'blind' until just set but not browned. Meanwhile cream the remaining fat and brown sugar with the finely grated lemon rind until soft. Gradually beat in the beaten egg and then fold in the self-raising flour with 1 tbsp lemon juice. Spread the cake mixture over the base of the pastry case, level the top and spoon over the well-drained cherries. Bake in the oven for about 35 minutes, covering if necessary. Serve warm or cold, dusted with icing sugar.

RASPBERRY CHEESECAKE TART
Serves 4

Pastry:
5 oz (175 g) plain flour
pinch salt
4 oz (110 g) butter

2 level tsp caster sugar
2 egg yolks, lightly beaten
3-4 tbsp cold water

Filling:
3 oz (75 g) cream cheese
1 tbsp milk
½ pt (300 ml) boiling water

1 raspberry jelly tablet
8 oz (225 g) raspberries, fresh or frozen
double cream to decorate

Preheat the oven to 400°F/200°C/Gas Mk 6. Sift the flour with the salt and lightly rub in the butter until the mixture resembles fine breadcrumbs. Stir in the sugar. Add the egg yolks, with 2–3 tsp cold water, if necessary, to bind the mixture into a firm but pliable dough. Leave to rest for about 30 minutes in the refrigerator. Roll out the dough on a lightly floured board to ⅛ in (3 mm) thickness and use to line a 9 in (23 cm) flan ring placed on a baking sheet. Press down gently with the fingertips. Leave the pastry rim a little higher than the ring to allow for shrinkage during cooking. Prick the case all over with a fork, line with kitchen foil and fill with dried beans. Bake 'blind' in the oven for 15 minutes. Remove the beans and foil and return to the oven for another 5–10 minutes, or until the pastry is cooked and golden. Cool. Beat the cream cheese and milk together until soft and smooth. Spread over the base of the cooled flan case. Pour boiling water over the jelly tablet and stir until dissolved. Add the raspberries and stir. Put in a cool place until the jelly is beginning to set, then pour into the pastry case and leave until completely set. Pipe whipped cream around the edge of the tart before serving.

RASPBERRY HAZELNUT PIE
Serves 6

8 oz (225 g) plain flour
4 oz (110 g) butter
2 oz (50 g) toasted hazelnuts,
 finely chopped
2 oz (50 g) icing sugar
4 tbsp cold water
8 oz (225 g) fresh raspberries,
 hulled

12 oz (350 g) cooking apples,
 peeled, cored and sliced
1½ oz (35 g) caster sugar
beaten egg for glazing
½ tbsp granulated sugar

Preheat the oven to 400°F/200°C/Gas Mk 6. Put the flour and butter in a bowl and rub together with the fingertips until the mixture resembles fine breadcrumbs. Add the hazelnuts and icing sugar and mix well. Add sufficient water to form a soft dough and chill in the refrigerator for about 30 minutes. Lightly grease a 10 in (25 cm) ovenproof pie dish. Place the dough on a floured flat surface and roll out half the pastry to form a large circle, 12 in (30 cm) in diameter. Lay the pastry in the pie dish and dampen the edges with water. Arrange the apples and raspberries on the pastry and sprinkle with caster sugar. Roll out the remaining pastry to form a circle of the same size and lay it on top of the fruit. Trim the edges and make a hole in the centre of the pastry lid. Brush the top with beaten egg, sprinkle over granulated sugar and bake in the oven for 30 minutes.

MISSISSIPPI MUD PIE
Serves 8

Pastry:

7 oz (200 g) plain flour
3½ oz (90 g) lightly salted butter
pinch salt

1 egg yolk
3 tbsp cold water

Filling:

4 oz (110 g) plain chocolate
4 tbsp cocoa powder
4 oz (110 g) butter, softened
9 oz (250 g) light brown sugar

3 eggs
¼ pt (150 ml) single cream
¼ pt (150 ml) double cream

Preheat the oven to 375°F/190°C/Gas Mk 5. Rub the butter into the flour and salt until the mixture resembles fine breadcrumbs. Add the egg yolk, and enough water to make a firm dough. Wrap in clingfilm and chill in the refrigerator for at least 30 minutes. Roll out and use to line a 9 in (23 cm) flan tin, pricking the pastry all over. Melt 3 oz (75 g) of the chocolate with 1 oz (25 g) butter and the cocoa powder in a large bowl set over a pan of simmering water. Cream the remaining butter with the sugar until it is light and fluffy, then beat in the eggs one at a time. Stir in the single cream and the cooled chocolate mixture and pour into the pastry case. Place on a preheated baking sheet and bake for 45 minutes. Remove from the oven and cool on a wire rack until the pie is at room temperature. Whip the double cream and swirl over the pie. Grate the remaining chocolate over the top. Chill until required.

STRAWBERRY CREAM FLAN
Serves 6

Pastry:
6 oz (175 g) plain flour
4 oz (110 g) unsalted butter
2 oz (50 g) caster sugar
1 egg yolk
1 tbsp cold water

Filling:
1½ lb (675 g) strawberries
12 oz (350 g) ricotta cheese
1 oz (25 g) caster sugar
¼ pt (150 ml) double cream
3 tbsp strawberry jam

Preheat the oven to 375°F/190°C/Gas Mk 5. Rub the butter into the flour and sugar until the mixture resembles fine breadcrumbs. Add the egg yolk, and enough water to make a firm dough. Wrap in clingfilm and chill in the refrigerator for at least 30 minutes. Roll out on a lightly floured board and use to line an 8 in (20 cm) fluted flan tin. Prick the pastry all over, put crumpled foil or baking paper and beans in the flan case and bake 'blind' in a preheated oven for 20 minutes. Remove the beans and paper and then bake for a further 10 minutes until the pastry is cooked. Leave to cool. Wash the strawberries and halve enough to cover the flan. Chop the remaining strawberries roughly and stir into the ricotta cheese with the sugar. Whip the cream to soft peaks and fold into the ricotta cheese. Put the pastry case on a serving plate and spoon in the cheese mixture, piling it up in the middle. Press the strawberry halves into the filling in a ring pattern. Melt the strawberry jam in a small saucepan and then sieve. Brush carefully over the strawberry halves.

APPLE AND APRICOT FLAN
Serves 8–10

Pastry:
3 oz (75 g) margarine, cut into small pieces
6 oz (175 g) flour
3 oz (75 g) cottage cheese

Filling:
3 large apples, peeled and cored
½ pt (300 ml) apricot purée

Make the pastry by hand or in a food processor. Rub together the margarine and flour until the mixture resembles fine bread crumbs. Add cottage cheese and quickly work into the dough. Leave to rest in the refrigerator for approximately 30 minutes. Preheat the oven to 400°F/200°C/Gas Mk 6. Roll out the dough and use to line a 10 in (25 cm) pie mould with removable base. Prick the dough base with a fork. Place in the refrigerator for 15 minutes. Bake blind the dough for 10 minutes. Cut the apples into thin wedges. Spread a thin layer of apricot purée into the base of the pastry shell. Place the apple wedges in an overlapping pattern on top. Spread the remaining apricot purée over the apples. Bake the flan in the lower part of the oven for about 15 minutes.

APPLE AND MARZIPAN TART
Serves 8

6 oz (175 g) hard margarine
10 oz (300 g) plain flour
2 level tbsp caster sugar

1 egg, beaten
1-2 tbsp water

Filling:
4 oz (110 g) marzipan
4 oz (110 g) soft margarine
2 oz (50 g) caster sugar

4 large cooking apples, peeled,
cored and grated
2 large eggs, separated

Preheat the oven to 425°F/220°C/Gas Mk 7. Rub the margarine into the flour and sugar until the mixture resembles fine breadcrumbs. Add the egg, and enough water to make a firm dough. Chill in the refrigerator for 1 hour. Roll out, and use to line a 10 in (25 cm) loose-bottomed flan tin. Keep the pastry trimmings for decoration. For the filling, grate the marzipan over the pastry base. Cream the margarine with the sugar until light and fluffy, then stir in the grated apples. Stiffly whisk the egg whites and fold in with a metal spoon. Spread the apple mixture over the marzipan. Cover with pastry strips to make a lattice. Brush the strips with beaten egg yolk. Bake for 35–40 minutes until the tart is a rich golden brown. Leave for a few moments before removing the base from the flan tin. Serve hot with custard, pouring cream or thickly whipped cream.

CUSTARD PIE
Serves 4

1 oz (25 g) lard
1 oz (25 g) margarine
4 oz (110 g) plain flour
¼ pt (150 ml) milk
1 x 6 oz (175 g) can evaporated milk
1 oz (25 g) caster sugar
2 large eggs
½ tsp vanilla essence
½ oz (10 g) butter
grated nutmeg

Preheat the oven to 400°F/200°C/Gas Mk 6 and put a baking sheet in the oven to heat. Rub the lard and margarine into the flour until the mixture resembles fine breadcrumbs. Stir in enough water to form a soft, not sticky dough. Knead lightly until smooth. Roll out on a floured surface and use to line a 9 in (23 cm) pie dish. Prick the base with a fork and chill in the refrigerator for 30 minutes. Line the pastry case with crumpled foil, place on the heated baking sheet and bake 'blind' in the oven for 15 minutes. Take out of the oven and reduce the oven temperature to 350°F/180°C/Gas Mk 4. Put the evaporated milk, milk, sugar, eggs and vanilla essence in a bowl and beat thoroughly. Remove the foil from the pastry case and strain the egg mixture through a sieve into the case. Dot butter over the top and sprinkle with nutmeg. Bake for a further 35–40 minutes until the filling has set.

ORANGE SPONGE TART
Serves 4

6 oz (175 g) shortcrust pastry
3 tbsp thin-cut orange marmalade
3 oz (75 g) butter
3 oz (75 g) caster sugar
2 tsp finely grated orange rind
1 egg, lightly beaten
1 oz (25 g) ground almonds
4 oz (110 g) self-raising flour
2 tbsp orange juice
1½ oz (35 g) blanched almonds

Preheat the oven to 425°F/220°C/Gas Mk 7. Roll out the pastry on a lightly floured board and use to line a 7 in (18 cm) ovenproof pie plate. Spread the orange marmalade over the base. Cream the butter and sugar together until light and fluffy. Add the egg, stir in the orange rind and ground almonds, and then fold in the sifted flour and orange juice alternately. Spread the mixture evenly into the prepared pastry case and decorate with the blanched almonds. Bake in the oven for 20 minutes and then reduce the heat to 325°F/170°C/Gas Mk 3 and bake for a further 20 minutes. Serve hot or cold.

RHUBARB AND ORANGE CHIFFON PIE
Serves 6

6 oz (175 g) digestive biscuits, crushed
2 oz (50 g) demerara sugar
3 oz (75 g) unsalted butter, melted
1 lb (450 g) rhubarb, trimmed and cut into 1 in (2.5 cm) lengths
grated rind and juice of 1 large orange
2 eggs, separated
2 oz (50 g) caster sugar
2 tbsp cornflour
½ tsp ground ginger
orange slices, for decoration

Put the biscuits and demerara sugar in a bowl and mix well. Mix in the butter. Press the mixture evenly on the base and up the sides of an 8 in (20 cm) fluted flan dish. Chill in the refrigerator. Meanwhile, place the rhubarb in a saucepan with 3 tbsp of water, cover and cook over low heat, stirring from time to time, until the fruit is soft. Purée in a blender, or by passing through a sieve, and pour into a bowl. Put the orange rind and juice in a heavy-based saucepan, and then stir in the egg yolks, caster sugar, cornflour and ginger. Cook over low heat, stirring constantly, until thick. Remove from the heat and add to the rhubarb purée, stirring well. Whisk the egg whites into stiff peaks and fold into the rhubarb mixture. Pour into the biscuit crust and chill in the refrigerator overnight. Decorate with the orange slices before serving.

WALNUT TREACLE TART
Serves 6

3 oz (75 g) wholemeal plain flour
5 oz (150 g) white plain flour
2 oz (50 g) ground walnuts
4 oz (110 g) butter
6 tbsp cold water
1 oz (25 g) bran flakes, crushed
6 tbsp golden syrup

Preheat the oven to 400°F/200°C/Gas Mk 6. Mix the flour and nuts together in a large mixing bowl and rub in the butter until the mixture resembles fine breadcrumbs. Add the water and mix to a soft dough. Chill in the refrigerator for about 30 minutes. Place about three-quarters of the dough on a floured surface. Roll this out to form a 10 in (25 cm) circle and place in a lightly greased 8 in (20 cm) flan dish. Sprinkle the bran flakes evenly over the pastry base and then pour over the syrup. Roll out the reserved pastry and cut into thin strips. Arrange in a lattice pattern over the syrup and bran flakes. Bake in the oven for 30 minutes until the pastry is golden brown.

MANCHESTER TART
Serves 4–6

4 oz (110 g) plain flour
pinch of salt
1 oz (25 g) margarine
1 oz (25 g) lard
3 level tbsp raspberry jam

2–3 tbsp desiccated coconut
3 level tbsp custard powder
2 level tbsp sugar and a little extra
1 pt (600 ml) milk
a little extra sugar

Preheat the oven to 400°F/200°C/Gas Mk 6. Sift the flour and salt into a bowl. Rub in the fats until the mixture resembles fine bread-crumbs. Stir in enough water to give a soft, not sticky dough. Roll out the pastry and use to line a 1½ pint (900 ml) pie dish. Line the pastry base with crumpled foil then bake blind for about 20 minutes or until the pastry is cooked. Remove the foil and leave to cool. Spread the jam over the pastry base, then sprinkle over the coconut. Put the custard powder and sugar in a bowl and blend to a smooth paste with about 3 tbsp of the milk. Heat the remaining milk to boiling point then pour onto the custard paste, stirring all the time. Return the custard to the pan and bring back to the boil, stirring, and cook for half a minute. Pour into the pastry case. Sprinkle sugar over the top to prevent a skin forming and leave until completely cold before serving.

PASTRIES & MERINGUES

CHOCOLATE CHINCHILLA
Serves 6

6 egg whites
pinch of salt
8 oz (225 g) caster sugar
2 oz (50 g) powdered drinking chocolate, sifted
1 tsp ground cinnamon, sifted

Preheat the oven to 350°F/180°C/Gas Mk 4. Grease a 2 pint (1.2 ltr) oven dish with a little butter. Whisk the egg whites and the salt together until they form stiff peaks, then beat in half the sugar. Fold in the remaining sugar in two batches. Fold in the chocolate powder and the cinnamon. Pile the mixture into the prepared dish and bake for 45 minutes or until well risen. Set the dish aside in a draught-free place to cool before serving

LEMON LAYER MERINGUE
Serves 8

4 standard egg whites
8 oz (225 g) caster sugar, plus 2 level tbsp
¼pt (150 ml) whipping cream
1 can condensed milk equivalent to 1¼ pt
2 large lemons, rind and juice

Preheat the oven to 250°F/120°C/Gas Mk 1/2. Whisk the egg whites until stiff and dry. Whisk in the 8 oz (225 g) of caster sugar a spoonful at a time. Mark out three 8 in (20 cm) circles on a sheet of greaseproof paper placed on baking trays. Spread the meringues in these circles. Dust with the remaining caster sugar. Bake until a pale biscuit colour. This will be about 3 hours. Remove from the paper and leave to cool. Combine the cream and condensed milk with the grated zest and juice of the lemons. Leave to thicken. Spread one meringue base with half of the lemon mixture, top with the second meringue and repeat. Top with the third meringue.

FRUIT PAVLOVA
Serves 10–12

margarine for greasing
plain flour for dusting
4 egg whites

1 tsp vinegar spirit
5 oz (150 g) sugar
1 tbsp cornflour

To garnish:
½ pt (300 ml) whipped cream
1 lb (450 g) strawberries

4 kiwi fruits
3 passion fruits

Draw an 11 in (28 cm) circle on a sheet of greaseproof paper. Grease the circle with a little margarine. Sieve plain flour on top and shake the paper to make sure the flour sticks. Place the paper onto a baking sheet. Preheat the oven to 300°F/150°C/Gas Mk 2. Beat the egg whites with vinegar spirit until very stiff. Add the sugar and continue beating until the mixture is thick and shiny. Stir in the cornflour. Spread the meringue mixture onto the circle, making a light indentation in the middle. Bake in the middle of the oven for 1½ hours. Turn off the oven and leave the cake in the oven for a few hours or overnight. Garnish the cake with whipped cream, berries and fruit.

STRAWBERRY MERINGUES
Makes 30

5 egg whites
8 oz (225 g) caster sugar
pinch salt

For the Frangipani:
1 egg, separated
3 oz (75 g) caster sugar
¼ pt (150 ml) milk
1½ tbsp plain flour
1½ oz (35 g) butter, cubed

¼ tsp vanilla essence
¼ tsp almond essence
2 oz (50 g) ground almonds
8 oz strawberries, washed and hulled

Make thirty 2 in (5 cm) meringue nests using the meringue method. For the Frangipani, put the eggs yolk and sugar in a bowl over simmering water and whisk until a ribbon trail is left when lifting the whisk. Scald the milk. Whisk in the sifted flour and then the milk. Pour into a heavy based saucepan and cook very gently, stirring all the time, until the mixture becomes thick. Beat for 3 minutes. Remove from the heat and beat in the rest of the ingredients apart from the strawberries. Cover and leave to get cold. Fill the meringue nests and decorate with slices of strawberry and a mint leaf.

CHOCOLATE MERINGUE
Serves 8

6 egg whites
12 oz (350 g) caster sugar
7 oz (200 g) plain chocolate
6 oz (175 g) marshmallows
1 tbsp sherry
½ pt (300 ml) whipping cream

Preheat the oven to 275°F/140°C/Gas Mk 1. Cover 3 baking sheets with non-stick baking parchment and mark out a 7 in (18 cm) circle on each sheet. Whisk the egg whites until they form stiff peaks, add half the sugar and continue whisking until shiny and smooth. Fold in the remaining sugar very gently with a metal spoon. Divide the mixture between the three baking sheets, smoothing the meringue out to fill the circles. Bake for about 3 hours until the crust is dry. Turn off the heat and leave in the oven with the door open to dry out. Melt 6 oz (175 g) of the chocolate together with the marshmallows in a bowl over a pan of simmering water. Stir in the sherry. Whisk the cream until it is stiff and fold into the chocolate mixture. Chill for 1 hour. Sandwich the meringues together with the chocolate mixture. Melt the remaining chocolate and drizzle over the top.

BLACKBERRY FLAN
Serves 10

For the pastry:
4 oz (110 g) oat flakes
4 oz (110g) flour
3 oz (75 g) sugar
3 oz (75 g) margarine
2 tbsp low fat cottage cheese

For the filling:
2 tbsp sugar
1 tbsp cornflour
9 oz (250 g) pkt frozen blackberries,
*   thawed*

Preheat the oven to 400°F/200°C/as Mk 6. Mix thoroughly all the ingredients for the pastry. Knead the dough until smooth. Roll out to fit a 9 in (23 cm) flan dish. Press firmly into the flan dish. Leave the mould to stand for a while. Thaw the blackberries. Mix together the sugar and cornflour. Layer the blackberries with the sugar mixture in the mould. Bake in the lower part of the oven for about 30 minutes.

PROFITEROLE RING
Serves 8

7 fl oz (200 ml) water
2 oz (50 g) margarine
7 oz (200 g) flour
3 eggs

Filling:
½ pt (300 ml) custard
vanilla essence to taste
1 lb (450 g) fresh strawberries or raspberries

Preheat the oven to 400°F/200°C/Gas Mk 6. Bring the water and margarine to boil in a saucepan. Add the flour a little at a time. Mix vigorously with a wooden spoon until the mixture comes away from the base and the sides of the saucepan. Allow to cool a little. Beat in the eggs, one at a time, beating well between each addition. Spoon or pipe the dough in a ring onto a baking tray lined with greaseproof paper. Bake in the middle of the oven for 25–30 minutes. Do not open the oven until the end of the baking time. The ring is ready when it has risen and is golden in colour. Leave to stand on a rack. Make the custard as directed on the packet. Add a drop of vanilla essence to taste. Leave the custard to cool. Rinse, hull and slice the strawberries. Using a sharp knife, slice the ring in half to make a top and base. Layer the custard and sliced strawberries onto the bottom half and then put back the top. Leave the ring to stand cold until serving.

HEDGEROW PAVLOVA
Serves 6

3 egg whites
3 oz (75 g) caster sugar
3 oz (75 g) soft brown sugar
2 tbsp cornflour, sifted
1 tbsp white wine vinegar
1 tsp vanilla essence
2 oz (50 g) hazelnuts, chopped
1 oz (25 g) walnuts, chopped
½ pt (300 ml) whipping
* or double cream*

1 eating apple, cored and sliced
1 pear, cored and sliced
2 tsp lemon juice
4 oz (110 g) fresh plums,
* stoned and quartered*
4 oz (110 g) fresh blackberries,
* washed and hulled*

Preheat the oven to 275°F/140°C/Gas Mk 1. Line a baking sheet with non-stick baking or greaseproof paper and mark out in pencil an 8 in (20 cm) circle. Whisk the egg whites until stiff. Mix the two sugars together and add to the egg whites a spoonful at a time, whisking well in between spoonfuls, until the mixture is stiff and glossy. In a small bowl blend the cornflour, wine vinegar and vanilla essence to a smooth paste. Using a metal spoon gently fold the cornflour mixture into the egg whites, together with the hazelnuts. Spoon the meringue onto the circle on the baking sheet, sprinkle over the walnuts and bake for about 1 hour or until dry and crisp. Leave on the paper on a wire rack to cool. When the meringue is completely cold, carefully peel away the paper and put the meringue on a serving plate. Whip the cream, until stiff and then spread carefully over the top of the meringue. Cover the apple and pear slices with lemon juice and when ready to serve, pile with the remaining fruit on top of the Pavlova.

MERINGUE RING
Serves 8–10

6 egg whites
4 oz (110 g) sugar

For the ring mould:
6 oz (175 g) sugar
2 tbsp boiling water

Serve with:
fruit salad or fresh strawberries
whipped cream (optional)

Preheat the oven to 400°F/200°C/Gas MK 6. Beat the egg whites until stiff. Add the sugar and continue to beat until the mixture is thick and shiny. Place the 6 oz (175 g) of sugar in a dry, clean frying pan and melt, stirring with a wooden spoon, until smooth and light brown. Add the boiling water and mix until the mixture is smooth. Pour immediately into a warm 2 pint (1.2 ltr) ring mould. Shake the mould until it is evenly covered with sugar. Pour the meringue mixture in the mould and place in a bain-marie. Bake for approximately 10 minutes until the surface has coloured slightly. Lower the temperature to 300°F/150°C/Gas Mk 2 and bake for 2 hours. Leave the mould to cool in the bain-marie. Turn out the ring onto a dish and decorate with fruit salad. Serve with fruit salad.

PROFITEROLES WITH CHOCOLATE SAUCE
Makes 24

butter for greasing
¼ pt (150 ml) water
2 oz (50 g) butter
2½ oz (60 g) flour

pinch of salt
½ tsp vanilla essence
2 eggs

Filling: ¼ pt (150 ml) double cream
1 tbsp caster sugar

Chocolate sauce:
4 oz (110 g) plain chocolate,
broken into small pieces
1 oz (25 g) cocoa powder

1 oz (25 g) butter
2 tbsp golden syrup
1-2 tbsp water

Preheat the oven to 400°F/200°C/Gas Mk 6. Lightly grease a baking tray. Heat the water and butter in a pan until the butter melts and the water comes to the boil. Quickly add the flour and beat in well over a low heat. Continue beating until the paste is smooth and starts to leave the sides of the pan. Add the salt, sugar and vanilla essence. Remove from the heat and beat in the eggs, one at a time, beating well after each addition until the paste is smooth and shiny. Spoon 24 small buns on to the baking tray, allowing room for spreading. Bake for 20 minutes then reduce the heat to 375°F/190°C/Gas Mk 5 for a further 10-15 minutes. Put the buns onto a wire rack and slit with a knife to let the steam escape. Leave to cool. To make the filling, whisk the cream with the sugar until fairly stiff. Spoon into the cold profiteroles and pile up on a serving plate. For the sauce, melt the chocolate in a heatproof bowl over a pan of simmering water. Carefully stir in all the remaining ingredients and pour over the profiterole mountain.

MINTY BLACKCURRANT MERINGUE
Serves 6

1 lb (450 g) fresh or frozen
blackcurrants
1 pt (600 ml) water

4 oz (110 g) caster sugar
1½ tbsp powdered gelatine
3 tbsp very hot water

For the fresh Mint Meringue: 3 egg whites
6 oz (175 g) caster sugar
1½ tbsp finely chopped fresh mint

To serve: ¼ pt (150 ml) double cream, lightly whipped
       clusters of fresh blackcurrants
       fresh mint sprigs

Put the blackcurrants in a pan with the water and sugar. Bring to the boil and then simmer, covered, for 10 minutes. Put in a food processor or blender and mix to a purée. Rub through a sieve to remove the pips. Sprinkle the gelatine over the hot water and stir until dissolved. Add to 1 pint (600 ml) of the blackcurrant purée and then pour into a lightly oiled 1 pint (600 ml) ring mould. Leave to set in the refrigerator overnight and pour the remaining purée into a jug. Preheat the oven to 275°F/140°C/Gas Mk 1. Whisk the egg whites, gradually adding three quarters of the sugar, until very thick and glossy. Mix the mint with the remaining sugar and fold into the meringue. Spread three-quarters of the meringue on a piece of Bakewell paper in a 9 in (23 cm) circle, and place on a baking sheet. Pipe or drop 12 small balls of meringue onto other parts of the paper. Bake for 2 hours, turn off the heat and leave in the oven until dry. Cool on a wire tray. Just before serving, place the meringue base on a serving tray. Ease the jelly from the edge of the mould and turn out on top of the base. Fill the centre hole with the 12 small meringues. Decorate with the clusters of blackcurrants and mint leaves and serve with the whipped cream and remaining purée.

ORANGE MERINGUE
Serves 6–8

6–8 oranges
2 egg whites
4 tbsp sugar
flaked almonds, to garnish

Preheat the oven to 400°F/200°C/Gas Mk 6. Peel the oranges removing all the pith. Segment them and remove the membrane with a sharp knife. Place the segments in an ovenproof dish or on 6 ovenproof portion plates. Beat the egg whites until they form stiff peaks beating continuously until the mixture is thick and shiny. Beat in the sugar. Place the meringue mixture on top of the orange segments, and sprinkle the flaked almonds on top. Bake in the upper part of the oven until the meringue has turned golden. Serve the orange meringue warm or cold with vanilla ice cream.

LIQUEUR PASTRIES
Makes about 30 double biscuits

1 whole egg
4 tbsp sugar
2 eggs, separated
4 tbsp cornflour

For the icing:
12 oz (350 g) icing sugar, sieved
2 tbsp red liqueur (alternatively water and red food colouring)
1 tbsp lemon juice
1 tbsp water

For the filling:
1/4 pt (150 ml) whipping cream
vanilla or liqueur to taste

Preheat the oven to 350°F/180°C/Gas Mk 4. Beat the egg with the sugar, and then add 2 egg yolks, stirring all the time, until light and fluffy. Mix in the cornflour. Beat the remaining egg whites (in a separate bowl) until stiff. Fold into the mixture. Place or pipe the mixture in walnut-sized balls onto greaseproof paper. Bake for 8–10 minutes. Allow the pastries to cool. Mix together the icing sugar, liqueur, and lemon juice. Add the water and stir until the icing is smooth and even. Spread the icing on top of the pastries and allow to set. Sandwich together with a little whipped cream, flavoured with vanilla essence and liqueur, if desired.

SORBET MERINGUES
Makes 8–10

3 egg whites
7 oz (200 g) icing sugar
flaked almonds
18 fl oz (500 ml) orange sorbet

Preheat the oven to 300°F/150°C/Gas Mk 2. Place the egg whites and icing sugar in a stainless steel container over a bain-marie and whisk with an electric whisk until the mixture is smooth, stiff and shiny. Spoon out the mixture onto two baking trays covered with greaseproof paper: 8–10 spoonfuls on each sheet. Flatten half of them with the back of a spoon, shape the remaining to peaks with the aid of two spoons. Sprinkle flaked almonds on the meringue peaks. Place both sheets in the oven. Change the baking trays around after 25 minutes, so that the one that started lower in the oven is now higher. Bake for an other 25 minutes. Lower the oven temperature and bake for another 40 minutes. Swop the sheets around once during this time. Turn off the oven. Leave the meringues to cool in the oven overnight. If this is not possible, remove them carefully and leave to cool on a rack. Leave the sorbet to stand at room temperature for a while to soften a little. Place a large spoonful of sorbet on top of the flat meringues and place the peaks on top. Serve the meringues immediately or place in the freezer.

OATY ICE CREAM LAYER
Serves 10

6 oz (175 g) oat flakes
2 tbsp sugar
3 oz (75 g) flour
¼ tsp baking powder
2 tbsp syrup
2 tbsp milk
4 oz (110 g) melted margarine

For the filling:
1¾ pt (1 ltr) low fat ice cream

Preheat the oven to 350°F/180°C/Gas Mk 4. Mix together the oat flakes, sugar, flour, and baking powder in a bowl. Stir in the syrup, milk, and the melted margarine. Cover two baking trays with greaseproof paper and mark out two equal-sized circles about 8 in (20 cm) in diameter. Divide the oat mixture between the two circles and spread the mixture out, using a palette knife, so that the whole of each area is evenly covered. Bake in the middle of the oven for 10–15 minutes. Leave the oat circles to cool, and carefully remove them. Place the bases onto a serving dish. Add a layer of ice cream to one and place the other base on top.

PANCAKES, WAFFLES AND OMELETTES

RICH KNIGHTS OF WINDSOR
Serves 4

8 oz (225 g) stale cake of any variety
1 large egg
¼ pt (150 ml) milk
1 oz (25 g) butter
caster sugar, for dusting
1 orange, thinly sliced, to garnish

Cut the cake into 8 slices about ½ in (1 cm) thick. Whisk the egg and milk in a bowl with a fork. Carefully dip each slice of cake into the mixture, taking care not to break the cake. Heat the butter in a heavy frying pan and fry the slices until golden brown, turning once. Dust with caster sugar and serve piping hot on a warmed serving dish with the orange slices.

POOR KNIGHTS OF WINDSOR
Serves 4

8 large slices white bread
butter
jam
oil for frying
1 egg
¼ pt (150 ml) milk
caster sugar for dusting

Make sandwiches in the usual way with the bread, butter and jam. Trim off the crusts. Cut each sandwich in half. Heat the oil (or butter and oil for a slightly better taste) in a deep frying pan. The oil is at the right temperature when a cube of bread turns golden brown in a few moments. Beat the egg and milk together and pour into a shallow dish. Coat the half sandwiches with the egg mixture and fry in the hot fat, turning once, until golden brown. Drain on kitchen paper, dust with a little caster sugar and serve at once. Whipped cream goes well with this dish.

STRAWBERRY SOUFFLÉ OMELETTE
Serves 2

8 oz (225 g) strawberries
2 tbsp Kirsch
3 tbsp caster sugar
3 eggs, separated
1 tbsp water
pinch of salt
¾ oz (20 g) butter

Set aside 5 strawberries for decoration. Chop up the remaining strawberries and sprinkle over them 2 tbsp of the sugar and the Kirsch. Cover with foil and place in refrigerator for 2 hours. Lightly beat the egg yolks, water and remaining sugar together until mixture is creamy and light. Whisk the egg whites for 30 seconds, add the salt and whisk until the mixture is softly peaked. Fold the yolk mixture into the egg whites, then set aside. Preheat the grill to a high temperature. Halve each of the reserved strawberries, then set aside. Melt the butter in an omelette pan over a medium heat. When the foam subsides, pour in the egg mixture. Cook for 90 seconds or until the bottom of the omelette is firm and golden and the top is runny. Place under the grill cooking for 30 seconds or until the omelette has risen. Make a well in the centre of the omelette, filling this with the chopped strawberries in Kirsch using a slotted spoon. Flip over the omelette and transfer to a warmed serving dish. Decorate with the reserved strawberry halves and serve at once.

BLACKCURRANT CRÊPES
Serves 8

3 eggs
3 oz (75 g) flour
12 fl oz (350 ml) milk
pinch of salt

2 tbsp melted margarine,
plus extra for greasing
1¾ pt (1 ltr) ice cream
½ pt (300 ml) black currant jam

To make the batter, whisk together the eggs and flour. Gradually add the milk while whisking and whisk until the mixture is smooth. Add the salt, and stir in the melted margarine. Use the batter to fry small pancakes in a greased crêpe pan. As you are cooking the crêpes, stack them on top of each other with a layer of greaseproof paper between them. Keep the crêpes warm on a plate over a saucepan of simmering water. Fill the crêpes with ice cream just before serving. Warm the blackcurrant jam in a saucepan and serve as a sauce.

FRUITY BATTER PUDDING
Serves 4–6

2 tsp butter
8 oz (225 g) can of pineapple rings,
    drained and quartered
15 oz (425 g) can of apricot halves,
    drained
2 x 7½ oz (210 g) can of red cherries,
    drained and stoned
2 oz (50 g) seedless raisins

½ pt (300 ml) water
2 oz (50 g) plain flour
½ tsp ground mixed spice
pinch of salt
3 oz (75 g) caster sugar
3 eggs
5 fl oz (150 ml) milk
5 fl oz (150 ml) single cream

Preheat the oven to 350°F/180°C/Gas Mk 4. Grease a 2 pint (1.2 ltr) ovenproof dish with the butter. Mix together the pineapple, apricots and cherries and spread over the bottom of the dish. Place the raisins and water in a saucepan over a low heat, bring to the boil and boil for one minute. Drain and sprinkle over the mixture in the dish. Set aside. Put the flour, salt and spice into a mixing bowl and stir in 2 oz (50 g) of the sugar, making a well in the centre. Beat the eggs into the well, mixing in the flour until smoothly blended. Gradually beat in the milk and cream little by little. Pour the batter over the fruit. Bake in oven for 1–1¼ hours until firm at the centre, golden brown all over and puffed at the edges. Set aside to cool for 15 minutes. Sprinkle the remaining sugar on top and serve warm.

BERRY PANCAKES
Serves 6

2 eggs
18 fl oz (500 ml) milk
5 oz (150 g) plain flour
½ tsp salt
2 tbsp margarine for frying
2 lb (900 g) mixed fresh berries

Whisk the eggs and add a little of the milk. Stir in the flour, add the remaining milk and salt and whisk until the mixture is smooth. Melt the margarine in a crêpe pan and fry the pancakes until both sides are golden brown on a medium heat. Serve the pancakes, freshly made, with the berries.

AMERICAN PANCAKES
Makes 12

1 oz (25 g) butter
2 level tbsp golden or cane syrup
1 egg
5 fl oz (150 ml) natural yoghurt
1 level tsp bicarbonate of soda
4 tbsp milk
4 oz (110 g) plain flour

Gently heat the butter and syrup in a small saucepan, stirring until the butter has melted. Beat the egg and yoghurt together. Dissolve the bicarbonate of soda in the milk, and add to the yoghurt mixture. Mix with the melted butter and syrup. Add the flour and mix lightly (the batter should not be completely smooth). Lightly grease a large, thick-based frying pan, and warm over a moderate heat. The frying pan is at the correct temperature when a drop of water just sizzles when dropped into the pan. Coat the base of the frying pan with 1 tbsp of the batter. Cook until bubbles begin to burst on the top of the pancake and the bottom is golden brown. Turn the pancake over with a fish slice and cook until golden brown on the other side. This will be about 3 minutes. Place on a warmed covered dish, while cooking the remaining batter in the same manner. Serve with a little butter and warm syrup.

JAM OMELETTE
Serves 4

4 eggs
1 oz (25 g) sugar
2 tsp single cream
few drops of vanilla essence

1 oz (25 g) butter
2 tbsp jam
chopped nuts
icing sugar

Place the eggs in a bowl and beat well. Blend in the cream, sugar and some vanilla essence. Melt the butter in a frying pan and pour in the egg mixture. When set, spread over the jam and fold in three. To serve, place on a warm dish and sprinkle with nuts and icing sugar.

FRIARS OMELETTE
Serves 4

1 lb (450 g) cooking apples, peeled, cored and sliced
2 oz (50 g) butter plus a little extra
2 oz (50 g) granulated sugar
grated rind of 1 small lemon
1 medium sized egg
4 oz (110 g) fresh white breadcrumbs

Preheat the oven to 375°F/190°C/Gas Mk 5. Place the butter in a
medium sized saucepan and heat until melted. Then add the apple
slices and sugar. Cover the pan and cook over a very low heat, stirring
from time to time, until the apple is thick and mushy. Remove from
the heat and stir in the grated lemon rind and the beaten egg. Place
half the breadcrumbs in a 1½ pint (900 ml) lightly buttered pie dish,
spread the apple mixture on top and cover with the remaining
breadcrumbs. Dot the top with butter and bake in the centre of
the oven for 45 minutes. Serve hot with custard.

APPLE AND BANANA FRITTERS
Serves 4–6

4 oz (110 g) plain flour
pinch of salt
6 tbsp lukewarm water
4 tsp vegetable oil
2 egg whites
1 large cooking apple, peeled,
  quartered, and cored

2 bananas
juice of ½ lemon
vegetable oil, for deep frying
caster sugar, to serve

Place the flour and salt into a bowl. Make a well in the centre. Add
the water and oil and beat to form a smooth batter. Beat the egg
whites in a clean dry bowl until they are stiff, then set aside. Slice the
banana thickly and sprinkle the banana and apple at once with lemon
juice to prevent discolouration. Fold the whisked egg whites into the
batter. Dry the fruit on kitchen paper and immediately dip in the
batter. Deep-fry the fritters a few at a time in hot oil until puffed and
light golden. Remove with a slotted spoon and pile onto a serving
dish lined with absorbent kitchen paper. Serve immediately sprinkled
with caster sugar.

CLAFOUTIS AUX CERISES
Serves 4

½ oz (10 g) butter
8 oz (225 g) black cherries,
  washed and stoned
2½ oz (60 g) plain flour
pinch of salt

2 oz (50 g) caster sugar
3 eggs, beaten
½ pt (300 ml) milk
few drops of vanilla essence
2 tbsp icing sugar, sifted

Preheat the oven to 350°F/180°C/Gas Mk 4. Grease a 7 in (18 cm) ovenproof dish with the butter. Cover the base with the cherries and set aside. Sift the salt and flour into a bowl and mix in the sugar. Make a well in centre and add the eggs. Pour in a quarter of the milk, whisking the eggs and milk together, slowly incorporating the flour. Add the vanilla essence to the remaining milk and then add the batter mixture. Pour the mixture over the cherries. Bake for one hour. When cooked set aside to cool for 15 minutes, then sprinkle icing sugar on top and serve.

ORANGEY APPLE FRITTERS
Makes 16–20

4 large cooking apples,
  peeled and cored
2 oranges, grated rind and juice
4 oz (110 g) plain flour
⅛ level tsp salt
1 oz (25 g) caster sugar

1 egg, separated
¼ pt (150 ml) milk
3 tbsp sherry
oil for frying
icing sugar for dusting
whipped cream

With a knife, cut the apples into ½ in (1 cm) thick rings. Put into a dish, pour over the orange rind and juice. Leave to stand for 30 minutes in a cool place or refrigerator. Combine the flour, salt and sugar in bowl. Pour over the egg yolk and sherry mixed together. With an electric mixer or rotary whisk, beat the milk into the mixture to make a smooth batter. Just before using the batter, stiffly whip the egg white and fold into the mixture. Dip the apple rings in the batter, coating them well on both sides. Heat the oil until bubbling and fry the rings until golden. This should take 3–4 minutes. Drain and keep hot while frying the remainder. Dust with icing sugar. Serve with whipped cream.

AMERICAN WAFFLES
Makes 8

4 oz (110 g) plain flour
2 tsp baking powder
pinch of salt
1 tbsp caster sugar

1 egg, separated
7 fl oz (200 ml) milk
2 tbsp melted butter
½ tsp vanilla essence

Warm a waffle iron over a low heat, turning occasionally. Sift the flour, baking powder and salt together into a mixing bowl. Stir in the sugar. Make a well in the centre of the mixture. Pour the egg yolk, milk, butter and vanilla essence into the well. Beat together, gradually incorporating the flour, until the batter is smooth and thick. Whisk the egg white until stiff and fold into the batter. Pour just enough batter over the surface of the waffle iron to cover it. Close the iron and cook for 2–3 minutes. Turn the iron and cook for a further 2–3 minutes. Cook all the remaining mixture in the same manner and serve immediately.

ENGLISH LEMON PANCAKES
Makes 12

4 oz (110 g) plain flour
¼ tsp salt
2 eggs
½ pt (300 ml) milk

1 tbsp melted butter
oil for frying
caster sugar
lemon juice

Sift the flour and salt into a bowl. Add the eggs and a little milk, beat to a smooth paste. Gradually add the remaining milk and the butter. Pour into a jug. Heat a lightly oiled 7 in (18 cm) frying pan. Pour in 1–2 tbsp of batter so it thinly coats the base of the pan. Cook until lightly brown on the underside. Flip the pancake over with a flat-bladed knife and cook the other side. Occasionally shake the pan gently from side to side to prevent the pancake from sticking. Place on a warm covered dish, while cooking the remaining batter in the same manner. Fold pancakes in half and serve sprinkled with sugar and lemon juice.

PINEAPPLE FRITTERS
Serves 4

4½ oz (120 g) plain flour
pinch of salt
1 egg
½ pt (300 ml) milk

2 tbsp water
14 oz (400 g) can of pineapple rings
oil for frying
caster sugar, for dusting

Sieve 4 oz (110 g) of the flour together with the salt into a basin. Break in the egg, beat well then gradually beat in the milk and water to give a thick coating consistency. Drain the pineapple rings, pat dry and lightly dust with the remaining flour. Heat the oil until a cube of bread turns golden brown within a short time. Dip the floured pineapple rings into the batter and fry until crisp and golden. Remove with a slotted spoon and drain on kitchen paper. Dust with caster sugar before serving hot. You may like a little squeeze of lemon juice with these. Rings of apple may be used instead but need a rather slower and longer cooking time. Pieces of banana are also good cooked in this way.

JENNIE'S JUMBLIES
Makes 12

2 oz (50 g) hard margarine or butter,
  cut into small pieces
6 oz (175 g) self-raising flour
2 oz (50 g) plain flour
1 level tsp ground cinnamon

4 oz (110 g) caster sugar
1 egg, beaten
¼ pt (150 ml) milk
oil for deep frying

Sift the flours and spice together, then rub the fat into the flour until the mixture resembles fine breadcrumbs. Stir in half the sugar, mix in the egg and enough milk to make a stiff dough. Divide the mixture into 12 equal parts. Roll each piece of dough into a sausage shape, twist and press ends together to form a ring. Heat the oil in a deep frying pan. The oil is at the right temperature when a cube of bread turns golden brown in a few moments. Deep fry the jumblies, 6 at a time, until golden brown. This should take about 4 minutes. Remove with a slotted spoon and drain well on kitchen paper. Toss the jumblies in the remaining sugar. Serve hot with apple sauce.

SOUFFLÉ OMELETTE AU LIQUEUR
Serves 2

3 eggs, separated
2 tbsp caster sugar
2 tbsp Grand Marnier
rind of 1 orange, grated
½ oz (10g) butter

Beat the yolks very well with the sugar, rind and liqueur. Whip the whites until stiff and fold into the creamy mixture. Melt the butter in a 10 in (25 cm) omelette pan, pour the omelette mixture in and cook for 1–2 minutes.

FRUIT OMELETTE
Serves 4

4 boiled pear halves
8 strawberries
1 kiwi fruit
3 eggs
3 tbsp orange juice

grated rind of ¼ orange
1 tbsp sugar
1 tbsp margarine
mint leaves or lemon balm leaves

Drain the pear halves and cut into wedges. Peel and slice the kiwi fruit. Rinse the strawberries if necessary. Whisk together the eggs, orange juice, rind and sugar. Melt the margarine until light brown in a frying pan. Pour in the egg mixture and fry the omelette on one side until it is almost set. Slide the omelette, unfolded, onto a plate and pile on the fruit. Decorate with the mint leaves.

ICE CREAMS & SORBETS

VANILLA ICE CREAM
Serves 4–6

3 egg yolks
4 oz (110 g) caster sugar
¾ pt (450 ml) milk
vanilla essence to taste

Whisk the egg yolks and sugar together in a large bowl over a pan of hot water until the mixture is thick and creamy. Scald half the milk, add the vanilla essence and pour over the eggs, stirring well. Continue stirring slowly over simmering water until the mixture is thick enough to coat the back of a spoon - about 10 minutes. Remove from the heat, pour in the remaining milk, stir and leave to cool. Pour into several undivided ice trays, cover, place in the freezer and freeze until firm. Using a fork beat 3–4 times during the freezing process to prevent ice forming. The freezing process should take about 3–6 hours. Before serving the ice cream, take it out of the freezer and put it in the refrigerator for 10 minutes to soften.

CHOCOLATE GRANITA
Serves 6

5 oz (150 g) cocoa powder
3 oz (75 g) sugar
1 pt (600 ml) milk
½ vanilla pod
2 tbsp whipping cream
orange rind, cut into strips

Mix together the cocoa powder, sugar and milk in a saucepan. Cut the vanilla pod lengthwise and scrape out the seeds into the saucepan, then add the pod. Bring to the boil and simmer for a few minutes, whisking all the time. Leave to cool. Remove the vanilla pod. Stir in the cream. Pour the mixture into a freeze-proof bowl and freeze for 1 hour. Whisk the mixture with an electric whisk or in a food processor. Re-freeze. Remove the granita from the freezer half an hour before serving. Divide the granita between 6 serving dishes and garnish with the orange rind.

KNICKERBOCKER GLORY
Makes 4

1 pt (600 ml) pkt raspberry jelly
8 oz (225 g) can of raspberries
juice of ½ lemon
2 oz (50 g) caster sugar
2 tsp arrowroot
2 large ripe peaches, stoned and sliced

2 bananas, peeled and sliced
¾ pt (450 ml) rich vanilla ice cream
2 oz (50 g) hazelnuts, finely chopped
¼ pt (150 ml) whipping cream,
  whipped
4 glacé cherries

Make up the jelly following the instructions on the packet and leave
to set. To make a Melba sauce, heat the raspberries, sugar and lemon
juice over gentle heat until the sugar dissolves. Remove from the heat
and rub through a sieve. Make this raspberry purée up to ¼ pt (150 ml)
with water if necessary. Mix the arrowroot to a smooth paste with a
little cold water. Put the raspberry purée into a small saucepan, stir in
the arrowroot and bring to the boil. Simmer, stirring, until the sauce
thickens. Leave to cool. Now chop the jelly into small chunks and put
1 spoonful into the bottom of 4 tall sundae glasses. Put a few peach
slices on top. Then put a few slices of banana on top of the peaches.
Then put 1 scoop of ice cream in each glass and pour over a little
Melba sauce. Continue with these layers until the ingredients are used
up. Pipe a swirl of whipped cream on the top of each glass and top
with a glacé cherry and the hazelnuts.

RASPBERRY REDCURRANT FREEZE
Serves 4–6

12 oz (350 g) fresh or frozen raspberries
8 oz (225 g) jar of redcurrant jelly
½ pt (300 ml) soured cream

Put the raspberries and jelly in a saucepan and heat gently, stirring
frequently, until the fruit is soft. Transfer to a blender or food
processor and work to a purée. Sieve to remove the seeds. Chill in the
refrigerator for about 1 hour until cold. Whisk in the soured cream,
then pour into a freezer container (not metal) at least 2 in (5 cm) deep.
Freeze for about 2 hours until firm but not hard. Turn the frozen
mixture into a bowl and break into pieces. Beat until smooth, creamy
and lighter in colour. Return to the freezer container and freeze for a
further 2 hours until firm. Allow to soften slightly in the refrigerator
for about 30 minutes before serving.

PINEAPPLE ALASKA
Serves 2

1 large pineapple
2 kiwi fruit
1 papaya
1 star fruit (carambola)
1 mango
3 tbsp dark rum

1 tbsp soft dark brown sugar
4 egg whites
7 oz (200 g) caster sugar
1 tsp vanilla essence
1½ pt (900 ml) coconut ice cream

Preheat the oven to 375°F/190°C/Gas Mk 5. Halve the pineapple lengthways and cut out the centre core. Do not remove the leaves. Cut a thin slice from the outside of each half so that they are stable when placed on a dish. Using a sharp knife, cut out the flesh from the skin and cut into cubes. Peel and slice the kiwi fruit and papaya. Slice the star fruit crossways to keep the star shape. Cut the mango in three thick slices, remove the skin and cube the flesh. Put all the fruit pieces in a bowl and cover with the rum and brown sugar. Chill for at least 2 hours. Whisk the egg whites until stiff and beat in half the sugar, a little at a time, and the vanilla essence. Fold in the remaining sugar, a spoonful at a time, until a stiff, shiny meringue is obtained. Divide the fruits between the two halves of pineapple and cover with scoops of ice cream. Immediately cover the ice cream with the whisked meringue, sealing it carefully so that no ice cream is visible. Use a fork to make peaks in the meringue. Cook in the oven immediately for 8–12 minutes or until the meringue is golden. Serve at once.

PASSION FRUIT SORBET
Serves 4

4 oz (110 g) sugar
4 fl oz (120 ml) water
pulp of 10 ripe passion fruit
8 fl oz (250 ml) still mineral water

In a large saucepan bring the sugar and the water to a gentle boil. Reduce the heat until bubbles just break the surface. Simmer for 10 minutes. Remove from the heat and cool. In a medium-sized bowl mix the passion fruit pulp, sugar syrup and mineral water. Pour into several undivided ice trays and freeze to a slush. Using a fork, beat vigorously. Cover and freeze until firm. Serve with fresh fruit.

BLUEBERRY SORBET
Serves 8

1 lb (450 g) frozen, unsweetened blueberries
2–4 tbsp honey
½ pt (300 ml) milk

Leave the berries to stand at room temperature for 5 minutes. Place the berries and honey in a food processor and blend for a few seconds. Add the milk through the mixer tube while the machine is running and blend for a few more seconds, until the mixture is thick and smooth. Spoon the sorbet into serving bowls and serve immediately.

ICED PEACH CREAM
Serves 3–4

4–6 fresh peaches, skinned and mashed
8 oz (225 g) caster sugar
8 fl oz (250 ml) double cream

Mix the peaches with the sugar and leave to stand for 2–3 hours. Whip the cream until it is really stiff. Fold into the fruit pulp and freeze.

CRANBERRY SORBET
Serves 8

1 lb (450 g) frozen cranberries
7 fl oz (200 ml) water
3 egg whites
2 tbsp sugar
a few fresh cranberries
lemon balm leaves

Purée the cranberries in a food processor together with the water. Freeze the purée for about 2 hours. Beat the egg whites until they form stiff peaks. Beat in the sugar a little at the time. Remove the cranberry purée from the freezer and whisk with an electric whisk. Stir in the egg white mixture. Freeze for another couple of hours. Stir occasionally. Spoon the sorbet into 8 individual serving dishes. Garnish with a few cranberries and lemon balm leaves.

CHOCOLATE NUT SUNDAE
Serves 4

2 oz (50 g) plain chocolate,
  broken into small pieces
½ oz (10 g) butter
1 tbsp milk

1 tsp vanilla essence
8 scoops of vanilla ice cream
¼ pt (150 ml) double cream, whipped
2 oz (50 g) chopped walnuts

Melt the chocolate and butter in a basin over a pan of hot water. Stir in the milk and vanilla essence to make a smooth, creamy sauce. Put two scoops of ice cream in each sundae glass and pour over the chocolate sauce. Pipe a whirl of cream on top and sprinkle with the chopped walnuts.

QUICK YOGHURT ICE CREAM
Serves 4

8 oz (225 g) frozen raspberries, strawberries or blackberries
2 tbsp icing sugar
1 tsp vanilla sugar
7 fl oz (200 ml) natural yoghurt
a few berries, to garnish

Purée the frozen berries in a food processor together with the sugar and vanilla. Add the yoghurt through the mixer tube while the machine is running. Blend for 30 seconds. Divide between 4 sundae glasses and serve with some extra berries.

BANANA RUM FREEZE
Serves 8

4 ripe bananas
4 oz (110 g) sugar
pinch of salt
4 fl oz (125 ml) pineapple juice

2 tbsp lemon juice
2 tbsp dark rum
8 fl oz (250 ml) double cream whipped
2 tbsp chopped almonds, toasted

Place the bananas, sugar and salt in a bowl and mash well. Stir in the pineapple and lemon juices and the rum. Gently fold in the cream. Pile into a freezer tray and freeze for about 3 hours until firm. Transfer the mixture to a bowl and break it up. Beat well until it is light and frothy. Mix in the almonds, return to the tray and freeze until set. Cut into slices and serve.

CHOCOLATE MOUSSE ICE CREAM
Serves 4

1 pkt chocolate mousse powder
milk
orange rind, grated finely

Mix the chocolate mousse powder and milk together as instructed on the packet. Pour the mousse into serving bowls and freeze for 2 hours. Take the bowls out of the freezer 15 minutes before serving and decorate with the orange rind.

FROZEN STRAWBERRY YOGHURT
Serves 4

13½ oz (360 g) can of strawberries in syrup
¾ pt (450 ml) plain yoghurt
4 fl oz (125 ml) whipping cream

Process the strawberries and syrup to a purée in a blender or food processor. Add the yoghurt and cream and blend until smooth. Pour into several undivided ice trays and place in the freezer. Cover and freeze until firm, beating with a fork at least twice during the freezing process. The freezing process should take about 3–6 hours. Before serving, take it out of the freezer and put it in the refrigerator for 10 minutes to soften.

FROZEN ALMOND CREAMS
Serves 3–4

½ pt (300 ml) double cream
2 egg whites
8 oz (225 g) caster sugar
pinch of salt
1 tbsp sherry
2 oz (50 g) chopped almonds, with extra to decorate

Whip the cream until it forms soft peaks. Whisk the egg whites until stiff, gradually adding the sugar and a pinch of salt, whisking all the time until the mixture is shiny and firm. Fold the chopped almonds into the egg whites, and then fold in the cream. Stir in the sherry and spoon into individual ramekins. Freeze. Decorate with chopped almonds.

LEMON CREAM
Serves 6

8 fl oz (250 ml) milk
8 fl oz (250 ml) double cream
8 oz (225 g) caster sugar
2 lemons, grated rind and juice
6 whole large lemons

In a bowl, mix the milk, cream and sugar until the sugar dissolves. Pour into a freezer tray and freeze for about 2 hours until the mixture is just set. Transfer the mixture to a bowl, stir in the lemon rind and juice and beat thoroughly until smooth. Return to the tray and freeze for 2 hours. Stir again and freeze until it is quite firm. Slice off the tops of each lemon and remove and discard all the pulp. Remove a small slice from the bottom of each lemon so that they stand upright. Pile the lemon cream mixture into each lemon and serve.

ICED APRICOT CREAM
Serves 6–8

1 lb (450 g) fresh apricots
1 tbsp water
thin strip orange rind
2 oz (50 g) caster sugar
½ pt (300 ml) double cream
1 oz (25 g) icing sugar

3 oz (75 g) almond macaroons or
ratafia biscuits, crumbled
2 egg whites
whipped cream
apricot halves

Place the apricots in a saucepan with the water, the orange rind and caster sugar. Cook very gently until the fruit is soft. Remove the orange rind, then press the apricots through a sieve to make a purée, which should be about ½ pint (300 ml). Cool. Whip the cream, and fold in the icing sugar, the cold purée and all but 1 tbsp of the biscuits. Whisk the egg whites very stiffly and gently fold into the apricot cream. Turn the mixture into a 2¼ pint (1.25 ltr) mould and freeze until it is set. Unmould the apricot cream and sprinkle the reserved biscuit crumbs over the top. Decorate with whipped cream and apricots.

SPARKLING SORBET
Serves 4

½ pt (300 ml) orange juice
2 egg whites
2 tbsp sugar
½ bottle sparkling white wine, chilled

Beat the egg whites until they form stiff peaks. Beat in the sugar until the mixture is thick and shiny. Mix in the orange juice. Freeze for about 2 hours. Remove the sorbet from the freezer. Whisk the sorbet until frothy with an electric whisk (leave to stand at room temperature for a while before whisking if thoroughly frozen). Freeze for another couple of hours. Whisk or stir occasionally during this period. Half fill 4 tall wine glasses with the cold wine. Add balls of sorbet until the glasses are full. Serve immediately before the wine stops sparkling and before the sorbet has melted too much.

PUDDINGS

RAILWAY PUD
Serves 8

12 oz (350 g) plain flour
3 level tsp baking powder
6 oz (175 g) butter,
    cut into small pieces

4½ oz (120 g) caster sugar
2 eggs, beaten
6 tbsp milk
6 level tbsp plum jam, warmed

Preheat the oven to 375°F/190°C/Gas Mk 5. Grease a 10 x 6½ x 2 in (25 x 17 x 5 cm) baking tin. Sift the flour and baking powder together into a bowl. Rub in the butter until the mixture resembles fine breadcrumbs. Add the sugar, eggs and milk. Mix to a soft consistency. Pour into the tin and bake for 30–40 minutes. Cool for 5 minutes. Remove from the tin. Cut the pudding in half and spread one surface with jam. Replace and sprinkle the top with a little sugar.

PEAR AND CINNAMON SPONGE PUDDING
Serves 6

1 lb (450 g) dessert pears
3 oz (75 g) sultanas
2 tbsp lemon juice
4 oz (110 g) butter or margarine
4 oz (110 g) caster sugar

2 eggs, beaten
6 oz (175 g) self-raising flour
1 level tsp ground cinnamon
2 tbsp milk
soured cream to serve

Grease a 2½ pint (1.3 ltr) pudding basin and a double thickness of greaseproof paper to cover. Peel, quarter, core and roughly chop the pears, then mix with the sultanas and lemon juice. Beat the butter or margarine until soft, then add the sugar and beat until light and creamy. Beat in the eggs little by little. Sift the flour with the cinnamon and fold into the creamed ingredients with the milk. Spoon a little of the pear mixture into the base of the prepared pudding basin and spread a layer of cake mixture over the top. Repeat this layering twice more. Cover with the double thickness of greaseproof paper and tie down the paper securely with string, making a loop over the top of the basin to form a handle. Place the basin in a saucepan of water which reaches half-way up the sides of the basin. Bring the water to simmering point, cover the saucepan with a tightly fitting lid and steam for about 2 hours. Add more water as required. Turn out onto a warmed plate and serve with soured cream.

SYRUP PUDDING
Serves 4–5

7 oz (200 g) self-raising flour
2 oz (50 g) fresh white
   breadcrumbs
4 oz (110 g) shredded suet
2 oz (50 g) caster sugar

1 egg
grated rind of 1 lemon
¼ pt (150 ml) milk
4 oz (110 g) golden syrup

Grease a 1½ pint (900 ml) pudding basin and a double thickness of greaseproof paper to cover it. Put the flour, breadcrumbs, suet and sugar in a bowl. Beat together the egg, lemon rind and milk. Add this to the dry ingredients and mix well. Put the syrup in the prepared pudding basin. Rotate the basin so that the syrup coats the inside of the basin. Put the suet dough in the basin and smooth the top. Make a pleat in the greaseproof paper to allow the pudding to rise. Cover the pudding with the paper and tie it down securely with string, making a loop over the top of the basin to form a handle. Steam for 2 hours. Turn out and serve with warmed golden syrup.

FIGGY PUDDING
Serves 6

8 oz (225 g) dried figs, chopped
8 oz (225 g) stoned dates, chopped
4 oz (110 g) raisins
4 tbsp brandy
8 oz (225 g) self-raising flour

6 oz (175 g) wholemeal breadcrumbs
6 oz (175 g) shredded suet
3 eggs, beaten
grated rind and juice of 1 lemon

Put the figs and dates in a bowl. Stir in the raisins and pour in the brandy. Mix well and put aside to soak for about 1 hour. Then add the flour, breadcrumbs, suet, eggs and lemon rind and juice and mix thoroughly. Grease a 2 pint (1 ltr) pudding basin and a double thickness of greaseproof paper to cover it. Place the mixture in the prepared pudding basin and cover with the greaseproof paper. Make a pleat in the greaseproof paper to allow the pudding to rise. Cover the pudding and tie down the greaseproof paper securely with string, making a loop over the top of basin to form a handle. Place the basin in a saucepan of water which reaches half-way up the sides of the basin. Bring the water to simmering point, cover the saucepan with a tightly fitting lid and steam for 4 hours until the pudding is firm. Add more water as required. When cooked, remove the cover and turn out the pudding onto a serving dish.

JAM ROLY-POLY
Serves 4

8 oz (225 g) self-raising flour
½ level tsp salt
4 oz (110 g) shredded suet
cold water to mix
8 oz (225 g) raspberry jam

Grease a double thickness of greaseproof paper about 12 in (30 cm) square. Mix together the flour, salt and shredded suet in a bowl and add sufficient water (about 7–8 tbsp) to make a soft, but not sticky, dough. Turn out onto a floured board and knead lightly. Roll out to an oblong, 12 x 8 in (30 x 20 cm). Brush the edges of the pastry oblong with water. Spread the pastry with the jam to within 1 in (2.5 cm) of the edges and roll up from the short side. Seal the ends and wrap loosely in greaseproof paper or foil. Steam for 1½ hours, replacing the water in the steamer, when necessary, with boiling water. Lift out gently, remove the paper or foil and place on a warmed serving dish.

BACHELOR'S PUDDING
Serves 4

4 oz (110 g) flour
pinch of salt
½ tsp baking powder
½ tsp ground ginger
2 oz (50 g) butter
4 oz (110 g) shredded suet

4 oz (110 g) seedless raisins, halved
4 oz (110 g) demerara sugar
4 oz (110 g) fresh white breadcrumbs
2 eggs, beaten
a little milk
extra brown sugar

Sift the flour, salt, baking powder, and ground ginger together and rub in the butter until the mixture resembles fine breadcrumbs. Mix in the suet, raisins, sugar, breadcrumbs, beaten eggs and milk. Mix thoroughly. Grease a 1½ pint (900 ml) pudding basin and a double thickness of greaseproof paper to cover it. Sprinkle enough brown sugar into the basin to cover the base and sides. Place the mixture in the prepared pudding basin. Make a pleat in the greaseproof paper to allow the pudding to rise. Cover the pudding with the greaseproof paper and tie down the paper securely with string, making a loop over the top of basin to form a handle. Place the basin in a saucepan of simmering water which reaches half-way up the sides of the basin. Cover with a tightly fitting lid and steam for 2–3 hours, adding more water as necessary.

STEAMED SULTANA PUDDING
Serves 4–6

8 oz (225 g) self-raising flour
½ level tsp salt
4 oz (110 g) margarine, cut into
   small pieces

3 oz (75 g) caster sugar
6 oz (175 g) sultanas
1 egg, beaten
5 tbsp milk

Grease a 1½ pint (900 ml) pudding basin and a double thickness of greaseproof paper to cover it. Place the flour and salt in a bowl. Add the margarine and rub in with the fingertips until the mixture resembles fine breadcrumbs. Stir in the sugar and sultanas. Add the beaten egg and the milk and mix well together. Place the mixture in the prepared basin and level the top with back of spoon. Make a pleat in the greaseproof paper to allow the pudding to rise. Cover the pudding and tie down the greaseproof paper securely with string, making a loop over the top of basin to form a handle. Place in the pan or steamer and cook for 1½–1¾ hours. Remove the greaseproof cover and turn out onto a warmed serving plate.

SPOTTED CHOCOLATE PUDDING
Serves 6

3 oz (75 g) butter
3 oz (75 g) caster sugar
2 eggs, beaten
6 oz (175 g) self-raising flour

2 oz (50 g) plain chocolate drops
grated rind of 1 orange
1 tbsp milk

Put the butter and sugar in a mixing bowl and beat until light and creamy. Beat in the eggs little by little, adding a teaspoonful of flour with each addition. Fold in the remaining flour. Mix in the chocolate drops, orange rind and milk. Grease a 1½ pint (900 ml) pudding basin and a double thickness of greaseproof paper to cover it. Place the mixture in the prepared pudding basin. Make a pleat in the greaseproof paper to allow the pudding to rise. Cover the pudding with the greaseproof paper and tie down the paper securely with string, making a loop over the top of basin to form a handle. Place the basin in a saucepan of simmering water which reaches half-way up the sides of the basin. Cover with a tightly fitting lid and steam for 2 hours, adding more water as necessary. Loosen the edges of the pudding from the basin and turn out onto a serving dish.

LIGHT FRUIT PUDDING
Serves 4–6

4 oz (110 g) butter
4 oz (110 g) soft brown sugar
2 eggs, beaten
1 tsp grated lemon rind
3 oz (75 g) mixed dried fruit

6 oz (175 g) self-raising flour
pinch of salt
1 tsp ground mixed spice
3 tbsp milk

Put the butter and sugar in a bowl and cream until fluffy. Beat in the eggs and lemon rind. Add the fruit and mix well. Fold in the flour, followed by the spice and salt. Gradually stir in the milk. Grease a 2 pint (1 ltr) pudding basin and a double thickness of greaseproof paper to cover it. Place the mixture in the prepared pudding basin. Make a pleat in the greaseproof paper to allow the pudding to rise. Cover the pudding with the greaseproof paper and tie down the paper securely with string, making a loop over the top of basin to form a handle. Place the basin in a saucepan of simmering water which reaches half-way up the sides of the basin. Cover with a tightly fitting lid and steam for 2 hours, adding more water as necessary. Remove the cover from the pudding and turn out onto a serving dish.

CHOCOLATE PUDDING
Serves 4–6

4 oz (110 g) butter
6 oz (175 g) caster sugar
1 tbsp golden syrup
2 eggs

6 oz (175 g) self-raising flour
2 tbsp cocoa powder
pinch of salt
4 tbsp milk

Put the butter and caster sugar in a bowl and beat until light and creamy. Stir in the syrup. Add the eggs, one at a time. Mix together the flour, cocoa powder and salt and gradually fold into the mixture alternately with the milk. Grease a 2 pint (1 ltr) pudding basin and a double thickness of greaseproof paper to cover it. Place the mixture in the prepared pudding basin. Make a pleat in the greaseproof paper to allow the pudding to rise. Cover the pudding with the greaseproof paper and tie down the paper securely with string, making a loop over the top of basin to form a handle. Place the basin in a saucepan of simmering water which reaches half-way up the sides of the basin. Cover with a tightly fitting lid and steam for 2 hours, adding more water as necessary. Remove the cover from the pudding and turn out onto a serving dish.

SAGO PLUM PUDDING
Serves 6

2 tbsp sago
8 fl oz (250 ml) milk
2 oz (50 g) butter
6 oz (175 g) sugar
1 tsp bicarbonate of soda

pinch of salt
4 oz (110 g) fresh breadcrumbs
6 oz (175 g) mixed dried fruit
2 tsp grated lemon rind
1 tsp ground mixed spice

Put the sago in a bowl, pour in the milk and leave to soak overnight. Put the butter and sugar in a bowl and beat until light and creamy. Stir in the sago and milk mixture, the bicarbonate of soda and the salt. Add the breadcrumbs, fruit, lemon rind and spice and mix thoroughly. Grease a 2 pint (1 ltr) pudding basin and a double thickness of greaseproof paper to cover it. Place the mixture in the prepared pudding basin. Make a pleat in the greaseproof paper to allow the pudding to rise. Cover the pudding with the greaseproof paper and tie down the paper securely with string, making a loop over the top of basin to form a handle. Place the basin in a saucepan of simmering water which reaches half-way up the sides of the basin. Cover with a tightly fitting lid and steam for 2 hours, adding more water as necessary. Remove the cover from the pudding and turn out onto a serving dish.

MINCEMEAT ROLY-POLY
Serves 6

6 oz (175 g) self-raising flour
pinch of salt
3 oz (75 g) shredded suet

2 oz (50 g) caster sugar
a little milk
4 tbsp mincemeat

Grease a piece of foil 12 in (30 cm) square. Sift the flour and salt into a bowl. Add the suet and sugar. Make a well in the centre and add enough milk to bind to a fairly soft dough. Roll out the dough to an oblong about 8 x 10 in (20 x 25 cm). Spread the mincemeat on the pastry, leaving a ½ in (1 cm) border on all sides. Roll the pastry from the short side. Moisten the edges to seal the roll. Place the roll on the greased foil and loosely wrap the foil around the roll, leaving room for the roll to expand during cooking. Seal the edges well. Lower the roll into a large saucepan, two-thirds full of boiling water, curling it if necessary to fit the pan. Cover the pan, lower the heat to a gentle boil and steam for 1½–2 hours. Serve hot with custard.

RICH CHRISTMAS PUDDING
Serves 8

4 oz (110 g) prunes, stoned and
  chopped
6 oz (175 g) currants
6 oz (175 g) seedless raisins
6 oz (175 g) sultanas
4 oz (110 g) plain flour
¼ tsp grated nutmeg
¼ tsp ground cinnamon
½ tsp salt

3 oz (75 g) fresh breadcrumbs
4 oz (110 g) shredded suet
4 oz (110 g) dark soft brown sugar
1 oz (25 g) blanched almonds,
  chopped
finely grated rind of half a lemon
¼ pt (150 ml) brown ale
2 eggs, beaten

In a large mixing bowl, mix together all the ingredients until they are well blended. Grease a 2½ pint (1.3 ltr) pudding basin and a double thickness of greaseproof paper to cover it. Place the mixture in the prepared pudding basin. Make a pleat in the greaseproof paper to allow the pudding to rise. Cover the pudding with the greaseproof paper and tie down the paper securely with string, making a loop over the top of basin to form a handle. Place the basin in a large saucepan of simmering water which reaches half-way up the sides of the basin. Cover with a tightly fitting lid and steam for 8 hours, adding more water as necessary. Remove the basin from the saucepan and leave to cool. Cover with foil and store in a cool place for about 2 weeks. When ready to serve, steam for 2½ hours, then turn out onto a warmed serving plate.

ALMOND FRUIT BAKE
Serves 4

1 pt (600 ml) milk
finely grated rind of 1 orange
1 oz (25 g) caster sugar
2 oz (50 g) fine semolina

2 oz (50 g) ground almonds
1 tbsp mixed peel, chopped
2 oz (50 g) dates, chopped
1 egg, beaten

Preheat the oven to 350°F/180°C/Gas Mk 4. Put the milk, orange rind and sugar into a saucepan and heat almost to boiling point. Gradually stir in the semolina until the mixture has thickened. Remove from the heat and add the almonds, peel, dates and the egg. Stir well and place in a greased ovenproof pie dish. Cook in the oven for 30 minutes until the top is golden brown.

SUSSEX POND PUDDING
Serves 6

12 oz (350 g) self-raising flour
½ tsp salt
6 oz (175 g) shredded suet
about 6 fl oz (175 ml) water

4 oz (110 g) butter, cut into pieces
4 oz (110 g) demerera sugar
1 large lemon

Put the flour and salt into a bowl, then stir in the suet and enough cold water to make a light elastic dough. Knead lightly until smooth. Roll out two-thirds of the dough on a floured work surface to a circle 1 in (2.5 cm) larger all round than the top of a 2½ pint (1.3 ltr) pudding basin. Use this circle to line the pudding basin. Put half the butter into the centre with half the sugar. Prick the lemon all over with a skewer. Put the whole lemon on top of the butter and sugar. Add the remaining butter and sugar on top. Roll out the remaining pastry to a circle to fit the top of the pudding. Dampen the edges and seal the lid. Cover with a double thickness of greaseproof paper and tie down the greaseproof paper securely with string, making a loop over the top of basin to form a handle. Place the basin in a saucepan of water which reaches half-way up the sides of the basin. Bring the water to simmering point, cover the saucepan with a tightly fitting lid and steam for about 4 hours until the pudding is firm. Add more water as required. Remove the paper and turn out onto a warm serving dish. During cooking the lemon inside the pudding bursts and produces a delicious lemon sauce. Each serving should have a piece of the lemon, which will be softened by the cooking.

VIENNOISE PUDDING
Serves 6

1 oz (25 g) lump sugar
½ pt (300 ml) milk
5 oz (150 g) stale bread,
  cut into small squares
3 oz (75 g) sultanas

Sauce:
yolks of 2 eggs
1 dessertspoon caster sugar

3 oz (75 g) caster sugar
3 oz (75 g) mixed peel, chopped
grated rind of 1 lemon
3 eggs
1 glass sherry (optional)

3 fl oz (75 ml) sherry, slightly warmed
strip of lemon rind

Put the lump sugar into a saucepan with 1 tbsp water and heat gently until the sugar becomes coffee coloured. Heat the milk and add carefully to the sugar mixture. Pour the caramelised milk over the bread cubes and leave to soak for 1 hour. Then add the sultanas, sugar, mixed peel and grated lemon rind. Beat the eggs well, add the sherry and mix into the bread mixture. Grease a 2 pint (1 ltr) pudding basin and a double thickness of greaseproof paper to cover it. Place the mixture in the prepared pudding basin and cover with the greaseproof paper. Make a pleat in the greaseproof paper to allow the pudding to rise. Cover the pudding and tie down the greaseproof paper securely with string, making a loop over the top of basin to form a handle. Place the basin in a saucepan of water which reaches half-way up the sides of the basin. Bring the water to simmering point, cover the saucepan with a tightly fitting lid and steam for 2 hours until the pudding is firm. Add more water as required. To make the sauce, put all the sauce ingredients in a small bowl and set it over a pan of simmering water. Whisk the sauce briskly for 10 minutes or until it becomes frothy. Do not let it get too hot, or the sauce will curdle. Remove the lemon rind and serve with the Viennoise pudding.

COFFEE UPSIDE-DOWN PUDDING
Serves 4–6

3 tbsp clear honey
2 x 14 oz (400 g) cans apricot
  halves in natural juice, drained
12 glacé cherries, halved
6 oz (175 g) butter, softened
6 oz (175 g) caster sugar
3 eggs, beaten

3 oz (75 g) wholemeal
  self-raising flour
4 oz (110 g) white self-raising flour
1 tbsp milk
3 tbsp coffee essence
¼ pt (150 ml) whipping cream,
  whipped

Preheat the oven to 350°F/180°C/Gas Mk 4. Put the honey in a small saucepan and warm over low heat. Lightly grease a 9 in (23 cm) shallow ovenproof dish and pour in the honey. Arrange the apricots and cherries on top of the honey. Cream together the butter and sugar. Beat in the eggs, little by little, adding one teaspoonful of flour with each addition. Fold in the remaining flour, milk and coffee essence and mix well until smooth. Spread over the apricots and bake in the oven for 45 minutes. Loosen the edges of the pudding and turn out onto a serving dish.

SPOTTED DICK
Serves 4

4 oz (110 g) fresh white breadcrumbs
3 oz (75 g) self-raising flour
pinch of salt
3 oz (75 g) shredded suet
2 oz (50 g) caster sugar

6 oz (175 g) currants
finely grated rind of half a lemon
5-6 tbsp milk
custard to serve

Put the breadcrumbs, flour, salt, suet, sugar, currants and lemon rind in a bowl. Stir well until thoroughly mixed. Add enough milk to the dry ingredients to bind together, cutting it through with a palette knife until well mixed. Using one hand only, bring the ingredients together to form a soft, slightly sticky dough. Turn out the dough onto a floured work surface. Dust lightly with flour, then knead gently until just smooth. Shape the dough into a neat roll about 6 in (15 cm) in length. Make a 2 in (5 cm) pleat across a fine-textured, colour-fast tea towel or pudding cloth. Alternatively, pleat together sheets of greased greaseproof paper and strong kitchen foil. Encase the roll in the cloth or foil, pleating the open edges of the cloth or foil tightly together. Tie the ends securely with string to form a cracker shape. Make a string handle across the top. Lower the roll into a large saucepan, two-thirds full of boiling water, curling it if necessary to fit the pan. Cover the pan, lower the heat to a gentle boil and cook for 2 hours. Top up with boiling water at intervals. Lift the roll out of the water. Snip the string and gently roll the pudding onto a serving plate. Serve immediately, with custard.

BAKED CHOCOLATE SAUCE PUDDING
Serves 4-6

2 oz (50 g) butter, cut into small pieces
3 oz (75 g) caster sugar
2 eggs, separated

12 fl oz (350 ml) milk
1½ oz (35 g) self-raising flour
5 tsp cocoa powder

Preheat the oven to 350°F/180°C/Gas Mk 4. Place the butter and sugar in a bowl and cream until fluffy. Gradually beat in the egg yolks and pour in the milk. Mix the flour and cocoa powder together then beat into the egg mixture until well mixed. Thoroughly whisk the egg whites and stir in the mixture. Arrange in a greased 2 pint (1 ltr) ovenproof dish and bake for 35-45 minutes until the sponge is set with the chocolate sauce on the bottom. Serve at once.

BREAD PUDDING
Serves 4

8 oz (225 g) brown or white bread
1 oz (25 g) caster sugar
2 oz (50 g) sultanas
2 oz (50 g) currants
1 oz (25 g) mixed peel, chopped

1 egg, beaten
½ level tsp mixed spice
2 oz (50 g) soft margarine
granulated sugar for sprinkling

Preheat the oven to 350°F/180°C/Gas Mk 4. Grease a 1½ pint (900 ml) ovenproof pie dish. Put the bread in a bowl and cover wth cold water. Leave for 5 minutes, then squeeze out the bread until most of the liquid has been extracted and beat until smooth. Stir in the caster sugar, sultanas, currants, mixed peel, beaten egg, mixed spice and margarine. Mix well. Spread in the pie dish and bake in the centre of the oven for 1 hour until firm and golden brown. Sprinkle the pudding with granulated sugar. Serve hot or cold.

DATE ROLY-POLY
Serves 8

10 oz (300 g) self-raising flour
4 oz (110 g) caster sugar
4 oz (110 g) shredded suet
water to mix

¼pt (150 ml) water
1 tsp lemon juice
1 carton plain yoghurt
2 level tbsp sugar

Filling:
6 oz (175 g) dates

Preheat the oven to 400°F/200°C/Gas Mk 6. To start the filling, chop the dates and put in a saucepan with the water. Simmer gently for about 5 minutes, stirring from time to time. When the dates are soft and thick, remove from the heat and stir in the lemon juice. Leave to cool. Stir the flour, sugar and suet together and add enough water to bind to a soft dough. Roll out on a floured surface to a 12 in (30 cm) square. Beat the yoghurt into the date mixture and spread over the pastry square. Roll up like a Swiss roll and cut into eight even slices with a sharp knife. Lay the slices in a shallow, oblong dish, approximately 9 x 6 in (23 x 15 cm), and brush with a little water. Sprinkle over the 2 tbsp of sugar and bake in the oven for about 50 minutes until cooked and golden on top. Serve with custard, a sweet white sauce or cream.

STEAMED APRICOT WALNUT SPONGE
Serves 6

6 oz (175 g) dried apricots
4 oz (110 g) light soft brown sugar
4 oz (110 g) butter or margarine
2 eggs
3 oz (75 g) walnut halves,
   roughly chopped

4 oz (110 g) self-raising flour
3 level tbsp clear honey
1 tbsp lemon juice

Soak the apricots overnight in plenty of cold water. Drain well, reserving the soaking water. Cream together the sugar and butter or margarine. Gradually beat in the eggs. Fold in half the walnuts and the flour. Spread 2 level tbsp of the honey over the base and sides of a 1½ pint (900 ml) pudding basin. Carefully arrange some of the apricots and the other half of the walnuts over the base and sides of the basin. Spoon in the creamed mixture. Cover with a double thickness of greaseproof paper and tie down the paper securely with string, making a loop over the top of the basin to form a handle. Place the basin in a saucepan of water which reaches half-way up the sides of the basin. Bring the water to simmering point, cover the saucepan with a tightly fitting lid and steam for about 2½ hours. Place the remaining apricots, honey and lemon juice in a saucepan with ¾ pint (450 ml) of the reserved soaking water. Bring to the boil, then simmer for 2–3 minutes. Purée then sieve. Serve warm with the sponge.

WALNUT AND ORANGE PUDDING
Serves 6

4 oz (110 g) soft margarine
2 oz (50 g) walnut pieces, chopped
3 oz (75 g) caster sugar
1 tbsp syrup
2 eggs

1 tsp vanilla essence
3 oz (75 g) self-raising flour
1 tsp baking powder
grated rind of 1 orange
4 tbsp fresh orange juice

Preheat the oven to 350°F/180°C/Gas Mk 4. Lightly grease six ovenproof ramekins. Put all the ingredients in a large bowl and mix together thoroughly until a smooth and creamy texture is obtained. Fill each ramekin about two-thirds full with the mixture. Place the ramekins on a baking sheet and bake in the oven for 20-25 minutes until the puddings are firm to the touch.

NELSON FRUIT PUDDINGS
Serves 6-8

8 oz (225 g) stale brown bread,
    crusts removed
½ pt (300 ml) milk
2 tbsp brandy
4 oz (110 g) dried fruit
2 oz (50 g) candied peel, chopped

grated rind of 1 lemon
2 oz (50 g) shredded suet
2 oz (50 g) soft brown sugar
2 tsp mixed spice
some grated nutmeg
2 eggs

Preheat the oven to 325°F/170°C/Gas Mk 3. Lightly grease 6–8 small ovenproof dishes. Break the bread into small pieces, place in a bowl and pour over the milk and brandy. Leave to stand for 30 minutes. Thoroughly mash the bread mixture, then add the dried fruit, candied peel, lemon rind and suet. Mix thoroughly and stir in the sugar and spices. Add the eggs and beat well. Divide the mixture evenly between the ovenproof dishes and bake in the oven for 30-40 minutes until the puddings are firm and brown. Loosen the edges with a knife and turn out onto serving dishes.

HOLYGOG PUDDING
Serves 6

8 oz (225 g) plain flour
4 oz (110 g) butter
2–3 tbsp cold water
5 tbsp golden syrup
milk

Preheat the oven to 400°F/200°C/Gas Mk 6. Sift the flour into a bowl, and rub in the butter until the mixture resembles fine breadcrumbs. Add sufficient water to form a firm dough. Place the dough on a lightly floured flat surface and roll out to a rectangle 10 x 7 in (25 x 18 cm). Carefully spread the syrup over the pastry and roll up the pastry from the short side. Grease a shallow, ovenproof dish and lay in the pastry roll with the seam side down. Pour in enough milk to reach a quarter of the way up the side of the pudding and brush milk over the top. Bake in the oven for 45 minutes until golden brown. Remove from the oven, cut into slices and serve.

GUARDS' PUDDINGS
Serves 4–6

4 oz (110 g) margarine
4 oz (110 g) soft brown sugar
1 heaped tbsp strawberry jam

½ level tsp bicarbonate of soda
4 oz (110 g) brown breadcrumbs
2 eggs, beaten

Sauce:
4–6 tbsp strawberry jam
1–2 tbsp lemon juice

Preheat the oven to 400°F/200°C/Gas Mk 6. Grease 4 large or 6 small old teacups or castle pudding moulds. Cream the margarine and sugar until soft and fluffy, then beat in the strawberry jam. Dissolve the bicarbonate of soda in 1 tsp of warm water, then beat into the creamed mixture. Add the breadcrumbs and eggs and mix well. The mixture should be of a very soft dropping consistency. Divide the mixture between the cups or moulds. Grease squares of foil and use to cover the cups or moulds. Press the edges into the side of the cup to form a cap (this holds in the steam and gives the pudding a light, airy texture). Place the cups on a baking sheet and bake above the centre of the oven for 25–30 minutes until well risen. Serve with strawberry sauce, which is made by gently heating the 4–6 tbsp strawberry jam with the lemon juice.

OSBORNE PUDDING
Serves 4

4 thin slices stale wholemeal bread
butter for spreading
orange marmalade for spreading
2 oz (50 g) sultanas
¾ pt (450 ml) milk

2 eggs
1 tbsp brandy
finely grated rind of 1 orange
1 tbsp soft brown sugar
grated nutmeg

Preheat the oven to 350°F/180°C/Gas Mk 4. Spread the bread with butter and marmalade and cut into triangles. Place the triangles buttered side up in layers in a greased ovenproof dish, sprinkling the sultanas between each layer. Heat the milk gently in a saucepan. Put the eggs in a bowl and beat well. Stir in the brandy and orange rind. Gradually pour in the warm milk, stirring constantly. Pour over the bread and set aside for 15 minutes. Sprinkle sugar and nutmeg over the top and bake in the oven for 30-40 minutes until the pudding is set and the top is brown. Serve at once.

DURHAM FLUFFIN
Serves 2

4 tbsp pearl barley, soaked overnight in water
¾ pt (450 ml) milk
1 tsp grated nutmeg
1 tbsp honey
candied fruit to garnish

Put the barley and milk in a saucepan and bring to the boil. Lower the heat and simmer for 45 minutes, stirring from time to time. Remove from the heat, stir in the honey and nutmeg and pour into individual serving dishes. Decorate with candied fruit to serve.

DATE AND BANANA UPSIDE-DOWN PUDDING
Serves 6

Caramel:
6 oz (175 g) granulated sugar
10 tbsp water

Topping:
2 bananas, quartered lengthwise
2 oz (50 g) dates

Pudding:
4 oz (110 g) butter or margarine
4 oz (110 g) caster sugar
2 large eggs
4 oz (110 g) self-raising flour
1 level tsp baking powder

Preheat the oven to 350°F/180°C/Gas Mk 4. Put the sugar and water in a heavy-based saucepan and stir over a gentle heat, without boiling, until the sugar has dissolved. Bring rapidly to the boil, without stirring, and boil gently until the mixture turns a caramel colour. Pour into a lightly greased 8 in (20 cm) sandwich tin. When the caramel is on the point of setting, arrange the bananas, cut side down, in the tin like the spokes of a wheel, with the dates in between each. Place all the pudding ingredients together in a mixing bowl and beat with a wooden spoon for a few minutes until well mixed. Spread the mixture over the bananas and dates and bake on the middle shelf of the oven for 35–40 minutes. Remove from the oven and turn out onto a plate. This pudding can be served hot or cold.

SPOTTED DATE PUDDING
Serves 5–6

4 oz (110 g) chopped dates
4 oz (110 g) self-raising flour
4 oz (110 g) fresh breadcrumbs
½ level tsp salt
3 oz (75 g) shredded suet

3 oz (75 g) caster sugar
grated rind of 1 lemon
1 egg
7–8 tbsp milk
1 tbsp syrup

Preheat the oven to 350°F/180°C/Gas Mk 4. Grease a deep 2½ pint (1.3 ltr) pudding basin. Press some dates against the side of the dish to give a spotted look. Mix together the flour, breadcrumbs, salt, suet, sugar, lemon rind and remaining dates. Beat the egg and add to the flour mixture with enough milk to give a soft dropping consistency. Spoon the syrup into the dish, then pour the date mixture on top. Bake for about 1 hour until firm and springy to the touch.

BANANA BREAD PUDDING
Serves 4

7 oz (200 g) French bread
5 oz (150 g) dried banana
2 oz (50 g) currants
¾ pt (450 ml) skimmed milk
3 eggs
2 level tsp caster sugar
¼ level tsp grated nutmeg
1 oz (25 g) butter or margarine

Preheat the oven to 350°F/180°C/Gas Mk 4. Cut the bread into 1 in (2.5 cm) pieces. Roughly chop the dried banana. Place both in a large mixing bowl with the currants. Whisk together the milk, eggs, sugar and nutmeg. Pour over the bread and fruit mixture. Stir gently to mix. Lightly grease a 3 pint (1.7 ltr) shallow ovenproof dish. Spoon in the contents of the mixing bowl. Dot the butter over the top. Bake for about 1 hour. Cover lightly towards the end of cooking time if necessary.

EVE'S PUDDING
Serves 4

1 lb (450 g) cooking apples, peeled,
cored and sliced
2 rounded tbsp granulated sugar
4 oz (110 g) margarine
4 oz (110 g) caster sugar
2 eggs, beaten
4 oz (110 g) self-raising flour

Preheat the oven to 350°F/180°C/Gas Mk 4. Layer the apples and granulated sugar in a 1½ pint (900 ml) ovenproof dish. Cream together the margarine and caster sugar until light and fluffy. Add the beaten eggs, a little at a time, beating well after each addition. Fold in the flour with a metal spoon, to make a soft dropping consistency. Spread this mixture over the apples and level the top with the back of a spoon. Place the dish on a baking sheet and bake in the centre of the oven for 1 hour. Test by pressing with the fingers. If cooked, the pudding should spring back. It should also have stopped bubbling and have begun to shrink from side of dish.

NOODLE FRUIT PUDDING
Serves 4

8 oz (225 g) broad flat noodles
1 large cooking apple, peeled
  and grated
4 oz (110 g) soft brown sugar
2 oz (50 g) sultanas

1 tsp cinnamon
pinch of grated nutmeg
1½ oz (35 g) butter, melted
3 eggs, separated

Preheat the oven to 350°F/180°C/Gas Mk 4. Bring a large pan of water to the boil, and add the noodles, stirring to separate. Cook for 12 minutes or until just tender. Drain in a colander, rinse with cold water and drain again. Place in a large mixing bowl and stir in the apple, sugar, sultanas, cinnamon, nutmeg and melted butter. Lightly beat the egg yolks and stir into the noodle mixture. Whisk the egg whites until stiff and then fold into the mixture. Place in a greased ovenproof dish, cover and cook in the oven for 45 minutes.

PRINCESS PUDDING
Serves 6–8

3 eggs, separated
7 oz (200 g) caster sugar
1 pt (600 ml) full-fat milk
vanilla essence
8 oz (225 g) fresh breadcrumbs
2 tbsp redcurrant jelly, melted
grated rind of 1 lemon

Preheat the oven to 350°F/180°C/Gas Mk 4. Whisk the egg yolks with 4 oz (110 g) of the sugar. Heat the milk and add to the egg yolks, whisking all the time. Add a drop of vanilla essence and the breadcrumbs. Allow to stand for fifteen minutes. Grease a 2 pint (1.2 ltr) soufflé dish and fill it with the mixture. Bake for 20–25 minutes until it is set but not brown. Spread the top with the melted redcurrant jelly. Whip the egg whites until they form stiff peaks. Add the remainder of the sugar and the lemon rind and spread over the pudding. Turn the temperature of the oven down to 325°F/170°F/Gas Mk 3. Bake for 10–15 minutes until golden.

INDEX